C000134897

Fishing for Souls

Fishing for Souls

The Development and Impact
of British Fishermen's Missions

Stephen Friend

L

The Lutterworth Press

Dedicated to
The Rev. Dr Roald Kverndal, 1921–2015,
Maritime scholar, mentor and friend;

and to my two children,
Ruth and Christopher Friend.

The Lutterworth Press
P.O. Box 60
Cambridge
CB1 2NT
United Kingdom

www.lutterworth.com
publishing@lutterworth.com

ISBN: 978 0 7188 9514 3

British Library Cataloguing in Publication Data
A record is available from the British Library

First published by The Lutterworth Press 2018

Copyright © Stephen Friend, 2018

All rights reserved. No part of this edition may be reproduced,
stored electronically or in any retrieval system, or transmitted
in any form or by any means, electronic, mechanical,
photocopying, recording, or otherwise, without
prior written permission from the Publisher
(permissions@lutterworth.com).

Contents

Illustrations and Charts

Illustrations

Charts

Abbreviations and Glossary

Abbreviations
Seafarers' Missions

Dates of the formation of seafarers' societies are shown in brackets.

ACM	Aberdeen Coast Mission (1858) (also known as the North East Coast Mission)
AOS	Apostleship of the Sea (1920)
BCM	Bristol Channel Mission (1837)
BCSM	Bristol Channel Seamen's Mission (1845) (formerly the BCM)
BFBS	British and Foreign Bible Society (1804)
BFSS	British and Foreign Sailors' Society (1833) (known as the Sailors' Society today)
BMS	Bristol Missions to Seamen (1855) (formerly the BCSM)
BSS	British Sailors' Society (renamed the Sailors' Society)
DSA	Destitute Sailors' Asylum (1827)
EFCS	Episcopal Floating Church Society (1825)
MDSF	Mission to Deep Sea Fishermen (1881)
MS	Missions to Seamen (1856)
NSCM	North Sea Church Mission (1896)
PHS	Port of Hull Society (1821) (later the SCS)
PLBUS	Port of London and Bethel Union Society (1826)
PLS	Port of London Society for Promoting Religion among Seamen (1818)
RNMDSF	Royal National Mission to Deep Sea Fishermen (1881–2) (formerly the MDSF)
SAWM	Saint Andrew's Waterside Mission (1864)

SAWCM	Saint Andrew's Waterside Church Mission (1892) (formerly the SAWM)
SCFS	Seamen's Christian Friend Society (1846)
SCM	Scottish Coast Mission (1853)
SCS	Sailors' Children's Society (formerly the PHS)
TCM	Thames Church Mission (1844)
UCM	Union Coast Mission (1850)
WCM	West Coast Mission (1855)

Literature

FEL	*Fisheries Exhibition Literature*
NSM	*New Sailors' Magazine* (1827)
SML	*Sailors' Magazine* (London) (1821)
TOD	*Toilers of the Deep*

Glossary

Beam trawl: An early trawl-net which has its net kept open by a long wooden spar.

Belgium Devil: A grapnel with sharpened blades that was used to cut the ropes of drift-nets.

Bumboat: See Coper.

Coper: A floating grog-shop common in the North Sea during the 1870s and 1880s; it was commonly spelt 'cooper' in the newspapers of the time.

Drift-nets: Nets which are suspended in the water with floats at the top and weights at the bottom.

Fleeting: A system of fishing, developed during the period 1850–1890, whereby fishing vessels sailed in a fleet under the direction of an 'admiral'.

Floating church: A hulk fitted out for Church of England services.

Floating chapel: A hulk fitted out for Nonconformist services.

Hospital ship: A vessel fitted out as a sailing hospital.

Maiden voyage: The first voyage of a ship.

Sailing church/chapel: A vessel fitted out as a sailing church/chapel used for visits to fishing vessels at sea.

Silver herrings: Herrings which had been salted and smoked for three to seven days.

Smack: A fishing vessel – a ketch-rigged trawler.

Wherry: A flat-bottomed barge common in the inland waterways, used for transporting coal and other bulky commodities.

Aknowledgements

For this study I am grateful to many people and organisations for their support and encouragement. After twenty-five years of research it is impossible to mention everyone, so I do apologise if I have missed anyone out.

Among the many individuals to whom I owe thanks are numerous colleagues and friends who have inspired my research. These include Rev. Dr Roald Kverndal, Dr Alston Kennerley, the Very Rev. Dr Paul G. Mooney, Rev. Dr Robert W. Miller, Rev. Clint Padgett (New York), Sue Handby (Vancouver) and all members of the International Association for the Study of Maritime Mission (IASMM). Academic supporters include: Professor Sebastian Kim, Professor Pauline Kollontai and Dr Sue Yore of York St John University; Professor David J. Starkey, Dr Rodney Ambler and Dr Robb Robinson of the University of Hull. Angela Bryan, Sue Parkes and Dr Julie Hirst were excellent research officers for the oral history project, and there were the many women along the Yorkshire coast who gave freely of their time for interviews. While there are too many individuals here to mention by name, I would like to draw particular attention, with gratitude, to Lindy Rowley MBE, Rachel Jenkinson and Margaret Taylor.

Others who in their various ways have been supportive and helpful include Kevin Duff (Landlord of the Short Blue pub in Gorleston, Norfolk), Mrs Karasek (granddaughter of R.M. Ballantyne), Malcolm Criddle, Derek Farman, Charles Lewis (Curator of the Yarmouth Maritime Museum), Patricia O'Driscoll, Deb Gillanders and Alan Stewart (grandson of W.F. Stewart of the Albatross Mission). Representatives of the maritime missions also provided help and support; these include Rev. Canon Bill Christianson and Ann Haines of the Mission to Seafarers; David Macmillan MBE, Bernard Clampton OBE and Paul Jarret MBE of the Royal National Mission to Deep Sea Fishermen; Father John McGuire of the Apostleship of the Sea; and the staff of the Sailors' Children's Society (Hull), and the Sailors' Society.

The staff of many libraries and archives have been enormously helpful in locating relevant materials for me. These include staff at the Royal Archives, Windsor; Lambeth Palace Archives; the GLC Archives (London); the National Library of Scotland (Edinburgh); York University Library; York St John University, Leeds University; Hull University; Grimsby Local Studies (Grimsby Library); and the British Library (London and Boston Spa); Northallerton Archives; Beverley Archives; and the North East Lincolnshire Archives, Grimsby. The public library staff at Barking, Norwich, Penzance, Brixham, Great Yarmouth, Gorleston, Filey, Whitby, Lowestoft, Grimsby, Scarborough and York. Also, staff at the Colindale Newspaper Library (now moved to Boston Spa). Hull History Centre (Hull University), Lincolnshire Archives, the archives of the Salvation Army, the National Archives, Kew, Lowestoft Library Archives, the Family Welfare Association files (now in the GLC Archives, London), Whitby Literary and Philosophical Society, Filey Museum, Norfolk County Council Library and Information Service, and numerous other local archives, especially in towns and villages along the Yorkshire coast. The staff of Adelaide Public Library (Australia) were also patient in helping me search for references to E.J. Mather's time spent in Australia during 1890.

Staff at the Head Offices of the major seafarers' missions have been very patient with my requests over the years for help in locating relevant materials, and have kindly allowed me to reproduce material from their various publications. These societies include: the Royal National Mission to Deep Sea Fishermen, the Mission to Seafarers, the Sailors' Society, the Apostleship of the Sea, the Sailors' Families' Society (Hull) and the Wesleyan Seamen's Mission.

Many organisations kindly provided support and funding, enabling me to visit a wide range of fishing communities. These include: the Winston Churchill Memorial Trust (which awarded me a Travelling Fellowship in 1999, thereby enabling me to spend several weeks visiting maritime mission organisations in the United States and Canada, including Newfoundland and Nova Scotia); York St John University provided funding for visits to fishing communities around the British coast, New England and Southern Australia. Support and funding for the oral history research project 'Women's Voices', conducted along the Yorkshire coast, was provided by the Local Heritage Initiative, Nationwide Building Society, the Countryside Agency, Scarborough Council, and York St John University.

Finally, I am most grateful to the many churches whose staff welcomed me and provided helpful insights and suggestions. Among these, and of especial note, are: Fr Edward J.R. Martin SSC, St Andrew's Church, Grimsby; St Andrew's Church, Gravesend; Fr Tony Cotson, St John the

Evangelist Church, Hull; staff at London Road Baptist Church, Lowestoft; staff at St Nicholas Church, Great Yarmouth; and staff at St Andrew's Church, Gorleston.

My grateful thanks to Dorothy Luckhurst, copy-editor, whose carefully annotated notes helped to make the text more readable.

Finally, my sincere thanks are due to Debora Nicosia, Editorial Assistant, for her careful and helpful typesetting of the text and her corrections to mistakes and misunderstandings.

Perhaps needless to say, any errors or infelicities are my own responsibility.

Introduction

This work seeks to establish an historical outline of the development of the churches' work among British fishing communities, and explores why a mission specifically concerned with fishermen was not initiated until the industry entered a period of economic decline during the early 1880s. The factors relating to the development of British fishermen's missions are complex, involving not only social and technological changes inside and outside the fishing industry, but also changing theological perceptions that had a significant impact on attitudes to social conditions. Although no organisation concerned solely with the welfare of British fishermen[1] existed until the advent of the Mission to Deep Sea Fishermen (MDSF)[2] in 1881-1882, some relevant work was undertaken by seafarers' missions, which included fishermen among their more general concerns. It should, however, be noted that, while some vessels sailed to Newfoundland to fish, the British fishing industry was generally carried on in sight of the land until the 1840s when new developments enabled the fishermen to sail further out to sea and to take advantage of the rich North Sea fishing grounds such as Dogger Bank and the Silver Pitts. Thereafter, developments gathered momentum and the numbers of men fishing increased dramatically. With the development of the railways, especially from Liverpool to Grimsby and thence to London, the market for fish quickly expanded. Ice, too, became an important commodity. Robb Robinson tells us that: 'Hewett's Barking fleet started the practice of taking ice to sea on smacks about 1847', although artificial ice was not used in the fish trade until 1874.[3]

---

1. Historically there were very few females working on British fishing vessels. Hence, the traditional terms 'fisherman' and 'fishermen' are used throughout this work, although the term 'fisherfolk' is used when referring to the wider fishing community.
2. The Royal National Mission to Deep Sea Fishermen received permission to use the term 'Royal' in 1897. In the preceding period the society was known as the Mission to Deep Sea Fishermen, initially as an aspect of the work of the Thames Church Mission.
3. R. Robinson, *Trawling: the Rise and Fall of the British Trawl Fishery* (Exeter: University

Prior to the English Reformation, confraternities, festivals and special shrines were central to the functions which later came under the domain of organised seafarers' missions and, until the advent of seamen's missions in the early nineteenth century, pastoral work with fishermen tended to be the responsibility of the local clergy. With the rapid development of the British fishing industry, during the middle years of the nineteenth century, there was perhaps little need for the development of fishermen's missions, as distinct from seafarers' missions. Given that Roman Catholic emancipation did not occur until 1829, the development of a modern Roman Catholic presence amongst British fishermen and seafarers was generally very limited – although some significant developments did take place in the later nineteenth century, which led, in the twentieth century, to the establishment of the Apostleship of the Sea (AOS). Some aspects of this development are discussed in Chapter 9 of the present work, although readers interested in the development of Roman Catholic maritime missions in Britain should consult R.W.H. Miller's book, *One Firm Anchor*.[1]

Early History and Symbolism

Despite the Jewish fear of the sea, perceived as a reservoir of evil forces, the Old Testament contains many maritime references, and several recorded events in the life of Jesus involved fishing. Christianity began with Jesus' invitation to some fishermen to become his disciples; he used fishing boats to cross the Sea of Galilee to talk to (or get away from) the crowds; he taught the disciples a lesson in faith by providing them with a coin from a fish's mouth; he cooked a meal of fish for the disciples following his resurrection; and most memorable among his words was his command to the first four disciples: 'Follow me, and I will make you fishers of men.'[2] Of Jesus' twelve disciples at least four were professional fishermen, three of whom formed the inner core of his friends, and it was to one, Simon Bar-Jonah (Simon son of Jonah), that Jesus said: 'You are Peter, and on this rock I will build my Church.'[3] It is possible that John the disciple was a cousin of Jesus in that Matthew infers that Salome was John's mother. And the gospel of John suggests that Salome was a sister of Mary, Jesus' mother.[4] If this was indeed the case, Jesus had an uncle (Zebedee), and at least two cousins (James and John) who were fishermen.

of Exeter Press, 1996), p.69.
1. R.W.H. Miller, *One Firm Anchor* (Cambridge: The Lutterworth Press, 2012).
2. Matthew 4:19; Mark 1:17.
3. Matthew 16:18.
4. Matthew 27:56; Mark 15:40, 16:1; John 19:25.

While there are several events in the Gospels to do with fishing, and there are accounts of Paul at sea in Acts, the remainder of the New Testament does not contain a great deal of note about maritime life. Nevertheless, given Peter's (and his relatives') status in the early Church, maritime symbols (such as the fish, anchor, net, ship and the sea) were a natural development and were among the earliest used by Christians – pre-dating cruciform symbolism by several centuries. C.R. Morley has noted that, while the fish symbol pre-dated Christianity and was adopted and given new symbolic meanings by the Christians, it still remains a matter of conjecture as to when it first became a generally accepted Christian symbol.[1] Peter, of course, is the symbol *par excellence* of the rough, tough working fisherman who was without any form of sophisticated education or social refinement, but who is held in great esteem by the Church and was the acknowledged leader of the early Christian community, taking precedence over Jesus' own siblings, despite James' leadership of the Jerusalem community. The Church Fathers developed this maritime symbolism further: Clement of Alexandria adopted the fish as a symbol in his ring; Tertullian called new converts '*pisciculi*' (little fishes);[2] and the Church itself became the 'ship' (nave) in which the faithful are safe and secure.[3] This use of maritime symbolism is natural given the importance of Peter and the number of disciples who were fishermen. Nevertheless, to suggest, as does Peter Anson, that the use of maritime symbolism implies an active maritime mission is misleading. There is no evidence to suggest that the early Church established specific 'missions' to seafarers, any more than to farmers and gladiators (the symbolism for both these groups is equally rich).

The Church and Fishing Communities
Prior to the Nineteenth Century

By the Middle Ages a rich tapestry of folklore and legend had grown up surrounding the saints of the early Christian era, and many of these were associated with the sea. Perhaps not surprisingly, chapels and shrines in fishing ports tended to be named after saints with a maritime connection, especially St Peter, St Andrew and St Nicholas. Mary, Jesus' mother, also achieved an honourable status quite early among fisherfolk with numerous chapels and shrines being erected in her name, and she was given the honorific title of Stella Maris (Star of the Sea). There were also important

---

1. C.R. Morley, 'The Origin of the Fish Symbol', *Princeton Theological Review*, viii (1910), pp.93-106.
2. Tertullian, *De Baptismo*, recorded in Morley, *op. cit.*, pp.403-406.
3. J. Danielou SJ, *Primitive Christian Symbols* (Dartmouth: Compass Books, 1961), ch.4, 'The Ship of the Church'.

annual festivals such as the 'Blessing of the Sea', 'Blessing of the Nets' and the 'Blessing of the Boats'. Fishermen were organised into guilds (often spelt 'gilds' in Medieval writings) and confraternities. In such a high-risk occupation the sense of communal support provided by guilds was of course important, and Roald Kverndal has made the point that membership of seafarers' guilds provided an important educational function through participation in processions, pageants and plays.[1] Membership required obedience to Church fasts, and those 'who neglected to fast on specific days, or who worked on Saturdays after the Vesper Bell had rung, were fined'.[2] Monks around the coast of Britain performed an important role in establishing warning lights at dangerous locations. The monks on St Michael's Mount in Cornwall, for example, displayed warning lights during the fishing season. The Church's aiding of shipping also led to an important role in the development of sea-laws, many of which were established during the Medieval period.[3]

During the sixteenth century the establishment of 'Fish Days' ensured an increase in the number of fishermen who were available to swell the ranks of the country's navy when this became necessary.[4] As well as being a natural alternative to expensive meat, fish also functioned as an important symbolic reminder of Christ's passion, and in 1549 the new legislation stated:

> No person or persons shall [. . .] willingly or wittingly eat any manner of flesh on Friday or Saturday, or the Embering Days, or on any day in the time commonly called Lent, nor at any such other as is or shall be at any time hereafter commonly reputed and accepted as a Fish Day.[5]

Those people who did not observe the Act were fined. Queen Elizabeth I later expanded the Act to include the statement that 'every Wednesday of every week should also be a Fish Day'.

Although the fishing industry experienced an expansion during the sixteenth and seventeenth centuries, the practice of religious observance at sea was rare, and by the late 1700s practically unheard of. Yet in the fishing ports we hear little of the moral degeneration that was later said to have

1. Roald Kverndal, *Seamen's Missions* (Pasadena, CA: William Carey Library, 1986), p.17.
2. Peter F. Anson, *The Sea Apostolate in the Port of London* (published posthumously, London: Apostleship of the Sea, 1991), p.3.
3. R.F. Wright, 'The High Seas and the Church in the Middle Ages, Parts 1 and 2', *Mariner's Mirror*, 1967, p.117.
4. 5 Eliz. Stat. I Cap. V, recorded in *The Nautical Magazine*, April 1974, p.203.
5. *Ibid.*

occurred among naval personnel. Given the stability of fishing communities up until the mid-nineteenth century, we can only conjecture that there was indeed little to compare the fishermen with their naval contemporaries. Daniel Defoe, on his tour around Britain, gave no indication that moral behaviour in fishing communities was in any sense outrageous, and of the various merchants and seafarers at Great Yarmouth he said:

> The merchants, and even the generality of traders of Yarmouth, have a very good reputation in trade, as well abroad as at home, for men of fair and honourable dealing, punctual and just in their performing their engagements, and in discharging commissions; and their seamen, as well master as mariners, are justly esteemed among the ablest and most expert navigators in England.[1]

One wonders to whom Defoe spoke! He went on to make the point that, despite the large population, there was only one parish church and one recently built church in the south end of town. Even so, of behaviour on the Sabbath, he remarked: 'I have nowhere in England observed the Sabbath-Day so exactly kept, or the breach so continually punished as in this place, which I name to their honour.'

By the beginning of the nineteenth century the Church's influence over the British seafaring population had declined to such an extent that many never entered a church. Horace Mann, in his report on the religious census of 1851, said that the 'habitual neglecters of the public ordinances of religion' belonged to the working class – although they were seen as indifferent rather than antagonistic.[2] But, as the working class generally complained that they felt excluded from attending church services, it is not surprising that seamen were seen as indifferent to religion. It was partly this attitude that had initially given rise to the establishment of organised missions to seafarers and the adaption of old hulks as 'floating churches', and with the rapid growth of the fishing industry after mid-century the various seafarers' missions began to develop work more actively within the fishing communities. Nevertheless, it has been too readily assumed that these missions were simply a response to a perceived lack of religious sensibility amongst fishermen. Economic and technological developments on the one hand and poor social conditions on the other were equally important factors in the development.

---

1. Daniel Defoe, *A Tour Through the Whole Island of Great Britain*, first published in 1724 (Harmondsworth: Penguin, 1971), p.91.
2. Hugh McLeod, *Religion and the Working Class in Nineteenth-Century Britain* (London: Macmillan, 1984).

Christian seafarers' organisations, which developed following the period of the Anglo-French wars after the French Revolution in 1789, employed missionaries to visit the fishermen in their home ports, and in some cases at sea, although little thought was initially given to help improve the social conditions of fishermen at sea. It was during the 1880s that the Mission to Deep Sea Fishermen undertook this task by providing literature, warm clothes, medical aid, religious services and in due course tobacco. While the MDSF, in the face of public criticism, regularly stated that its primary objective was to evangelise, it is significant that the words 'Preach the Word' and 'Heal the Sick' were emblazoned on the bows of their vessels, although in the mid-1880s an emphasis was increasingly placed on its medical work. This example of concern for the fishermen's physical well-being was followed in the 1890s by other organisations, especially those represented by the Anglo-Catholics, and as a result there tended to be some conflict between the Nonconformists and the Ritualists.

Records, Documents and Publications

It is ironic that the social and economic aspects of the British fishing industry began to interest historians at a time, especially since the 1970s, when the industry experienced a sharp decline. Although many records and documents have been lost or destroyed, there are numerous extant documents carefully preserved and indexed in specific institutions, for example, the Hull History Centre, Greenwich Maritime Museum and the Liverpool Maritime Museum.

The task, however, is made more difficult because there is no comprehensive history of the sea fisheries in Britain. Peter Heath, writing in 1965, for example, pointed out that: 'None of the general histories of the fishing industry at present available can be called satisfactory.'[1] Some recent publications have helped to fill the gap, such as Starkey, Reid and Ashcroft's book, *The Commercial Sea Fisheries of England and Wales since 1300*.[2]

Many of the maritime missions have produced their own histories, sometimes with the help of outsiders, and each society has kept minutes and other important documents, which have helped to inform these histories. There are also newspaper articles, letters and official reports. Alongside this material there are other publications, such as: the Rev. George Charles Smith's *Sailors' Magazine and Naval Miscellany* (1820–1827) and his *New Sailors' Magazine and Naval Chronicle* (1827–), which eventually metamorphosed

1. P. Heath, 'North Sea Fishing in the Fifteenth Century: the Scarborough Fleet', *Northern History*, vol. 3 (1968), fn p.53.
2. D.J. Starkey, C. Reid and N. Ashcroft (eds), *England's Sea Fisheries* (London: Chatham, 2000).

into the British and Foreign Sailors' Society (BFSS) magazine, the *Chart and Compass* in 1879; the Thames Church Mission (TCM) published *Light from Aloft*; the Missions to Seamen (MS), the *Word on the Waters*; and the MDSF published *Toilers of the Deep*. Each society also produced an annual report, giving details of its work, expenses, accounts *etc*. These and other publications help to fill in many of the gaps and provide an insight into the overall early work of such missions, although, perhaps inevitably, they do tend to exaggerate the positive side of the work. There were also some early attempts at a general history of seafarers' missions, notably those by the Rev. G.C. Smith and later by his son, Theophilus, but these were never completed.[1] Hence, despite the losses, there still remains a wealth of material that researchers can utilise (and which is becoming more easily accessible), so long as great care is taken with the interpretation of this data.

While popular histories were produced by the various maritime mission societies, it was not until the mid-twentieth century that a more thorough approach began to materialise. The pioneer here was the English Benedictine oblate, Peter Anson, who wrote in an unpublished manuscript that: 'For reasons difficult to understand, maritime missiology – to use a clumsy expression – has never attracted historians.'[2] Even he encountered problems and never published his major work on maritime missions, although he did publish several relevant books and articles. For example, his *The Church and the Sailor* (1948) contains some interesting material on missions among fishing communities.[3]

There have been a few short biographies of Anson, and he wrote about his life and work in several of his books (especially in *Life on Low Shore*), but there has not been any attempt at a major biography – although Miller's book, *'One Firm Anchor' (2012), includes an important chapter* on Anson's work (as does his MPhil thesis).[4] Miller has pointed out that, while 'succeeding authors have depended heavily upon Anson's work, his writings are not always reliable and are usually unsourced'.[5]

---

1. See the preface to Kverndal's *Seamen's Missions*, 1986.
2. Peter Anson, Foreword, in an unpublished typescript entitled *The Church Maritime*, c.1974. (The British *Apostleship of the Sea* archives, including works by Anson, have now been relocated at the Hull History Centre.) Unfortunately, much of Anson's material in *The Church Maritime* is now very out of date, and his personal views do not always sit comfortably with present-day attitudes.
3. Peter Anson, *The Church and the Sailor* (London: John Gifford, 1948).
4. Miller, *op. cit.*, ch. 15 (*One Firm Anchor* is a significant update of Miller's earlier work, *From Shore to Shore*, 1989); Miller, 'Ship of Peter', MPhil Thesis, Institute of Marine Studies, University of Plymouth, April 1995. But see especially Peter Anson, *Life on Low Shore* (Banff: The Banffshire Journal Ltd, 1969).
5. R.W.H. Miller, 'The *Société des Oeuvres de Mer*', *Newfoundland and Labrador Studies*, no.

Peter Anson (1889-1975).

Anson's pioneering work was taken up in the 1970s and 1980s by several scholars who found themselves working on different aspects of maritime mission history: Roald Kverndal, Alston Kennerley, Robert Miller, Stephen Friend and Paul Mooney all completed university theses on maritime missions, and all have published their work in a variety of forms. Kverndal pointed to the difficulty of undertaking such research in that the primary and secondary sources were widely disseminated and often difficult to locate and view – not to mention the many documents lost or destroyed. Nevertheless, a significant development took place in 1990 when Kverndal met with other scholars who together founded the International Association for the Study of Maritime Mission (IASMM), listing its aims as follows:

1. To promote the study and research of maritime mission;
2. To catalogue, encourage presentation and publicise sources for research in maritime mission;
3. To encourage the interdisciplinary integration of maritime mission in places of learning;
4. To provide a forum for debate and discussion by conferences and publications;
5. To stimulate and facilitate publications on maritime mission.

After successful meetings, a popular newsletter and biannual conferences, a meeting was organised in 1996 on the topic of 'Maritime Mission Archives: Problem or Opportunity', chaired by Bishop Bill Down. Members of IASMM subsequently worked hard to ensure the preservation of these archives and many have now been relocated with relevant archives in Britain and the USA.

Since 1970 there have been five major threads in the scholarly approach to maritime mission studies and, while there is a good deal of overlap between these threads, the paradigm will help us to explore the overall

---

20 (2005), 2, n.49. There are currently two biographies of Anson: Stanley Bruce and Tina Harris, *Back to the Sea* (Bard Books, 2009); and Michael Yelton, *Peter Anson: Monk, Writer and Artist* (Anglo-Catholic History Society, 2005).

development. It should also be noted that the following is a selective list as numerous articles have appeared in various journals by the stated authors and others.

The first thread saw publications and theses about the history of the Church maritime by Alston Kennerley, Roald Kverndal, Robert Miller and Stephen Friend.[1] Kennerley completed his Master's thesis in 1978, entitled

Founding members of the International Association for the Study of Maritime Mission at IASMM's First Biannual Conference at Tilbury, at the Stella Maris Hostel, Essex, 5 April 1988.
Back Row: Dr Stephen Friend, Rev. Dr Roald Kverndal, Fr John McGuire
Front Row: Stephen Twycross, Rev. Dr Robert Miller, Howard Bloch and Dr Alston Kennerley.

'The Education of the Merchant Seaman in the Nineteenth Century', and followed this in 1989 with a doctoral thesis, 'British Seamen's Missions and Sailors' Homes, 1815–1970', which explored the various aspects of voluntary welfare provision for seafarers. The results of Kverndal's doctoral work were published in 1986 under the title, *Seamen's Missions: their Origin and Early Growth*. Miller published his general history of seafarers' missions in 1989 under the title, *From Shore to Shore: a History of the Church and the*

---

1. Robert Miller, *From Shore to Shore*, published privately (Newmarket: Ladycroft, 1989); Alston Kennerley, 'British Seamen's Missions and Sailors Homes, 1815–1970', PhD thesis, CNAA, September 1989; Stephen Friend, 'The Rise and Development of Christian Missions Amongst British Fishing Communities during the Nineteenth Century', MPhil thesis, University of Leeds, January 1994.

Merchant Seafarer, and in 1995 he completed a Master of Philosophy thesis, entitled 'Ship of Peter: the Catholic Sea Apostolate and the Apostleship of the Sea'. In 2002 Miller also completed his doctoral thesis with an exploration of the work of the Medieval Church with seafarers entitled 'The Man at the Helm: the Faith and Practice of the Medieval Seafarer'. This was followed in 2012 with an update and expansion of his earlier publication, entitled *One Firm Anchor: the Church and the Merchant Seafarer, an Introductory History.* In 1994 Friend completed a Master of Philosophy degree with a study about the rise and development of fishermen's missions in Britain. Some aspects of this thesis were later explored further in Friend's PhD in 2010, which examined the relationship between identity and religion in three Yorkshire fishing communities.[1]

A second thread resulted in a number of studies exploring the work of particular individuals and organisations: Kverndal provided various studies of significant seafarers' missionaries in his book on *Seamen's Missions,* and more recently published a biography about the Rev. George Charles Smith.[2] In 1992 Miller offered an assessment of the work of the life and work of Charles Plomer Hopkins in his MA thesis, entitled 'Charles Plomer Hopkins and the Seamen's Union with Particular Reference to the 1911 Strike', then published a book on this topic in 2010 entitled *Priest in Deep Water.* His most recent book is a biography of Rev. Dr John Ashley;[3] Ronald Rompkey examined the life and work of Wilfred Grenfell;[4] and Sinclair Oubre completed a Licenciate in Canon Law thesis in 1998 on the topic of 'The *Apostolatus Maris:* its Structural Development Including its 1997 Reorganisation';[5] Friend examined the life and work of Ebenezer Joseph Mather, the founder of the Mission to Deep Sea Fishermen;[6] and Miller, in his recent book, *One Firm Anchor,* provided a helpful analysis of Peter Anson's work.[7]

1. Stephen Friend, 'A Sense of Belonging: Religion and Identity in Yorkshire and Humber Fishing Communities, c.1815–1914', University of Hull, May 2010.

2. Roald Kverndal, *George Charles Smith of Penzance* (Pasadena, CA: William Carey Library, 2012).

3. Robert Miller, *Dr Ashley's Pleasure Yacht: John Ashley, the Bristol Channel Mission and All that Followed* (Cambridge: Lutterworth Press, 2017).

4. Ronald Rompkey, *Grenfell of Labrador* (Toronto: University of Toronto Press, 1991). Grenfell was a doctor at the London Hospital who trained under Frederick Treves. Treves was on the Committee of the Mission to Deep Sea Fishermen and encouraged Grenfell to spend some time at sea doing medical work among the fishing fleets.

5. Sinclaire K. Oubre, 'The *Apostolatus Maris:* its Structural Development Including its 1997 Reorganisation', in part-fulfilment of the Licenciate in Canon Law thesis, Catholic University of America, Washington DC, 1998.

6. Stephen Friend, see the biography of 'Ebenezer Joseph Mather' in the *New Dictionary of National Biography* (Oxford: Oxford University Press, 2004).

7. R.W.H. Miller, 'Charles Plomer Hopkins and the Seamen's Union with Particular

The third thread explores the work of maritime missions in various countries. For example, Jonah Won Jong Choi and David Chul-Han Jun explored the role of maritime missions in Korea;[1] Vincent Yzermans published a study of *The American Catholic Seafarers' Church*;[2] and Michael L. Hadley provided a history of the Columbia Coast Mission in Canada, called *God's Little Ships*.[3] Alain Cabantous has examined maritime missions in France;[4] and Kverndal has provided a history of the Nordic seamen's missions in the *Norwegian Yearbook of Maritime History*.[5]

Fourthly, Bishop Bill Down, the Very Rev. Paul Mooney and the Rev. Dr Roald Kverndal have focussed on developments in the twentieth century, especially the work of the International Christian Maritime Association (Down); and Mooney has taken a lead from Liberation Theology by providing a helpful analysis of a new paradigm that puts greater emphasis on the pastoral and mission role of seafarers themselves.[6] Kverndal has also edited a collection of articles on aspects of maritime mission, entitled *The Way of the Sea: the Changing Shape of Mission in the Seafaring World*.[7]

A fifth thread covers a range of meetings, conferences, discussions, talks, presentations and displays. All the people mentioned above, and numerous others, have actively engaged in discussion and the presentation of maritime mission topics in a range of countries, including England, Ireland, the US, Spain and South Africa. There has also been some involvement with organisations concerned with relevant aspects of seafaring.

Reference to the 1911 Strike', MA thesis, University of Warwick, 1992; 'The Man at the Helm: the Faith and Practice of the Medieval Seafarer', PhD thesis, University of London, 2002.

1. Jonah Won Jong Choi, 'Shalom and the Church Maritime', 9 May 1996, DMin thesis, New York Theological Seminary; David Chul-Han Jun, 'An Historical and Contextual Approach to Seafarers by Korean Churches with Special Reference to Muslim Seafarers', 7 June 2001, DMiss thesis, Fuller School of World Mission, Pasadena, California.

2. Vincent A. Yzermans, 'American Catholic Seafarers' Church: a Narrative History of the Apostleship of the Sea' (The National Catholic Conference for Seafarers in the United States, 1995). Sinclair Oubre, *op.cit., 1998*.

3. Michael L. Hadley, *God's Little Ships* (Madeira Park, BC, Canada: Harbour Publishing, 1995).

4. Alain Cabantous, 'Religion et monde maritime au Havre dans la seconde moitié du XVIIIe siècle', *Annales de Normandie*, 33 (1983), p.3.

5. Kverndal, 'The Origin and Nature of Nordic Missions to Seamen', in the *Norwegian Yearbook of Maritime History* (1977), pp.103-134.

6. Bill Down, *On Course Together* (Norwich: The Canterbury Press, 1989); Paul Mooney, *Maritime Mission* (Zoetermeer, the Netherlands: Uitgeverij Bockencentrum, 2005).

7. R. Kverndal, *The Way of the Sea* (Pasadena, CA: William Carey Library, 2008).

There is, of course, a good deal of overlap between these strands. For example, Rompkey's study discusses not only Grenfell's work in Britain and Labrador with the Royal National Mission to Deep Sea Fishermen (RNMDSF), but also the development of the International Grenfell Association. However, each of these strands provides a scholarly balance to the more subjective approaches taken by the various societies and their supporters.

Following the establishment of the International Association for the Study of Maritime Mission in 1990, a twice-yearly newsletter was published until 2010. The work under the secretaryship of Stephen Friend (1990–2010), and now under the caretaker role of the Rev. Clint Padgett in New York, provided the growing number of researchers with an opportunity to explore issues and publish short accounts of their work and research.[1]

Despite this encouraging activity there is still much to be published on the development of missions amongst fishing communities. Hence, the present study is concerned specifically with this development during the nineteenth century and confines itself mainly to mission work in Britain. Nevertheless, Chapter 10 offers a brief overview of some of the maritime missions, influenced by the work of the RNMDSF, and developed in France, Germany, Scandinavia and the US. Given the complexity of the relationships between the many maritime missions in Britain a helpful one-page chart has been included in Appendix 1a.

Views from the Deck

The maritime mission societies have not unnaturally tended to paint a positive picture about their work, although there are a few instances that suggest a less than positive image. Anson has provided some dissenting examples. For example, he commented: 'On one occasion [the chaplain] had a dog set on him, and on another was pelted with pieces of pork rolled up in his own tracts.'[2] Kennerley also came across the following extract in a book written by a seaman (the spelling and grammar are original and retained; the words are generally written as they sound):

> [We] shuve in to the cost, drops the hook and work in this boar like a fiar engine, swet and swet next thing i knowed it this mishuonry come Down on you. i knowed he would soon as you was to give him a chanse but I did not give him anney chanse but they come At you without one. i packs up, I was mearly going forward and

---

1. The website for the IASMM is now: www.iasmm.org.
2. Peter F. Anson, *op.cit.*, 1974, p.165.

come by some pawk and beens from cookie, comes down on you which he said it is a nise evining isent it. says i didant like the looks of it soe much Why not he said. tells him I do not know but it looks omnerous. he said ar yes, they do say ar a lot these mishuonries. says ar twise, shuve his head Up and Down, says i suppose you sailors can tell by the heavonley boddies. replyes which bodies. which he said the stars and cetra, well god damnit i thort he meaned some angels as was loombing into vieuws some wheres. goes on says you can tell the weather by the stars carnt you. Tells him not if the sun is Up they goes Out then, ar yes he said. which come a stop in the conversashin, i did think i might of got of, come by my pawk and beens but they inter lope in your live, he said well my young friend it is a fine live. what is i said because i knowed what he were after, but mersey on us i do not see why this specious of mithooselumb should be aloud to go and say it is a fine live and never done a hands turn scrubbing decks onley with their foot and Durtey it.[1]

Such written views are uncommon, although there are a few hints given by writers on aspects of maritime history. The following comments were written by Ole Mortensøn reflecting on a paper read by Alston Kennerley at Stavanger, Norway, in 1992:

Kennerley hints at the conflict between missionaries as social workers or as guardians of established morals. And he also touches on a related issue – how effective were the missionaries? [. . .] I have interviewed many Danish seamen from the days of sail and they generally seem little impressed by the missions. Zealous missionaries were scorned or at least left in a social vacuum when they boarded the ships. Many seamen disliked the well-fed, complacent missionary as well as the learned, fanatical delegate of God. Most successful were the missionaries who knew life at sea from experience. 'God's own donkeyman' was a well-known and beloved missionary, a former fireman. The seamen visited seamen's churches, but more often to speak to countrymen, read national papers and get a good cup of coffee sitting in a chair than to listen to the word of God.[2]

1. William P. Taplow, in Hamish Maclaren (ed.), *The Private Opinions of a British Bluejacket* (London: Peter Davies, 1929).
2. Alston Kennerley, 'British Seamen's Missions in the Nineteenth Century', in *The North Sea: Twelve Essays on Social History of Maritime Labour* (Stavanger, Norway: Stavanger Maritime Museum/The Association of North Sea Societies, 1992),

Walter Wood has also provided an indication of some attitudes of fishermen who visited the Mission ship during a religious service:

> At one meeting I attended, after a deputation had waited upon me with a request that I would play the harmonium for them, I could not help being amused at the attitude of a smacksman who evidently was not considered by the others to be 'converted'. A fellow-skipper was praying earnestly for him by name, a fact which did not disconcert him in the least, for all through the prayer he conversed with a friend in his normal voice, evidently about the course of some vessel, for at intervals I could plainly hear such expressions as 'nowth-east by nowth', and 'lost his gear', showing very decidedly that the fears for his soul's safety expressed by his seafaring brethren were not shared by him.[1]

There were, of course, also many seamen who welcomed the maritime missions, and there were many who benefited from the medical help provided at sea, the free literature, services, refreshment and entertainment. But Mortensøn's observation is pertinent and more research needs to be undertaken in this area in order to gain a balanced view.

Women in Fishing Communities

Another under-researched topic is the role of women in fishing communities. While many books concentrate on fishermen, their vessels and catches, there is very little on the women of the fishing communities, other than photogenic young women, such as those recorded by Frank Meadow Sutcliffe, and other nineteenth-century photographers, who portrayed fishwives in traditional dress often carrying very heavy fish baskets. There is very little on the ordinary, everyday lives of the women.

The present author, and his research assistants, over a four-year period has tried to redress the balance by conducting an oral history project along the Yorkshire coast that allowed women to tell their own stories. An initial study was produced as chapter 11 in Kim and Kollontai's book, *Community Identity*[2] in 2007. A DVD was also produced, and other similar research projects have since appeared in print, especially *The Women They Left Behind*, by Nick Triplow, Tina Bramhill and Jade Shepherd.[3] Nevertheless, the culture of the fishing

---

pp.79-95.

1. Walter Wood, *North Sea Fishers and Fighters* (London: Kegan Paul, Trench, Trubner & Co. Ltd, 1911), p.218.

2. Sebastian Kim, Pauline Kollontai (Eds.), *Community Identity: Dynamics of Religion in Context* (London: T&T Clark, 2007).

3. Nick Triplow, Tina Bramhill and Jade Shepherd, *The Women They Left Behind*

A Whitby fishwife.
Photograph by Frank Meadow Sutcliffe, c.1880.

industry is male dominated and the role of the womenfolk within that culture is perhaps most underrated This is usually by omission in that most books about the fishing industry tend to concentrate on men and boats. Indeed, until recently many memorial statues only featured fishermen – although this seems to be being rectified in some communities where women have been portrayed in various roles (for example, at Fleetwood a mother and her two children are looking out for the returning fishing vessels, at Bridlington a girl is knitting a gansey, and at Stornoway a herring girl is portrayed).

There were, however, a number of women who owned businesses associated with the industry, including Baroness Burdett-Coutts who established the short-lived Columbia fishing fleet and the Columbia fish market (1881–1884), and opened a fishing school for boys at Baltimore. In some cases

(Fathom Press, 2009).

Mrs Clark on her fish stall in 'The Vaults', Scarborough, c.1950.

women were responsible for their own Christian missions, including Dame
Agnes Weston, who, along with her colleague Sophia G. Wintz, established
the Royal Sailors' Rests in Portsmouth and Devonport. The Hon. Elizabeth
Waldegrave was involved in work among seafarers at Southsea, and Sarah
Robinson at Portsmouth. Agnes Hedenstrom was also appointed by the
Swedish Free Church as a missionary to the London Docklands in 1875.
Other Scandinavian women, such as Emma Leijonhelm (1847–1937) and
Andrea Franks (1857–1942) also ran sailors' homes.[1]

    There were also the wives of fishermen who took over their husband's
business following his death. One example is Mrs Clark who ran her
stall in 'The Vaults' at Scarborough for many years in the mid-twentieth
century. Several fishermen's wives also ran crab stalls at Scarborough. These
are modern examples of nineteenth-century labour where the wives of
fishermen trundled from village to village with heavy baskets full of fish for
sale. Hence, the women, from the highest to the lowest classes were very
much involved in the economic activity of the fishing communities.

    There were even a few women who engaged in fishing at sea, such as Jane
Witty of Hull during the 1850s and 1860s[2] and Dora Walker who built
her own boat, the *Good Faith*, and fished off Whitby between the 1930s

---

1. Kverndal, *op. cit.* (1986), p.606; 'Women on the Waterfront', *Maritime Mission Studies*,
   vol. 2 (Spring 2000), p.21.
2. Robinson, *op. cit.* (1996), p.44.

and the 1950s. While Walker initially experienced opposition from the local fishermen, she eventually earned their respect and became known as 'Skipper Dora'. In later years, she was actively involved in the Whitby Literary and Philosophical Society and was a member of the local Committee of the Missions to Seamen.[1]

Paul Thompson has referred to the fisherwomen who worked on the *She Cruiser* in County Down, Ireland, during the 1980s, and the female fishing skipper at Helvik, Waterford.[2] A few women also occasionally crewed for their husbands, such as the fisherman's wife at Hastings, when the male crew members failed to turn up.[3] But British women were generally absent from fishing work on the vessels, and indeed many fishermen held it a poor omen should a women step on board their vessel before it left for the fishing grounds.

Ironically, perhaps, many of the Christian missions among fishing and other seafaring communities were initiated by women, who provided the necessary finance to get the societies off the ground or to support the founders of maritime missions. An important example here is Lady Mary Grey (the wife of the Commissioner of the Portsmouth Naval Dockyard) who sponsored the early career of the Rev. G.C. Smith.[4] Others provided the funds to purchase vessels. There was also an army of women who provided knitted items and raised funds for the missions via drawing-room meetings and charity events. In most cases these women remain anonymous, and much of the credit for the work has been given to the men who are usually cited as founders of the various societies. Yet other women became scripture readers. Anson has pointed out that Mother Lydia Sellon's Sisters appear to have been the 'first female ship-visitors'. Miss Sellon established several organisations including, in 1848, a Church of England Sisterhood of Mercy of Devonport and Plymouth and, the following year, she founded two 'Houses of Peace' as refuges for 'fallen women', where they could be looked after and trained for domestic service. Other developments followed including St George's College for Sailor Boys. The boys were taught to dance the polka and hornpipe and were encouraged to engage in play-acting, and she 'regaled them with tales of wild adventure' – activities that shocked and upset the local evangelicals! Another aspect of her work included a Home for Old Sailors and their Wives.[5]

1. Marian Durrans, *The Life and Times of Miss Dora Walker, F.R.S.A., 1890–1980* (Whitby Literary and Philosophical Society, 1998).
2. Paul Thompson, 'Women in the Fishing', *Comparative Studies in Society and History*, vol. 27 (1985), p.7.
3. Beatrice Cloves MA, *Loving the Fishing* (Old Hastings Preservation Society, October 2003).
4. Kverndal, *op. cit.* (2000), p.19.
5. Anson, *op. cit.* (1974), pp.40-41.

There were also countless women who worked as fishergirls in the herring industry, travelling around the coast with their relatives to work in the ports where the fishermen brought in the herring. Much has already been written about this group, although mission work with the herring girls (and the individuals and organisations involved, such as the Scottish Episcopal Mission to Fisherfolk) has not been to any great extent examined. The material here is sparse although some brief notes have been included in Chapter 5.[1]

Finally, it should not be forgotten that the wives of the fishermen took on the main responsibility for the family and home, including looking after the finance. And, before the advent of a universal welfare system, the women lived daily with the fear that their husbands might be lost at sea, leaving them destitute, apart from the small claims that might be made to a relevant charity. Paul Thompson, in his book, *Living the Fishing*, devotes a chapter to the women in fishing communities, this he begins with the words: 'Fishing is commonly thought of as a man's trade. In fact, it is an occupation peculiarly dependent on the work of women.'[2] His study explores, *inter alia*, the role of women leading demands for better pay and conditions, especially during the twentieth century.

British Seamen's Missions after 1850

As the British fishing industry began its rapid expansion in the mid-nineteenth century, especially in the North Sea, the increase in social problems and abuses led to a concern for practical intervention by seafarers' missions. It was also the period during which significant innovations and discoveries led to the development of the modern British fishing industry. An overview in this study is also offered of the example and influence of seafarers' missions in the early part of the nineteenth century, in that methods used by later, more specialised missions to fishing communities drew upon the work and techniques of this earlier activity.

By 1900 the nature of fishermen's missions was changing from a predominantly sea-centred enterprise to shore-based work, although the process had already begun in the early nineteenth century with Rev. G.C. Smith's various organisations and societies for seafarers. With the rising costs of obtaining an appropriate vessel by the end of the nineteenth century, it became increasingly difficult for the various fishermen's

---

1. The only references viewed so far come from comments in the correspondence of the Missions to Seafarers Archives, Hull History Centre; and Peter Anson's paper entitled *Seamen's Welfare Work in Scottish Ports*, c.1949, Apostleship of the Sea Archives, Hull History Centre, U DAPS/12/1/HIST.
2. Paul Thompson, Tony Wailey and Trevor Lummis, *Living the Fishing* (London: Routledge & Kegan Paul, 1983), p.167.

missions to maintain their work at sea, or indeed to maintain their work at all. Hence, by the beginning of the twentieth century, while all the main organisations were in place – despite some times of crisis and innovations in organisational procedures – some inevitably fell by the wayside. The fleeting system (a system of fishing developed by Hewett in the 1850s, which involved vessels sailing for the fishing grounds together and working there under the control of an 'admiral') was abandoned, a fact symbolised by Hewett's disbanding of their 'Short Blue Fleet' c.1902, and, although smaller fleets continued to work the Dogger Bank for several years after, the heady days of fleeting had come to an end.

Late Victorian Britain saw a period during which the sea-fishing industry developed to such a remarkable extent that it was acknowledged as the largest and most successful the world had ever known. It was no accident, therefore, that during this period the Church and the public began to take an interest in the welfare of the men and women who were employed by, and dependent upon, this industry. This interest, however, did not take place in a vacuum, and we must note the marked changes in social, economic and theological perspectives that occurred throughout the Victorian era, and the influence these changes had upon the attitudes of those engaged in ministering to the members of fishing communities.

The structure of this study therefore explores the development of the various organisations established to look after the spiritual and physical welfare of fishermen and their families. Chapter 1 looks briefly at the development of the British fishing industry. Chapter 2 examines the nature of the social and theological contexts in which a concern for the physical and spiritual welfare of fishermen was generated. Chapters 3 to 5 examine the development of maritime missions in Britain, with particular emphasis on their involvement with fishing communities, and provide an overview of the development of seafarers', especially fishermen's, missions throughout the nineteenth century. The period is divided for convenience into three sections: 1800–56, 1856–80, 1880–1900 – although Chapter 5 also examines some of the main developments in the early years of the twentieth century. While in this section we will examine in detail the first ten years of the Mission to Deep Sea Fishermen, 1881–91, it is important to remember that the MDSF has very few documents in its archives relating to its formative years, and the correspondence between the MDSF and the Family Welfare Association has sadly been destroyed. In Chapter 6 there is an examination of the development and demise of the copering trade. Chapter 7 follows with an examination of the MDSF's medical work at sea. The resignation of the society's founder, Ebenezer Joseph Mather, is examined in Chapter 8. He was similar in many ways to founders of other seafarers' organisations, and his relationship with his Committee, and his eventual downfall, reflects the problems faced by earlier seafarers' missionaries, the Rev. George Charles Smith and the Rev. Dr John Ashley.[1] Chapter 9 offers a brief overview of the Roman Catholic work at sea; and Chapter 10 identifies briefly those missions influenced by the work of the RNMDSF.

Inevitably, later writers tend to simplify complex issues, and often telescope and juxtapose events that originally bore no such direct relationship. From this arises the 'myth'. This is no less true of the RNMDSF than it is for other organisations, and some published accounts of the early days of the RNMDSF have created much that is fictitious. Fictions are relatively easy to discredit; truth is never easy to ascertain, facts are always interpreted by the participants and later researchers, and we are left to make judgements as to the most likely course of events. The difficulty is in simplifying events without losing contact with reality. The myth, of course, serves a useful purpose in giving a sense of identity and uniqueness to the beginning of an organisation or movement and reinforcing its role. But there are times when it is necessary to reflect upon the origins, and to attempt to recapture a clear sense of the early vision if reconstruction and future development are to occur. This process is often painful – many people would prefer to continue living with a myth, but when the myth loses contact with reality it is in danger of becoming meaningless or irrelevant. This study, therefore, is an attempt to offer a coherent outline of the development of missions to fishermen in Britain and to analyse some of the events which led to and influenced this missionary activity.

---

1. Miller, *op. cit.* (2017).

Chapter 1
The Development of
the British Fishing Industry

British Fisheries before the Nineteenth Century
One of the earliest accounts of fishing in Britain comes from the Greek mariner, Pytheas, who visited these islands (Brython) in 324BC where he observed how the 'primitive islanders fished the inshore waters of the innumerable shallow bays and inlets from their coracles of plaited, hide-sheathed withies'. Two hundred years later the Greek voyager, Posidonius, noted the development of more sophisticated vessels, which could venture into deeper waters, although the fisheries were mainly restricted to the more predictable waters off the south coast.[1] While the British sea fisheries appear to have developed under the influence of the Romans, Dion Cassius, in the late second century AD, said that although fish in abundance was to be found in Britain's northern seas the natives had not tasted them.[2] But significant developments took place during the next few hundred years and by the eighth century sailing ships were commonly used for offshore fishing, although still mainly on the southern coasts.

Exactly when the move northwards commenced is unknown, although by the eleventh century there was a thriving international trade centred on Great Yarmouth in herrings and dried cod imported from Iceland.[3] Great Yarmouth was formally recognised by charter in 1208 when King John granted the town the status of self-governing borough. This independence was capitalised on by the institution of a 'Herring Fair' – an event previously dominated by the Cinque Ports (Sandwich, Romney, Dover, Hythe and Hastings). In 1277, Great Yarmouth and the Cinque Ports agreed to administer the Fair jointly, although this situation led to a good deal of rivalry, animosity and violence. Even so, it was only in 1663 – when the

1. Major Reginald Hargreaves, 'Fisherfolk', *The Nautical Magazine*, April 1974, p.199.
2. Cassii Dionis Cocceiana, *Historiarum Romanarum Quae Supersunt*, U.P. Boissevain (ed) (Berlin: 1901), vol. III, p.367 (quoted in Colin Matheson, *Wales and the Sea Fisheries* (National Museum of Wales, 1929), p.13).
3. Hargreaves, *op. cit.*

Cinque ports began their decline – that the Fair ceased to be administered as a partnership. The importance of the Herring Fair for medieval Europe can be gauged from the amount of herring shipped abroad: in just five days, during 1344, 'sixty foreign vessels, including ten from Lombardy in Italy, loaded cured herrings at Yarmouth'.[1] The sixteenth-century historian, Damet, recorded the importance of the herring fishery:

> great numbers of the fishermen of Fraunce, Flaunders, and of Hollande, Zealande, and all the lowe countryes yerelie, from the feaste of Sainte Michaell the Archangell, untyll the feaste of Sainte Martine, (were involved in) the takinge, sellinge and buyenge of herringes.[2]

The opening up of the Newfoundland cod fishery in the sixteenth century also gave impetus to the British and European fisheries as a result of the quantity and size of the local fish.[3] During the seventeenth century Great Yarmouth remained the most important fishing port in Europe, such that John Speed wrote in 1611, 'there is yearly in September the worthiest herring fishery in Europe which draweth great concourse of people, which maketh the town much the richer all the year following, but very unsavoury for the time'.[4] And in 1697, Daniel Defoe wrote of 1,123 vessels belonging to the town.[5]

The expansion continued into the eighteenth century, although this was overshadowed to some extent by the Dutch who came to dominate the North Sea and Icelandic fisheries when they developed vessels capable of carrying large quantities of fish.[6] Nevertheless, it was still only possible to transport fresh fish a little way up the rivers and estuaries; heavily salted fish was transported to inland markets via pannier ponies. It was not until the advent of the railways and the development of artificial ice in the nineteenth century that it became possible to supply fresh sea-fish in large quantities to inland populations.

The Nineteenth Century

During the early-nineteenth century fishermen adapted their methods according to the seasons, as the following report on the Newlyn fishermen during the 1820s demonstrates:

1. Charles Lewis, *Great Yarmouth: History, Herrings and Holidays* (Poppyland Publishing, 1981), p.13.
2. *Ibid.*
3. Ronald Hope, *A New History of British Shipping* (London: John Murray, 1990), p.85.
4. C. Lewis, *op. cit.*, p.14.
5. Defoe, *op. cit.*, p.91.
6. Hope, *op. cit.*, p.174.

During the winter all are at home, but in summer they go on the mackerel fishery; in the spring they run to Plymouth or Bristol, and in the autumn they visit Ireland, or fish for herrings off the Isle of Man, in the Irish Channel, or attend the pilchard fishery at home in Mount's Bay or St Ives' Bay. Their life is hazardous, fatiguing, dreary, and comfortless.[1]

Fishing methods included the use of a seine net, line fishing and trawling. Exactly when trawling came into use in Britain is conjectural, although it seems likely that some form of trawl-net (perhaps the drag-net of New Testament times) was in use following the Romanising of Britain.[2] With the development of the North Sea fisheries in the nineteenth century the beam trawl came very much into its own; the invention of the steam winch reduced the time it took to haul in the nets from several hours to thirty minutes; and the development and commercial use of artificial ice in 1874 meant that vessels could stay at sea longer and still supply fresh fish to the markets. A convenient overview of developments is provided by Mr G. Alward:

> The period 1825 to 1850 might be considered to be a new era in the fishing industry, particularly so far as trawling is concerned. The West country and Barking men were indulging in new methods of capturing fish and its conveyance, mainly to Billingsgate. New and improved methods were immediately found to produce better results, more particularly financially, both to the investors, who had built the vessels, and to those who managed them, and this alone was an incentive to proceed further in the attempt to produce even better methods and gear. So far as the development of the great British fisheries is concerned, from this time onwards the greater part should be placed to the credit of the Devonshire and Thames fishermen.
>
> It was not until about the middle of the century that the rapid growth of the trawl fishery commenced. The charts of the North Sea, which were published in 1847, gave a very imperfect description as to the depth, and the rough grounds where it was impossible to work the trawl nets.[3]

These developments came at a time of increasing public demand for fish. The influx of Irish Catholics in the 1840s was important in that as Catholics they ate fish on Fridays. And the beginning of fish and chip shops

---

1. *Sailors' Magazine (London)*, 1824, p.48.
2. Anon., 'The History of Trawling', *Fish Trades Gazette*, 19 March 1921, p.21.
3. G.L. Alward, *The Development of the British Fisheries during the Nineteenth Century* (a lecture published by Grimsby News Co. Ltd, February 1911), pp.14-15.

in the 1860s helped to further increase the demand.[1] Economic problems in the late 1870s, however, encouraged vessel owners to experiment with alternative methods and innovations. In November 1877 William Purdy, of North Shields, fitted trawl gear to the paddle tug, *Messenger*. In the same year David Allen, in Scotland, converted the *Pioneer* as the first steam drifter; and a year later, in January 1878, the Grimsby steam tug, *United*, was also adapted for trawling.[2] The experiment clearly had a marked effect and, in retrospect, hailed the end of the sailing smacks.

With the many developments in fishing equipment and techniques, an efficient and comprehensive infrastructure and the discovery of new fishing grounds, all-year-round fishing became commonplace – but this new situation soon gave rise to other problems, as F.G. Aflalo has noted:

> The Anglo-Saxon perpetually jeopardises his own welfare by over-production, and the fishing industry holds out greater temptations to over-produce than most. Shareholders in the big northern syndicates are human and look for dividends. [. . .] The captains and mates employed on their fleets are paid by results, and therefore they bring ashore as much fish as they can cram in their holds.[3]

This situation was exacerbated by the development of the fleeting system.

The Fleeting System

As the sailing smacks moved further out into the North Sea, the problem arose of getting the catches to market while the fish were still fresh. The fleeting system was a direct response to this situation. The idea was simple: a group of vessels would engage in catching fish, which could then be put onto larger and faster carrier ships for transportation to the fish market. The fishing industry, therefore, like many others, shared in a quarter century of economic prosperity, c.1850–c.1875. The fleeting system appears to have commenced in 1847, the initiative of two Barking companies.[4] Robb Robinson says fleeting 'had originated at Barking back in 1828, and by the mid-1830s the smacks trawling off the Isle of Man often worked in a similar manner, with one of them acting as a cutter to take their catches into Liverpool'.[5]

---

1. John K. Walton, *Fish and Chips and the British Working Class, 1870–1940* (London: Leicester University Press, 1992).
2. Robinson, *op. cit.* (1996), pp.85-87.
3. F.G. Aflalo, *The Sea Fishing Industry of England and Wales* (London: Edward Stanford, 1904), pp.32-33.
4. Trevor Lummis, *Occupation and Society: the East Anglian Fishermen 1880–1914* (Cambridge: Cambridge University Press, 1985), p.20.
5. Robinson, *op. cit.* (1996), p.71.

One of the owners, Samuel Hewett, came to dominate the industry when he introduced Scandinavian ice onto his carrier ships in c.1847, a lead reinforced by the introduction of steam-cutters to his fleet in 1864. Hewett's success was noted by others and by the 1870s there were numerous fleets of varying sizes:

> Each of the larger and better organised fleets has its definite fishing ground, varying perhaps with the season of the year. Three of the four Yarmouth fleets, for instance, will be found in summer fishing off the Dutch coast between Terschilling and Heligoland, while in winter the 'Blues' take up their position at the east end of the Silver Pits; the 'Leleu' and the 'Columbia' in Botney Gut. At the same season 6,000 men of Hull and Grimsby are trawling in the exposed and stormy waters off the Dogger Bank.[1]

Fleeting continued twenty-four hours a day throughout the year, the work being controlled by an 'admiral' who decided where and when to fish, using a system of coloured flares to indicate the lowering and hauling of nets. The largest fleet (Hewett's 'Short Blue Fleet') had up to 200 sailing smacks, and the smaller fleets had 50 to 60 vessels – the number in all cases fluctuating with the arrival and departure of individual fishing smacks. Each vessel fished with the fleet for about eight weeks followed by two or three days in the port. The work at sea was demanding and highly dangerous as each trunk of fish (weighing a hundredweight) was loaded on to the carrier vessel by hand from a small rowing boat.[2] The fleeting system peaked c.1879–83 with 12,000-15,000 fishermen employed night and day on the North Sea alone.[3] By the 1890s the innovation of steam-powered vessels transporting the fish to market from the fleets, led to the system's decline: once the carrier ships were seen to run well on steam it was not long before individual owners began experimenting with steam for their fishing smacks. Fish could then be quickly transported by individual vessels to the nearest port with a railway line and dispatched around the country. By the beginning of the twentieth century fleets were no longer the dominant force in the fishing industry and, given the conditions in the fleets, there was little incentive for fishermen to adhere to the system. By 1899 Hewett was laying up smacks, and with the sale

1. *Toilers of the Deep*, 1887, p.20.
2. *Toilers of the Deep*, May 1887, pp.120-121 (also May 1887, pp.94-101; Dec 1887, pp.246, 264).
3. Personal correspondence with Derek Farman, Norfolk, whose extensive research into the history of the fishing community in East Anglia has demonstrated that the number of vessels engaged in fleeting reached a peak during the period c.1879–83.

of the Short Blue Fleet about 1905 the fleeting system effectively came
to an end – although a few vessels continued fleeting until well into the
twentieth century.[1]

Conditions at Sea

Among the wider population there was a general ignorance about the
lives of fishermen, of where the fish came from and how it was caught. A
correspondent writing in the Mission to Deep Sea Fishermen's monthly
magazine, *Toilers of the Deep,* in October 1887, said: 'So many people to
whom I speak of the Mission to Deep Sea Fishermen seem quite surprised
to hear that all the fish eaten in England is not caught on the coast.'[2] Even
fewer were aware of the conditions in which these men worked:

> The deck, the bulwarks, the boats, the benches, the cooking
> vessels and even the bed clothes are slippery with the material
> which, however valuable for manure, is decidedly out of place
> under one's feet. The cabin is a kennel as small, as damp, and not
> so well lighted, as a coal cellar. Here the skipper and his crew eat,
> sleep, cook, smoke, and pass the wet hours, until after working
> day in and day out, resting as they can, and eating what they have,
> they complete their cruise. For weeks at a time, except for the
> opportunities they have of 'hailing' other fishermen, or fighting
> with them, the trawlers are unable to communicate with their
> species. Every now and then the owner's 'cutter' calls for their
> fish, and is itself towed in over the bar by the tug dispatched for
> that purpose. Finally, after enduring this kind of existence for
> two months at a stretch, or rather longer than it takes a clipper
> to steam to China and back, the skipper gropes his way home
> again, mainly by the unassisted light of reason, a steady course of
> soundings, a few well-known landmarks and 'the look of things'.
> For these services, and the worse than a dog's life he has to lead,
> his average earnings are only from twelve shillings to twenty-four
> shillings per week, with rations of the least luxurious description.
> A week is usually allowed for refitting, and then they are off again
> to the old routine. The only relief to the tedium of their lives is a
> battle with a Belgium *pecheur,* who has swept a scimitar-like 'devil'
> through the Englishman's nets, or a visit to one of the floating
> bumboats too well known as 'coopers'.[3]

---

1. *Toilers of the Deep,* July 1937.
2. *Toilers of the Deep,* October 1887, p.222.
3. 'The Woes of Smacksmen', *Toilers of the Deep,* October 1887, p.241.

Loading fish onto the carrier ship.

Cuts and injuries from fish bones, boils, broken limbs, crushed bodies, plus a whole range of illnesses, were regular occurrences at sea, and gales caused havoc among the fleets.[1] There was little medical help and, if injured fishermen were brought into port on a carrier ship, they were often forced to spend an extended period undergoing medical treatment, were often maimed for life and some might have simply died before reaching home. There was little respite from the perennial round of work and sleep, and when rest came it was often the result of a calm. Crews would visit one another's boats for company or would hail and visit passing vessels. Prior to the 1880s, they had little in the way of reading material, very few games on board and little opportunity for socialising. Then, the appearance of a 'coper' or 'cooper' (a floating grog-shop selling tobacco, liquor and other goods) was a welcome diversion. The effect of the liquor was often devastating, partly because the men had drunk little or nothing for many weeks and tended to drink far more than was good for them, and partly because the quality of the liquor was generally very poor. (See Chapter 6 for a brief overview of the rise and fall of the North Sea copering trade.)

---

1. *Toilers of the Deep*, January 1888, p.29.

Fishing Apprentices

Apart from the difficulties the fishermen experienced at sea, there were also problems in the ports. The lack of accommodation for visiting and stranded fishermen, and the lack of a central meeting-place in most fishing ports prior to the 1870s, left fishermen and apprentices to wander around the streets, usually gravitating towards the pubs and brothels and often ending up in gaol.[1]

When fishing was essentially a local industry, most boys began their work as apprentices, often going to sea for the first time with their fathers and uncles. With the rapid expansion of the fishing industry, in the second half of the nineteenth century, there were insufficient new recruits from this traditional source, and fishing smack owners began to look to orphanages, reformatories, workhouses, training ships and poor homes for boys aged about twelve years to be bound as apprentices (cabin boys) to the fishing industry. By the 1870s apprentices made up nearly a third of the crews sailing on Grimsby smacks and outnumbered indentured fishermen by 1,350 to 1,150. (In his inquiry on the treatment of apprentices in the Grimsby fishing trade in 1873, Baldwin Fleming put the figure for apprentices at 2,000.[2])

The recruitment of poor and underprivileged children as apprentices had gone on since the Elizabethan Poor Law Act of 1601, and conditions appear to have improved little since Jonas Hanway investigated the apprenticing of pauper children from the workhouses in the 1760s. Hanway's conclusion that 'apprenticeship was often little more than thinly-disguised slavery' could well have been applied to the apprenticing of boys to the fishing industry one hundred years later.[3] Prior to 1870 there was very little provision for the welfare of apprentices, each new boy being expected to lodge with the skipper's or mate's family when on shore, or with someone recommended by the skipper, master or owner. This lack of care gave rise to many problems, and the growing awareness of the situation led to responses from several directions. For example, a Fisherlads' Institute was opened in Grimsby in 1879 by the owners of large fishing companies.[4] Other responses came from local clergy, national seafarers' missions, the

1. *The Word on the Waters*, 1874, p.101.
2. Edward Gillet, *A History of Grimsby* (Hull: University of Hull Press, 1969), p.247; Baldwin Fleming, *The Treatment of Pauper Apprentices to the Grimsby Fishing Trade*, 19 June 1873 (Report drawn up for the Government and submitted to the Rt Hon. James Stansfeld MP, President of the Local Government Board), copy in the Local History section of the Grimsby Public Library, PRO MH/32/99.
3. Robinson, *op. cit.* (1996), p.53.
4. G.L. Alward, *The Sea Fisheries of Great Britain and Ireland* (Grimsby: Albert Gait, 1932), p.197.

general public, the newspapers of the day and the Government.[1] Mr Alward, the owner of a fishing company, drew attention to the problem at Grimsby in the 1870s:

> With so many young boys roaming around the fishing ports the owners recognised the need to have some controlling influence over them. Attempts were made at first to have the boys meet in the evenings for educational tuition, as few could read or write. Then Hostels and Fisherlads' Institutes were opened.[2]

Other facilities were quickly opened around the country. These included a Fishermen's Institute at Great Yarmouth in 1876, which incorporated a home for fishing apprentices, and there was a Smack Boys' Home in Ramsgate in 1878. But there were also earlier examples of the care and concern for orphans and sailor boys, such as the Rev. G.C. Smith's recommendation of a floating school for the Religious and Professional Improvement of Apprentices, and the foundation of St George's College for Sailor Boys by Mother Lydia Sellon in the 1850s (she hired a small cutter for the boys to use during their holidays). Also, in 1859, she opened an orphanage for the sons of mariners.[3]

Formal meetings for the Grimsby fisherlads were begun in 1871 with the establishment of a society in a room in the Temperance Hall:

> We have to go back to the year 1872 for the inception of the Fisherlads' Institute. [. . .] Mr Bradley, together with the late Mr George Brown, and one or two others talked the matter over, and decided to ask lads to come to classes. They took a room at the Temperance Hall as it was then called, now the King's Hall, and here they taught the lads reading, writing and arithmetic, and endeavoured to win their confidence and so gain a little control over them.[4]

As the numbers grew, larger premises were sought and an agent was appointed to devote his time to the apprentices. Local people were encouraged to subscribe to the establishment of a 'Fisherlads' Institute', which was subsequently opened in 1879. The venture proved highly successful with 10,870 fisherlads using the Institute in 1886 – although many of this number must have been regular visitors.[5]

---

1. Institutions, orphanages *etc.* were established in all the major fishing ports and many of the smaller ones. The Walrond Institute at Great Yarmouth, for example, was established by the Missions to Seamen.
2. Alward, *op. cit.* (1932), p.195; see also D. Boswell, *Sea Fishing Apprentices at Grimsby* (Grimsby Public Libraries, 1974), p.26.
3. T.J. Williams, *Priscilla Lydia Sellon* (London: SPCK, 1965), p.70.
4. *Grimsby News*, 27 January 1911.
5. Alward, *op. cit.* (1932), pp. 257-8.

Despite such developments, the ill-treatment of apprentices by some skippers and crew members gave rise to mounting concern. When two particularly nasty cases of ill-treatment in Grimsby and Hull came before the courts during the early 1880s, the details were widely disseminated in the newspapers, and this situation, along with growing concern about the general social conditions at sea and on shore, led to moves within the existing seafarers' missions to respond to the problems.[1]

Statistics

With the rapid development of the fishing industry during the mid-1800s, there was a massive growth in support industries, including fishmarkets, coopers, engineers, shipbuilders, rope-makers, net-makers and goods wagons on the railways. Yet with all this activity there appears to have been little interest in keeping statistics. His Excellency Spencer Walpole, then Lieutenant Governor of the Isle of Man, writing in 1883, bemoaned the lack of reliable and comprehensive statistical information: 'There are now no means of ascertaining with precision such simple facts as the number of persons engaged in the sea-fisheries of England and Wales.'[2] Mr Walpole, however, provided statistics for the year 1881 (see Chart 1 below).

Taking the full-time and part-time fishermen together these figures imply an average of four or five fishermen per boat (three or four in England and Wales, five or six in Scotland), but by the 1880s many vessels were regularly carrying between six and eight, and, in some cases, ten, fishermen. In 1885, for example, Staithes, on the North Yorkshire coast, had a fishing fleet of over 120 smacks and cobbles – each of the smacks carrying a crew of ten.[3] Other statistical sources do not help a great deal as the methodology is not standardised and this makes it impossible to estimate the number of vessels, fishermen and dependent workers with any accuracy. Nevertheless, if we estimate an average of only five or six fishermen per boat, the figure for Britain would be 200,000 (and at least one source suggests the figure should be 300,000[4]). Assuming 200,000 fishermen around 1880, it is possible, when we add dependent workers, the growing number of fish and chip shops, families and children, there may well have been in the region of one million people directly dependent on the British fishing industry.

1. Boswell, op. cit. (1974), pp.105-6.
2. Spencer Walpole, The Fisheries Exhibition Literature (London: Wm Clowes & Son, 1884), vol. I, pp.4-5.
3. The Times, 1885.
4. G. Holden Pike, Among the Sailors during the Life and Reign of the Queen (London: Hodder & Stoughton, 1897), p.234.
[38] Walpole, op. cit. (1884), pp.9-10.

Chart 1
Fishermen and Dependent Workers in Britain, 1881[38]

	Date	Fishing vessels	Fishermen F/T	Fishermen P/T	Dependent Workers
England and Wales	1881	15,000	42.000	14,000	35,000
Scotland	1881	14,809	48,121	48,000	48,000
Ireland (Plus 4,614)	1881	1,844	7,534	16,994*	
Isle of Man	1881	450	2,872		
Channel Isles	1881	300	1,000		
Totals:	1881	37,017	101,527	78,994	83,000

* The figures for Ireland, the Isle of Man and the Channel Islands are incorporated with the figures for England and Wales.

Chapter 2
The Social and Theological Context

Introduction

The 1851 Census of Religious Activity in Britain undertaken by Horace Mann has been criticised for its emphasis on church attendance as the yardstick of religious commitment. The concept of popular religion was largely ignored (the term used in the nineteenth century was 'diffusive Christianity') and, perhaps inevitably, the working-classes, who were thought to make up the bulk of non-attenders, found themselves viewed as, at best, 'unconscious secularists' and, at worst, as pagans in need of salvation.[1] After the census the number of Christian organisations established with the aim of winning the souls of working-class people multiplied; although increasing prominence was given to social welfare, spiritual welfare remained an important factor, especially for evangelicals. Nevertheless, the general assent to the social gospel during the second half of the nineteenth century opened the way for social and political activities by Christians, which would have previously been considered unacceptable.

During the mid-Victorian era in Britain the many social changes affected and reflected, at least in part, changing theological perspectives, all of which had a dramatic effect upon Christian missions. This was no less true of missions among seafaring people than in other areas of Victorian life and labour. What is surprising is that, while the British fishing industry experienced a massive expansion during the 1840s and 1850s, with the shift from inshore to deep-sea fishing and an improving infrastructure, remarkably little concern was shown for this workforce at sea until the 1880s, although there was some preparatory work undertaken during the early part of the century.

Among the pioneers, the Revd. Carl Gustav von Bülow and William Henry Angus both obtained vessels in the early 1820s, the former for work along the Scandinavian coast, while the latter visited the coasts of Holland

---

1. For a brief discussion of 'diffusive religion', see G. Parsons, *Religion in Victorian Britain: Vol II Controversies* (Manchester: Manchester University Press for the Open University, 1988), pp.77-79.

and Germany. Both visited seafaring, especially fishing communities, and both were supported by the British and Foreign Sailors' Society. In 1839, the Rev. Dr John Ashley, supporting himself financially, obtained a vessel named the *Eirene* and established his work among fishing communities on the islands and among the fishing fleets in the Bristol Channel. Ashley's work subsequently influenced the founders of the Thames Church Mission in 1844 and the establishment of the Missions to Seamen in 1856. Other pioneers, such as Thomas Rosie and Henry Cook, were also supported by the BFSS. Rosie inaugurated the Scottish Coast Mission (SCM) working with fishing communities during the 1850s in his vessel; and Cook established his Portsmouth and Gosport Seamen's Mission in 1869, maintaining several vessels that worked along the south coast of England and the French coast and canals. There were also some individual clergy who, in their boats, occasionally visited the fishing fleets just off the coast of their parishes, including the vicar of a parish at the mouth of the Thames, who sailed in his boat the *Kingfisher*.[1]

Despite these and other early developments, it is surprising that seafaring communities have since been neglected in studies concerned with the religion of the working-classes. When it is considered that seafarers (including fishermen) and their dependents might account for over two million individuals by 1881 (over five per cent of the population), we cannot write off this group of predominantly working-class people with respect to their religious/spiritual beliefs and practices. Kennerley has estimated that during the nineteenth century there were well over 100 Christian maritime missions in Britain concerned with seafarers, to which could be added innumerable Sailors' Bethels, Sailors' Rests, Fishermen's Reading Rooms, Smack Boys' Homes, facilities for apprentices and a wide range of religious and secular benevolent societies.[2] Yet historical and theological studies show an almost complete disregard for this significant and important group. Gerald Parsons, for example, makes only one brief reference to fishermen in his study of *Religion in Victorian Britain, Vol I*; and Kenneth Scott Latourette in his mammoth study on the expansion of Christianity has only a passing note about the founder of the Royal National Mission to Deep Sea Fishermen – and gets the details wrong![3]

---

1. J. Scarth, *Into All the World* (London: Griffith, Farran, Okeden & Welsh, 1890), p.28.
2. Kennerley, *op. cit.* (September 1989), App. 5.
3. Parsons, *op. cit.* (1988) p.215; Kenneth Scott Latourette, *A History of the Expansion of Christianity*, *Vol. 4* (London: Harper & Row, 1970), p.149. Latourette says that: 'the MDSF was begun by a clergyman of the Church of England.' Far from being an Anglican clergyman, the founder, E.J. Mather, was a member of the Plymouth Brethren until 1883 when he joined the Church of England as a layman.

Unfortunately, the number of nineteenth-century British seafarers is notoriously difficult to obtain, although from various sources it is possible to suggest some estimated figures. The fishing industry alone employed over 200,000 men and boys at sea in the early 1880s, plus at least 100,000 dependent workers on shore, and numberless others who were indirectly involved.[1] If we add to these figures labourers' families, we reach a rough estimate of approximately one million people dependent on the British fishing industry. This figure can be more than doubled if we include those people directly and indirectly dependent on the work of merchant and naval seafarers.[2] Kennerley, for example, has estimated the number of seafarers employed on merchant vessels in the UK in 1881 as 192,900. Given these figures, it is indeed very odd that seafarers have received so little attention in studies on working-class religion. Nevertheless, more recent research into the development of the Church's work among fishing communities in the nineteenth century shows that there were many independent factors that influenced this work, and that we cannot talk of the origin of fishermen's missions without considering the changing circumstances that precipitated the need for an appropriate response.

What was the Government doing in terms of social welfare for the fishing communities? While some societies were established by Christian groups and individual philanthropists working in the fishing industry, there was little in the way of government intervention in seamen's welfare, and no national coordinated attempt to oversee seamen's welfare work, until Mr Ernest Bevin, Minister of Labour and National Service, established the Seamen's Welfare Board (SWB), in 1940. A report on the implications of the board's work was published in 1944 by R.J.P. Mortished, although his comment on the work of seafarers' missions was somewhat insensitive and patronising:

> It may therefore be necessary for the voluntary organisations to reconsider the part they should play in the lives of merchant seamen and to concentrate their activities on catering for the religious needs of the men, with entertainment and charitable work figuring only as incidental activities.[3]

Unfortunately, the tone of this comment was not uncommon in SWB publications, and Kennerley has explored the attempts of the 'SWB to regulate the voluntary sector outside statutory control'. While some of

---

1. Walpole, *op. cit.* (1884), pp.9-10.
2. Kennerley, op. cit. (September 1989), App. 1b.
3. R.J.P. Mortished, 'Developments in Welfare Work for British Seamen', *International Labour Review*, September 1944, p.333.

the criticisms were no doubt valid, especially regarding the poor standards within some of the institutions, the major religious maritime missions took exception to the content of the SWB reports. But this mid-twentieth-century development is outside the range of the discussion for the present work.[1] Despite the Government's lack of practical intervention in seamen's welfare during the nineteenth century, several government reports were produced during the 1870s and 1880s about the problems within the fishing industry and these gave rise to greater public concern, especially about the men's conditions at sea. This present study of fishermen's missions in Britain supports in part the view that such missions were essentially a response to social, economic, political and technological changes. But this does not convincingly account for the apparently late development of an organised, dedicated fishermen's mission towards the end of the fishing-fleet boom in the early 1880s. We must also take into account changing theological perspectives and the increasing emphasis placed upon an incarnational theology, which in turn affected the nature of Christian missions.

Missions to Fishing Communities

In the case of the Mission to Deep Sea Fishermen, the initiative for the development of its organised work at sea came not from the established seafarers' missions, but from a fishing fleet owner who was concerned ostensibly about the spiritual state and the welfare of his employees (and certainly about their productivity). He in turn may also have been influenced by Government reports on conditions at sea in the fishing fleets. It is important to remember that practically all the methods used by the Mission to Deep Sea Fishermen and other maritime missions during the last two decades of the nineteenth century had been in use since well before the advent of the Victorian era. As Donald Lewis has noted, a number of historians have tended to argue that the urban slums were evangelised almost exclusively by the Ritualists, thus ignoring the significant work of other groups.[2] The evangelicals were especially active among seafaring communities in the early years of the nineteenth century – although, apart from the work of a few individuals, much of the work tended to be shore-based, on converted hulks refitted as chapels and churches stationed in ports around the country, and by means of small launches in the docks and rivers.

While the BFSS and the MS sent individual missionaries to visit the fishing fleets at sea during the 1860s and 1870s, later organisations equipped sailing chapels and churches for work at sea among the fishing fleets

1. Kennerley, *op. cit.* (1989), pp.227-37.
2. Donald M. Lewis, *Lighten Their Darkness* (London: Greenwood Press, 1986).

throughout the 1880s and 1890s. The organised response was dominated by representatives of the Church of England evangelicals, represented by the Mission to Deep Sea Fishermen (1881), an offshoot of the Thames Church Mission (1844–1939), and the Anglo-Catholics, represented by the St Andrew's Waterside Church Mission (SAWCM)(1864–1939), along with its offshoot the North Sea Church Mission (NSCM)(1896–1906). Of these two groups (evangelicals and Anglo-Catholics), it was the evangelicals who eventually dominated the work, while the Anglo-Catholic societies gave up their work at sea and eventually threw in their lot with the more liberal Missions to Seamen (1856–) during the early years of the twentieth century.[1]

The rise and development of these organised Christian missions at sea was motivated by three major factors. First, the rapid expansion of the British fishing industry from c.1840 to c.1880, with more men at sea for long periods of time, as a result of the 'fleeting system', led to concern about the spiritual and physical welfare of fishermen and their apprentices. Second, an increase in public awareness of social, economic and moral abuses led to a sense of urgency in responding to these issues, especially as the fleeting system reached its peak c.1879–80. Third, as theological perspectives within Victorian religion began to change during the second half of the nineteenth century (from an emphasis on the Atonement to an emphasis on the Incarnation), a more general concern with social, economic and political issues began to emerge. While each of these factors does not alone offer a sufficient explanation for the rise of dedicated fishermen's missions during the 1880s and 1890s, the combination of factors can provide some insight into the development of fishermen's missions in general and the Mission to Deep Sea Fishermen in particular.

The 1880s also saw increased focus on the degree and nature of poverty, especially in London and other major cities, and the MDSF leadership cannot but have been influenced by the work of the Christian Socialists during the 1880s – such as that undertaken by Rev. Samuel Barnett whose East End constituency encompassed the London Docks. Barnett and his wife established Toynbee Hall in 1884 with a small number of educated volunteers who lived and worked amongst the poor of London's East End. In the same year, the Rev. Stewart Headlam established his Guild of St Matthew in the slums of Bethnal Green.

---

1. The Missions to Seamen has gone through several changes of name. It began as the Missions to Seamen Afloat at Home and Abroad in 1856. It's founder was W.H.G. Kingston and his wife and his sister designed the 'Flying Angel' logo which has been used for the society since that date. In 1858 its name was changed to the Missions to Seamen, and in 2000 to the Mission to Seafarers.

There were also several influential publications that brought the social condition of the poor to the notice of the public. Kathleen Heasman has argued that a general Christian social concern was especially motivated following Andrew Mearns' publication of his pamphlet *The Bitter Cry of Outcast London* in 1883.[1] In 1886 Charles Booth began his investigation into the *Life and Labour of People in London*; and in 1890 the Salvation Army leader, William Booth, published his *In Darkest England and the Way Out*. These and other publications, especially the Government reports of the late 1870s and early 1880s, had a significant impact on the churches' response to the needs of the poor.[2] To these published concerns should be added some very practical action on the part of the poor – not least the London Match Girls' Strike in 1888, and the London Dockers' Strike in 1889.

While many people were sympathetic to the work of maritime missions, much early criticism was levelled at the TCM, the MDSF and Mather for not giving credit to the already long history of the various seafarers' missions, even if it had been sporadic. The publicity literature of the MDSF gave the impression that it was initiated as a mission to fishermen without precedent, although this was manifestly not the case. All aspects of the work of the society had their antecedents (Bethel ships, ship visitation, services at sea, literature distribution, tracts, Bibles, woollens, employment of seafarers as mission staff, the sending of mission staff to visit the fishermen at sea, and the recording of statistics). Mather demonstrated his knowledge of this earlier work in October 1881, when he addressed the Newcastle Church Congress (Appendix 4), but his genius lay in his ability to unite all these various elements to meet a specific need, and in his willingness to take risks where others would not. He also had a good eye for publicity, and a charismatic personality, which paid dividends in terms of fund-raising.

When the fleeting system reached its peak around 1880 there was already a growing public interest in the social and economic problems faced by the fishing communities, as well as among the working class generally, and, when cases of abuse and the murder of apprentices came before the courts in the late 1870s, calls for action led to the Payment of Wages Act in 1880. This Act, which referred to the apprentices' lack of pay, ill-treatment by their employers, and their excessive imprisonment, brought the issues to the attention of the public although other problems were beginning to surface and a report of 1883 had a more far-reaching effect. Other

1. Kathleen Heasman, *Evangelicals in Action* (London: Geoffrey Bles, 1962), p.48.
2. Andrew Mearns, *The Bitter Cry of Outcast London* (London: J. Clark & Co., 1883); Charles Booth, *Life and Labour of the People in London* (London: 1889); William Booth, *In Darkest England and the Way Out* (London: 1890).

Government action came in the form of an 1881 report that examined 'Outrages Committed by Foreign upon English Fishermen in the North Sea' (referring to the so-called 'Belgium Devil', a sharpened implement towed through the nets of British trawlers by foreign fishing vessels). Other reports were also in progress, such as the 1882 inquiry into the need for legislation regarding 'Relations between the Owners, Masters, and Crews of Fishing Vessels'.[1] The rising militancy of fishermen also began to worry the fishing companies.

Three issues particularly drew sympathy from middle-class Victorians: the abuses of drink, sex and children. When the MDSF came into existence, it was mainly based on outrage at abuses in these categories, although it is intriguing that the TCM did not capitalise in its publicity about the liquor trade of the copers (vessels that sailed among the fishing fleets selling, especially, tobacco, liquor and pornographic items) until well after the establishment of the MDSF. Indeed, Mather's diary notes from his first trip to the North Sea fleets, make no mention of the copers, nor is there any mention of copering activities in his address to the Newcastle Church Congress in 1881. He did, however, provide a brief account of the copers' activity in his earliest publication, 'Trust Christ More' (making use of the Thames Church Mission acronym, TCM), which initially appeared in *Sunday at Home*, c.1882, and subsequently as a booklet in 1884.[2]

After 1884, the 'fight against the copers' became an important publicity item when public funds were needed – the society publicised its activities against what it called the 'Devil's Mission ships' (see Chapter 6) when it became obvious that fishing alone was not going to ensure sufficient funds for the Bethel ships, and the effect of the economic recession during the early 1880s began to bite.

After the initial success of the first TCM/MDSF Bethel ship, the *Ensign*, several businessmen came forward to offer support for the purchase of further vessels. The development of a fleet of Bethel ships, therefore, appears to have been the result of an economic opportunity that presented itself to several businessmen, rather than Mather's own idea. And later, when Mather eventually found himself solely responsible for the growing fleet of vessels, this was the direct result of economic difficulties faced by the growing band of businessmen who had invested in the purchase of Bethel ships on the basis that they would each personally, including

1. Sources for the Acts are as follows: Merchant Seamen's (Payment of Wages, &c.) Act 1880, 43 & 44 Vict. c.16. BPP LXXXII, 1881. BPP, XVII, 1882.
2. Mather's diary notes were printed in the TCM Annual Report for 1881 and are reproduced in Appendix 5.

Mather, receive a percentage of the profits. When the vessels became a financial liability, the businessmen sold their shares to Mather and left him with the sole responsibility for the work. This situation led to a crisis in 1884, which resulted in the eventual separation of the TCM and the MDSF, and the re-establishment of the MDSF on a new basis in 1886. After the reorganisation, the work prospered and other organisations began to take note of the development. The MDSF, during its restructuring as an independent organisation, formally disassociated itself from the Thames Church Mission and declared itself to be an un-denominational society, although it retained close links with the Church of England. By the early years of the twentieth century, the MDSF (which had now been given permission to use the title 'Royal') found itself with a monopoly of work amongst fishermen at sea. As social, economic and technological changes continued to affect the British fishing industry, the Royal National Mission to Deep Sea Fishermen expanded its shore-based work by developing mission stations and hostels with accommodation for fishermen who were working in ports other than their own.

While the loss of life at sea resulting directly from alcohol abuse is extremely difficult to assess (as is the amount of financial loss incurred by owners and fishermen, and the subsequent suffering of families on shore), there were sufficient cases of injury and death to supply journalists and the various seafarers' missions with a steady source of material for publication during the 1880s. That the extent of the abuses directly related to alcohol was overplayed by the MDSF and other mission agencies cannot be in doubt, but the resulting income from public subscriptions provided the society with a means of helping meet other needs such as medical aid.

The society's change of emphasis from concern with combatting alcohol abuse to the provision of professional medical aid at sea after 1886 was due partly to the ban on the sale of liquor at sea agreed by European governments at the Hague Conference of July 1886, and partly to the involvement with the MDSF of Sir Frederick Treves, the eminent Victorian surgeon. Treves and his doctors (one of the most notable being Wilfred Grenfell), who volunteered to spend time among the fishing fleets, pioneered the work of sailing hospitals and helped change the emphasis of the MDSF from that of a primary focus on evangelism to a joint one on spiritual and social welfare. Nevertheless, while the early development of the MDSF can be directly linked to rapid changes in the economic situation, this fact alone does not explain the public's willingness to support the work, hence more general changes in attitudes within the churches towards the causes and effects of poverty must have played a part.

During the 1890s, representatives of the Victorian Anglo-Catholics (notably the St Andrew's Waterside Church Mission and the North Sea Church Mission) objected to the proliferation of evangelical Bethel ships and developed their own 'sailing churches' for work amongst the fishing fleets. This action heralded a period of competition between the various Anglo-Catholic and evangelical missions. The situation, however, resolved itself when the SAWCM and the NSCM found that financial constraints made it increasingly difficult to sustain their work at sea, and both societies sold their vessels. The NSCM ceased to exist, and the SAWCM eventually amalgamated with the Missions to Seamen. The Salvation Army's Salvation Navy (which had four vessels by 1900) also curtailed its British work in the North Sea by the beginning of the First World War, although the Salvation Army continued its work along the British inland waterways and in other countries, including Iceland and Newfoundland (see Chapter 5).

It is difficult at this stage to determine the extent of the success of the sailing chapels and churches. The SAWCM and the NSCM objected to keeping statistics regarding attendance at services on board their sailing churches. The RNMDSF, on the other hand, has always kept copious statistics, and used these to great effect in gaining public support. Unfortunately, there are inconsistencies in the various versions of the published statistics, and no complete set now exists for the 1880s and 1890s. Even so some information can be gleaned from those available, especially about the society's annual meetings when figures were published in local and national newspapers. For example, the number of prayer books given out by the TCM diminished considerably when Mather took over as Secretary, and the number of tracts given out increased dramatically. This would appear to reflect the growing evangelical influence within the society. Other statistics, such as those that relate to medical aid, cause more problems. Here the often very high figures do not distinguish between new cases and those fishermen returning for follow-up treatment.

Fishermen's Benevolent Societies

Given the constant dangers faced by fishermen, many local initiatives in the form of benevolent societies sprang up to respond to the tragic loss of life at sea by providing financial support for those left behind. In most cases fishermen were asked to give a small sum to one of these societies to ensure support if or when it was needed. Many of these initiatives were established by local clergy for the members and parishioners under their care. One of the earliest such initiatives, the Seamen's Box, also known as the Shipmasters' Society of Aberdeen, was established in 1598 and 'founded for the auld, agit and decrepit maisters and mariners of the Burgh of Aberdeen', the funds being kept in an old seafarer's chest known as the 'sure and lockit box'. That the society remained popular is shown by a later comment that in 1670 the society was permitted to establish a loft (gallery) in the Kirk of St Nicholas, Aberdeen, for the sole use of seafarers.[1]

Over subsequent years other such societies were developed around the British coast. One of the earliest nineteenth-century benevolent societies specifically for fishermen was the Flamborough Fishermen's Fund. Established on 7 September 1809, it was run by a committee of nine people who were elected at the Annual General Meeting in Flamborough. Members were to be Flamborough fishermen and, following admission to membership, they were expected to pay two shillings per month, but were not entitled to benefits for the first three years. Benefits were various: four shillings per week during periods of unemployment, as the result of illness or other reasons not resulting from misconduct; and, on the death of a fisherman, twenty shillings to his widow, plus a weekly payment of one shilling per child.[2]

As these initiatives gathered momentum, other developments began to follow, including the Destitute Sailors' Asylum (DSA), opened in 1828, and the Well Street Sailors' Home, opened in 1829. Both were developed by the Rev. G.C. Smith and his friends. Smith also recognised the need for more specialised organisations to help different categories of seamen, including a junior department for boys. This latter development was later copied for fishing apprentices, and several religious and secular institutes and societies for these sprang up around the coast during the latter part of the nineteenth century.

By the 1830s initiatives to improve the lot of fishermen as a class were emerging, for example, the Fishermen's Refuge in Yorkshire, formed in January 1834 and possibly influenced by the work of the Flamborough Fishermen's Fund. The Refuge, a Church of England charity, was initially established to benefit the fisherfolk of Staithes and Runswick, with aims including: alleviating 'sad and afflicting loss of life'; giving ten shillings and six pence to those who sought to save the lives of others by 'affording compensation for the loss of property at sea'; and by supporting and providing 'for their wives and children' when the fishermen were drowned. The idea soon spread and the work was expanded to embrace the whole of the Yorkshire coast. Fishermen were invited to pay two shillings and six pence as admission to membership, and then one shilling a month for the first year, after which they were eligible for the benefits of the society. Under its more extended form of

---

1. Alexander Clark, *A Short History of the Shipmasters Society* (Aberdeen: William Smith & Sons, 1911) (source: *The Aberdeen Newspaper Weekly Journal*, Thursday 3 April 1947, p.1).

2. See 'Flamborough Fishermen's Fund, 1809', in Robinson, op. cit. (1996), p.20.

a *General Charity* for the equal benefit of all Fishermen on this dangerous Coast, it has obtained the high and special Patronage of their Royal Highnesses the Duchess of Kent and the Princess Victoria, and also of His Grace the Archbishop of York, and of many of the principal Noblemen and Ladies of the neighbourhood, the Clergy, and other charitable and distinguished persons interested in its welfare.[1]

Until the establishment of the Refuge, fishermen (apart from a few exceptions) received little in the way of financial benefit other than parish relief. The Rev. W.T. Wild of Lofthouse, the founder of the Refuge, however, impressed on the fishermen that, although this benefit would not be affected, they should not claim two benefits when they could manage on one. The option, nevertheless, remained open for those suffering particular hardship, and a committee was established with a jury of seven to twelve fishermen to decide on individual cases. The scheme appears to have succeeded well, as a pamphlet was published two years later giving details of the charity and requesting further support.

Despite the concern shown by Rev. Wild, there was no Anglican Church in Staithes until the school room was licensed for worship in 1849 (later being rededicated as the Mission Church of St Peter). But the Anglicans did not fare well, and in 1885 a *Times* correspondent commented on the religious situation in the village: '

Many of the local fishermen — the majority indeed — have gone over to dissent, the primary cause for this inclination being, as in the case of the Durham pitmen, that the Church has left them greatly to themselves.[2]

Other developments had already taken place on the south-west coast aimed at providing seafarers with Christian reading. For example, the Bristol Marine Bible Association, established by Wesleyan Methodists and some Anglican clergymen, had been active since 1820.[3] Marine Bible Associations had also been developed in the north of England, including the Tyne Union Bible Committee (1814), the Whitby Auxiliary Bible Society (1812), the Whitby Bible Association and the Whitby Religious Tract Society (both in 1813), the Sandsend and Blyth Bible Association (1813), the Hull Marine Bible Association (1817); and, among others, associations at Liverpool (1818), Aberdeen (1817) and the Shetland Islands (1818).

---

1. *The Fishermen's Refuge* (1836), pp.3-4 (a small booklet in the Leeds Reference Library, Ref. 361 F53Y); and *The Yorkshire Gazette*, 18 January 1834.
2. Quoted in D Clark, between Pulpit and Pew (Cambridge: Cambridge University Press, 1982), p.58
3. *Sailors' Magazine (London)*, 1820, pp.341-2; also Kverndal, *op. cit.* (1986), p.224.

Societies were also established in the nineteenth century with various benevolent objectives, including the benefit of orphans and apprentices, such as the Port of Hull Society for the care of orphans and, later in the century, the Sailors' Orphan Society of Scotland established at Glasgow University in 1889.[1] A number of late nineteenth-century churches and organisations also opened and ran orphanages, for example, the Grimsby and Cleethorpes Orphanage for the Daughters of Fishermen and Sailors, established in 1898 by St Andrew's Church – although this orphanage struggled financially and closed two years later.[2]

There were hospitals and hospices founded specifically for seamen and fishermen, such as the Seamen's Hospital, Whitby, in 1676,[3] and the Fishermen's Hospital at Great Yarmouth, founded in 1702 by the Great Yarmouth Corporation for old and decayed fishermen.[4] Such institutions served an important purpose, but they could not meet the medical needs of fishermen at sea, especially those working among the fishing fleets in the nineteenth century.

Many charitable organisations, such as the Rechabites, Shepherds and the Royal Antediluvian Order of Buffaloes (RAOB, known as the BUFFS to its members), as well as churches and chapels, also ran benevolent societies of various kinds in the country's fishing ports. In addition, there were various secular societies established to provide financial, medical and residential support for fishermen and other seafarers. For example, the Shipwrecked Fishermen and Mariners' and Royal Benevolent Society was founded in 1839 to provide help for those former merchant seamen, fishermen and their widows who were experiencing need. The Royal Alfred Seafarers' Society, founded in 1865, still has a home in Surrey where it provides residential, respite and dementia nursing care for elderly, sick and disabled seafarers, including fishermen. In 1877, the villagers of Marshside, near Fleetwood, developed a slightly different benefit scheme called the Fishermen's Provident Association; members paid a subscription that helped local fishermen to buy and insure their own vessels. This was an especially important approach for fishermen, given the growing cost of fishing vessels.[5] Other 'provident' schemes provided homes for retired fishermen, such as the Royal Provident Homes in Grimsby erected in 1897.

---

1. Archive material is located at the Centre for Business History in Scotland, University of Glasgow.
2. SAWCM Minutes, 13 October 1900.
3. Rev. George Young, *A Picture of Whitby and its Environs* (1840), p.230.
4. Notice on the wall at the entrance to the Gt Yarmouth Fishermen's Hospital.
5. Thompson, Wailey and Lummis, *op. cit.* (1983), Ch. 5.

Some individuals and groups in the fishing industry also established institutions for the benefit of the fishing community, although Kennerley has made the point that such initiatives generally came from people of some social standing. He observed that 'initiatives from serving seafarers, due to the nature of their sea employment, were predictably rare'. But he has drawn attention to one significant case: the Great Yarmouth Shipwrecked Sailors' Home, which was initiated and established by the fishermen and boatmen of Great Yarmouth in 1858, with support from the local authority. Facilities included a school, library, museum and refreshments for which members paid one penny per week. Kennerley has also provided some statistics for this initiative showing that the average annual usage of the premises and facilities for the years 1859–64 was 219 members, and 2,400 visitors.[1] Other initiatives included the provision of educational facilities, especially for the growing number of apprentices; Messrs Orby Bradley and George Brown of Grimsby were foremost in establishing some educational classes for fishing apprentices in 1871, developing this into a Fisherlads' Institute in 1879.

Thus, in the nineteenth century there was a wide range of religious and secular initiatives established for fishermen and their families. Many of these were developed by people with strong spiritual and religious leanings, such as the 200-bed, new, model Sailors' Home in Poplar, opened in 1841 by George Green of Blackwell, and the Sailors' Orphan Society for fifty boys and fifty girls established by the Episcopal Floating Church Society (EFCS).[2] Other seafarers' homes were to follow in the country's ports.

Theological Developments in Victorian Britain
The Bethel societies, which grew up in the 1820s, were primarily concerned with winning converts, and little thought was given to the social conditions of the seamen – although there were some significant exceptions, such as the Rev. G.C. Smith's innovations, especially his sailors' homes. But the missions, including the major societies like the British and Foreign Sailors' Society, were initially primarily focussed on the spiritual aspects of the work.[3] By mid-century, however, this situation was beginning to change, influenced by several theological issues, including the Anglo-Catholic revival of the 1840s and later by the number of Anglo-Catholics working in inner-city parishes.

---

1. Kennerley, *op. cit.* (1989), p.85 (details from Norfolk Record Office, SO4/1.Minute Book 1, 1858–66).
2. BFSS Report (1942), p.22.
3. There have been several name changes over the years: from British and Foreign Sailors' Society to British Sailors' Society in 1925, the British and International Sailors' Society in 1995 and the Sailors' Society in 2007.

The period of rapid growth of the British fishing industry, 1840–80, was marked in the earlier years by the so-called Crisis of Faith in Victorian religion, and by a more tolerant attitude and pervasive pluralism by the 1880s. The traditional view, that the crisis was between the churches and the scientific community, has been challenged by J.L. Atholtz, who argued that the struggle of faith was essentially a crisis within Victorian religion, rather than one against outside foes.[1] However, while the educated laity took an interest in the growing importance of Biblical Criticism and the challenges of scientific knowledge, and began to have doubts about traditional views on the causes of poverty, there were many evangelicals who simply longed to see the numbers of Christian converts grow.[2]

Although much social concern was evident among evangelical Christians, from the mid-nineteenth century onwards, the primary concern was usually evangelism, and this was no less true of evangelicals in seafarers' missions than in other spheres. The Mission to Deep Sea Fishermen, like its contemporary the Salvation Army, could claim regular converts, and this in turn ensured evangelical support. In this sense, the society was part of the general missionary concern and, in reaching out to fishermen at sea, it had a great deal in common with overseas missions – an impression that was reinforced when Wilfred Grenfell established the work of the MDSF in Labrador, following his first visit there in 1892. By the 1880s a shift was discernible within Victorian Christianity away from an emphasis on prayer, patronage and paternalism, towards a recognition that the churches should first help in the alleviation of poverty and its subsequent problems before expecting the working classes to respond to evangelism. This shift was especially linked to changing theological perspectives: from an emphasis on the Atonement in the 1830s to an emphasis on the Incarnation by the 1880s – a situation that owed much to the Anglo-Catholics and Christian Socialists. Gerald Parsons has argued that this shift of emphasis 'was neither the product nor the property of any one theological tradition', although the new view had been forcefully argued by F.D. Maurice and the Christian Socialists.[3] The influence of the Roman Catholics, not least of Cardinal Manning who had successfully acted as the arbitrator during the London Dock Strike of 1889, must also have goaded many non-Catholics into taking a more practical interest in the welfare of the poor and underprivileged.

---

1. J.L. Atholz (ed.), *The Mind and Art of Victorian England* (Minneapolis: University of Minnesota Press, 1976).
2. A.D. Gilbert, *Religion and Society in Industrial England* (London: Longman, 1976), pp.54-5.
3. Parsons, *op. cit.*, Vol. II (1988), p.59.

The growing emphasis on social welfare became a means of answering those who attacked the Church as being narrow and unconcerned. The earlier marked contrast within evangelicalism, between dogmatism on the one hand and a high moral sensitivity on the other,[1] left many evangelicals ambivalent about their response to social welfare. But as the century progressed, and the nature of poverty and its consequences became part of daily public reading, even the most conservative evangelicals could not ignore the issues, despite being divided over the causes. This ambivalence was mirrored in the Mission to Deep Sea Fishermen where there were constant requests for, and reaffirmations that, the work was essentially spiritual and primarily concerned with evangelism. Despite the rising awareness of the need for Christians to be engaged in economic, social and political reform, the growing number of evangelicals were nevertheless keen to support those successful missions with evangelistic motives. Faced with growing pluralism, the results of the 1851 census (plus the local censuses of 1881) and fears of a more pervasive secularism, the success of the MDSF must have appealed to many frustrated evangelicals.

Perhaps significantly, E.J. Mather and his Thames Church Mission colleagues were able to cash in on the wave of optimism raised by Moody and Sankey's London Revival Meetings of 1883 and 1884, and Mather and the TCM Committee talked initially only of spiritual work amongst the deep-sea fishermen. That the work was 'spiritual' in nature was also emphasised by the fishing fleet owner, Samuel Hewett, who invited members of the TCM to visit his North Sea fleet in 1881. It is unlikely that Hewett would have encouraged the TCM to engage in social work at sea as this would have implied criticism of his fishing company. Even so, by the mid-1880s Mather recognised the need to appeal to a broader spectrum of the populace and he began moving towards the reformation of the MDSF. The years 1885–86 therefore saw a growing emphasis on philanthropic concern – a change that had been preceded in his own life when he moved from the Plymouth Brethren to the Church of England in 1883. (Although, he may have been influenced to make this move partly by events, such as increasing secession, within the Brethren movement.)

Evangelicals caught up in the frenzied round of 'doing good' did so partly to avoid condemnation and eternal punishment. The growing emphasis on a theology that played down the concept of eternal punishment was an important aspect of the evangelical need to redefine their *raison d'être* for doing good works. That Mather managed to retain the support of evangelicals and liberal Christians, whilst at the same time developing a mission that appealed to the philanthropic spirit of the wider public,

1. Atholz, *op. cit.* (1976).

was a credit to his publicity skills. This wide-ranging support was an important factor in the MDSF's continued development and, if the society had not modified its theological stance in this direction in 1886, when a new Council was convened, it is unlikely that it would have survived the initial stages of its development. The two aims of spiritual and social welfare, however, caused problems not only for evangelical supporters, who objected to the perceived growing emphasis (at least in the publicity) on social welfare, but also for supporters of the High Church, Saint Andrew's Waterside Mission (SAWM), who objected to what they saw as an undue emphasis on evangelism and a foregoing of the responsibilities entailed in parochial ministry.

The inauguration of the SAWM along ritualistic lines in 1864 inevitably precipitated confrontation with the Thames Church Mission when both organisations engaged in ship visitation at Gravesend. The former society proposed an amalgamation with the latter in 1867, but the offer was curtly rejected. By the 1870s some members of the Church of England, especially supporters of the SAWM, were pressing for a direct response to the problems facing fishermen – as may be seen from Church Congress reports calling for ships to be sent to visit fishing fleets. In 1886, the British and Foreign Bible Society lamented 'the prevailing spirit of antagonism between the Anglo-Catholics and the Nonconformists' – a situation that was becoming more visible in the country's fishing ports, as the MDSF began to be more successful in its work. Anglo-Catholics objected to the proliferation of lay-workers and the

> Salvation Army kind of service, which, if [the fishermen] attend, they are invited to make a declaration that they are saved, so that the return of souls saved may be tabulated, added up, and sent in with the fish we have for breakfast.[1]

But the situation is not as clear-cut as this comment suggests. To take Grimsby as just one example of the churches supported by the SAWM, we find that the mission curate, the Rev. H.T. Harte, provided, at least from 1878, some statistics about his work in the port. During the winter season, for example, an average of twenty fisherlads attended evening services.[2] His later reports provide more detail about the work, such as: 'During the past year [1879] I have supplied 361 vessels with books, tracts, illustrated papers *etc.*' When Mr D. Henry Lee was appointed Missioner in 1884, he kept a diary of the number of visits made to the Mission Room. With Mr Lee's retirement in 1888, the various statistics cease to appear except for

1. Report of the Church Congress, Norwich, 1895, 350.
2. SAWM Report, 1884.

occasional references to the success or otherwise of the work. Nevertheless, the statistical data provided by Messrs Harte and Lee help us to see the general growth and success of the work (see Appendix 7).

While the SAWM objected to the keeping of detailed statistics, the Nonconformists objected to this society's authoritarian attitude and the use of elaborate ritual and ceremonial. The SAWM also argued for local parochial initiatives rather than the absolute control of a centralised organisation, while the non-denominational and centralised MDSF put its main efforts into work at sea. But this situation was never clear-cut; the SAWM acknowledged the value of time spent at sea by local clergy, and the MDSF acknowledged the importance of pastoral work on shore. Nevertheless, there were also constant complaints about the MDSF's high expenditure on advertising, although these comments did not always come from the Anglo-Catholics. The British and Foreign Sailors' Society also strongly objected to what it saw as a waste of large sums of money.

The Anglo-Catholic model, and the successful work of the Roman Catholics, of clergy living and working with the urban poor whom they sought to serve, was applied by the SAWM in the major ports such as Grimsby, Brixham and Hastings. Unfortunately, the SAWM's reluctance to advertise its work widely, and make full use of publicity opportunities, presented the committed local clergy with constant financial worries. While they won the respect of their parishioners for their practical involvement with their community, funding for the various projects they developed was always a problem. When the MDSF began developing shore-based missions more widely in the early twentieth century, the SAWM could not compete other than in a few of the major fishing ports, where the situation was far from harmonious. The MDSF complained of opposition encountered in the communities, especially where local clergy worked on behalf of the SAWM, and the SAWM complained that the MDSF was encroaching on its territory. But, despite the occasional opposition onshore, when the respective vessels of both societies met at sea or in port, there were mutual congenial visits by the crews.

The changes in the fishing industry after 1900 and the decline of the fishing fleets meant that the whole approach to fishermen at sea had to be reassessed. The now renamed St Andrew's Waterside Church Mission found itself unable to maintain the use of vessels as sailing churches, and the now renamed Royal National Mission to Deep Sea Fishermen had to concentrate on developing its shore-based work, although the RNMDSF's highly sophisticated fleet of hospital ships still retained a presence at sea. While the SAWCM managed to survive into the twentieth century, it could not compete with the RNMDSF in its national work amongst fishermen, and much of its work in this area was curtailed. The SAWCM eventually amalgamated with the Missions to Seamen in 1939.

It is somewhat ironic, therefore, that, while Anglo-Catholicism made significant inroads with a good deal of success in working-class parishes, it failed to capitalise on this in its work at sea. The evangelicals who appear to have had less success among the working class on shore, except for a few notable exceptions, managed to succeed admirably at sea. Part of the reason for this was no doubt the use of fishermen as evangelists, and the very great social care, especially medical aid, provided among the fleets. While the Anglo-Catholics also used seafarers for much of the primary work, the time of the fleets was rapidly coming to an end with the approaching dawn of the twentieth century. With the RNMDSF's ten-year start among the fishermen at sea, the SAWCM and the North Sea Church Mission were always going to have an uphill struggle. It may, however, be significant that, where the SAWCM's work in the ports was long-standing (for example, at Grimsby, Brixham and Hastings), the society achieved a much greater degree of success.

Working-Class Religion in Fishing Communities
Hugh McLeod has argued, in the 1980s, that the prevailing view of working-class religion (derived from the studies of E.R. Wickham, K.S. Inglis and A.A. MacLaren) is that the working classes have always been indifferent to religion and felt alienated from the churches. Nevertheless, McLeod has pointed out that there is little real agreement on this issue, and a range of views can be drawn from a variety of studies: (a) that the working classes never attended churches in great numbers; (b) that the predominantly middle-class, nineteenth-century churches neglected the interests of the working classes; (c) that there has been an over-readiness to accept middle-class definitions of religion; and (d) that more recent studies have demonstrated that the working classes attended Sunday services in greater numbers than had previously been supposed. The contradictions inherent in these assumptions were acknowledged by McLeod.[1] If the working classes are divided into three types, lower, radical and respectable, fishermen would appear to belong mainly to the 'lower' group.[2] It has further been argued that downwardly mobile social groups have little interest in religion, while upwardly mobile groups do. There

---

1. McLeod, *op. cit.* (1984), p.15.
2. A.D. Gilbert has noted that: 'Nonconformity in the later eighteenth and early nineteenth centuries appealed much more strongly to artisan than to the poorest sections of the working class.' (Cited in McLeod, *op. cit.* (1984), p.24).

was little opportunity for fishermen to rise in society, apart from those few who could purchase their own vessels and gradually move on to become owners and employers. At the same time, fishermen appear to have been less directly affected by downward mobility, except in times of economic recession, when large numbers of fishermen were on shore together (and were then able to engage in trade union activities – a situation epitomised by the London Dock Strike of 1889). The very nature of their occupation, with long periods at sea, generally prevented them from engaging in such radical actions (although there was an increasing number of fishermen who did so in the late nineteenth and early twentieth centuries). Hence, fishermen were, perhaps of necessity, generally conservative and, as members of a stable group within the working class, they may be seen as inherently religious.

Despite Horace Mann's conclusion, the national religious census of 1851 and the local censuses of 1881 appear to show attendances above average in some seafaring communities such as Bristol and Plymouth. As several mining communities are also recorded as having over sixty per cent attendance in 1851 we may be justified in hypothesising that communities dominated by long-standing traditional occupations, such as agriculture, mining and fishing, were more likely to have had a high commitment to the churches than new and fluctuating communities, such as those found in expanding urban centres. There are, of course, important exceptions, such as the influx of religious groups, especially among the Irish and Jewish immigrants – but even this would seem to bear out the point that identifiable communities with long traditions and history tend to have a higher commitment to religious institutions. Gerald Parsons confirms this general point when he says that 'agricultural communities and mining and fishing villages were the customary strongholds of Primitive Methodism'.[1]

As the fishing industry went through a period of rapid expansion and change during the third quarter of the nineteenth century, and some communities became dominated by new recruits to the industry, such as the huge influx of apprentices, it is likely that as the century progressed fewer people held allegiance to local churches. This view seems to be borne out explicitly by Trevor Lummis, who argued that 'religion did not play a very central role in the lives of the fishermen or their families' in East Anglia during the later years of the nineteenth century, and implicitly by David Clark, who demonstrated a high degree of religious commitment among the isolated and very insular fishing community of Staithes in North Yorkshire.[2]

1. Parsons, *op. cit.*, Vol. II (1988), p.215.
2. D. Clark, *op. cit.* (1982).

Lummis's comments, however, suggest that he is talking about *institutionalised* religion, and his observations on aspects of popular religion such as superstition are revealing:

> Evidence on the practice of and belief in superstitious ritual, however, has a very different quality. It not only reveals a much deeper commitment to its practice than in the case of (institutionalised) religion but the degree to which it was practised can be related directly to the work situation.[1]

By this he meant that the greater the economic risk, the greater the level of superstition. This form of religious belief has been identified as having the character of 'popular Christianity', which not only embraces superstition but uses institutionalised religion in a functional manner. John Kent put it succinctly:

> the working man who rejected the revivalist system, according to which he was under the wrath of God [. . .] often lived in terms of a simpler religion of his own. He accepted, for example, the idea that certain rituals were needed for the 'blessing' of life, or perhaps for the prevention of disaster.[2]

Clark made a similar point by demonstrating that superstition and institutional religion were intimately bound up with each other in a Yorkshire fishing community:

> For villagers, the two cultures (folk religion and sacred religion) became a seamless web. Methodist doctrine, superstitious observance or denominational prejudice were all 'religion' and were inextricably intertwined in symbol, rite and belief.[3]

Perhaps one major issue here is that the life of the Church did not always relate in a total sense to the lives of its members. Religious festivals and rites of passage were generally well catered for, but the fisherman tended to leave his institutionalised religion behind on shore along with his family when he set sail for the fishing grounds.

The insistence of some fishing communities, such as those at Staithes, Scarborough, Filey and Newlyn, that the fishermen should be at home on Sundays suggests a strong link with traditional religious practices. But, with the passage of time, growing pluralism in the churches, technological change and economic demands on younger fishermen (from non-traditional

---

1. Lummis, *op. cit.* (1985), p.147.
2. John Kent, *Holding the Fort* (London: Epworth Press, 1978), p.360.
3. D. Clark, *op. cit.* (1982), p.66.

backgrounds) who began to rise to be skippers and owners, there was a gradual erosion of such traditional practices. Perhaps not surprisingly, it was the fishermen in the major fishing ports, especially in East Anglia and the newer centres such as Grimsby, who began to break with traditional taboos. In other longer established fishing communities, such as that in Scarborough, Filey, Brixham and Newlyn, there was initially strong local opposition to some aspects of change.

When Lummis pointed to the high attendance at some mission halls and church services, he indicated that attendance was for a variety of reasons other than religious observance. Entertainment, meeting of prospective partners, the obtaining of goods such as clothes and food, and so on, were all enticing factors. He also pointed out that allegiance to the churches was not very strong; attendance at some festivals such as Thanksgiving Services at the end of the herring season were poorly attended, although the vicar may have been popular (as was the Rev. Tupper Carey of St Margaret's Church, Lowestoft). Even so, when attendance was good, allegiance tended to be to the vicar rather than the Church. This was certainly the case at Grimsby (the Revs W. Marples, J. Spawforth and R. Meddings), at Gorleston (the Rev. F. Phillips) and at Brixham (the Rev. A.G. Stallard). Given the anomaly between the relative lack of success in terms of attendance figures at church services by such figures as the Rev. Tupper Carey, we are left asking why some churches achieved successful attendance figures and others did not – despite the popularity of the vicar. Two points may be pertinent here. First, proximity – St Margaret's Church, Lowestoft, was some distance away from the main body of the fishing community, while another Anglican Church (Christ Church) was right in the heart of the nineteenth- century fishing community and had been built in the wake of the 1859–60 international religious revival. Second, ownership of the church – while St Margaret's Church was committed to welcoming fishermen and their families to the services, there appears to have been little sense of 'ownership' of the church by the fishing community.

The practices of Bible-reading and family prayers do not seem to have been much engaged in in the average fisherman's home – not least, perhaps, because relatively few could read, but also because of the fisherman's considerable amount of time away from home. It is possible, however, that women prayed regularly with their children for their men's safe return. But the evidence here is sparse and it remains an area that needs further investigation. We have, for example, to rely on interviews conducted during the 1960s by researchers such as Thompson, Lummis and Clark, although the oral evidence here only reaches back to the 1880s.[1] The

---

1. Thompson, Wailey and Lummis, *op. cit.* (1983).

situation is not clear; Kennerley has argued that religion for seafarers was marginal but he, too, has acknowledged the need for more research. This is no less true for those fishermen at sea than for the fishing communities on shore, especially during the period 1840–80, for which no first-person oral evidence is available, although Thompson's and Lummis's interviewees, while reflecting back to the 1880s, have presumably implicitly drawn upon the influences of their Victorian forebears.

Many fishermen would attend services on board the Bethel ships for reasons other than worship. While services were lively and warm, there was also the attraction of entertainment in the form of lantern-slide shows, lectures and boxing matches – plus, welcome supplies of literature, woollens, medical aid, cheap tobacco and catching up with gossip. It has also to be remembered that there was little in the form of state intervention in the lives of fishermen before the establishment of the Seamen's Welfare Board in 1940. Fishermen were therefore highly dependent upon charitable aid and much of this was provided by the missions and the churches. Even charities which were run by fishermen themselves, such as the Fishermen's Refuge on the Yorkshire coast, tended to have been established and overseen by the clergy. While the churches began to acknowledge the limitations of what they could achieve, given the extent and size of the social problems, there was little real aid for those at sea. Prior to the MDSF and Government reports highlighting these problems during the 1880s, people appear to have viewed fishing as an idyllic occupation, and seafaring was generally perceived through romantic eyes. But, once roused from their ignorance the Victorians responded in droves by fundraising, knitting, collecting woollens, providing literature and financially supporting the missions. Many also (men and women), especially journalists, took the opportunity to visit the fishermen at sea on board the Mission vessels. Nevertheless, while fishermen did visit the Bethel ships in large numbers, the statistics are misleading in that simple numbers do not give any indication of religious commitment; and conversions at emotionally charged services are of little statistical value, given that most conversions in such circumstances are likely to be short-lived – especially if the new convert returned to his fishing vessel to be confronted with taunts from his skipper and fellow crew. On the positive side, however, converted fisherman would find warm support from a Christian skipper and crew who would help nurture the new Christian's faith.

While the present study tends to support the general results of previous researchers into the nature of working-class religion, it also seeks to open up new areas for future study by providing a framework within which such research can be undertaken. Such research could, for example, focus on:

the extent and nature of religious commitment in fishing communities; the short-term and long-term influence of missions in the fishing ports; the nature and success of the different missions (including later Roman Catholic developments such as work among Catholic fishing apprentices); and further study of the nature and development of popular religion in fishing communities and its relationship with evangelical, Anglo-Catholic and Roman Catholic mission agencies. The publicity machine of the MDSF gave the impression that many thousands of fishermen were converted or at least influenced by the mission's work at sea. The example of the link between spiritual and physical improvement must have added considerably to the late Victorian view that Christian missions ought to incorporate a concern to improve social conditions.

Chapter 3
Fishing for Souls
1800–1856

Many nineteenth-century men and women from various Christian traditions were dedicated to providing spiritual and social welfare for fishermen and their families. Some were individual clergy who held a specific concern for their fisherfolk parishioners, others were laymen and women. The initiative for such work, however, was generated by the Bethel movement, which was concerned primarily with making converts and tended to be the preserve of evangelical individuals and groups. At the beginning of the nineteenth century the Church of England was experiencing a difficult period, with many claiming it would not survive. By contrast, the Evangelicals, in the form of the New Dissent, composed mainly of Methodists, Congregationalists and Baptists, were undergoing a period of revival.

3.1. Nonconformist Missions

The Bethel Movement

The impetus for the Bethel movement arose at the end of the Napoleonic Wars, when large numbers of seafarers, including 90 per cent of the naval officers, found themselves unemployed.[1] This religious revival began on the Thames during the summer of 1814 under the influence of several Methodists: a young shoemaker, Zebedee Rogers, Captain David Simpson, of the brig *Friendship*, and Samuel Jennings, a local timber merchant who encouraged Rogers in his ship-visiting and helped finance the work. Others soon joined the group and by 1816 ships on the Thames were being regularly visited. Prayer meetings were held on the vessels and there was a shore-based Seamen's Mission in Samuel Jennings' grounds. This work was, as Roald Kverndal has pointed out, 'the first organised, ongoing programme of preaching known to have been established specifically for sailors'.[2] The revival along the Thames continued throughout 1816, the numbers of men

---

1. Kverndal, *op. cit.* (1986), p.131.
2. *Ibid.*, p.156.

attending the meetings grew and it became necessary to use some form of signal during the winter evenings to identify the vessel on which meetings would take place. This signal was initially a lantern hoisted to the topgallant masthead or placed high in the rigging but, with the approach of lighter evenings, it was inappropriate. Zebedee Rogers and his friends discussed the situation and decided upon the use of a flag. Captain Wilkins collected some blue material and Peter Hunt, a sailor, cut out the letters B E T H E L

Hoisting the Bethel flag.

in white, Rogers' sister did the sewing and, on 23 March 1817, the flag was hoisted on the collier brig, *Zephyr*.[1] Other similar flags were later made including some with a dove and star added.

In 1818 the Bethel movement took on a more formal appearance with the establishment of the Nonconformist Port of London Society (PLS). The PLS opened a floating chapel (the *Ark*) on the Thames on 27 November 1818 and it quickly became a popular venue for visiting seafarers. The subsequent history of the Bethel movement, however, was one of infighting and the formation and demise of numerous groups and organisations within it. The eventual establishment of two national Nonconformist seafarers' missions, the British and Foreign Sailors' Society in 1833 and the Seamen's Christian Friend Society (SCFS) in 1846 (both arising out of the earlier work of the Bethel movement), was followed by a period of consolidation during which many of the provincial societies were drawn under their wings. There were, however, some notable exceptions, such as the Port of Hull Society (PHS) and the Bristol Channel Mission (BCM), which retained their independence.

Early Nineteenth-Century Missions to Fishermen

During the first half of the nineteenth century fishermen were not seen as a distinct group for evangelisation but were subsumed under a general concern for seafarers. Even so, missionaries were active in fishing communities, amongst inshore fishermen and those who worked on British lakes and rivers. Indeed, the Rev. G.C. Smith regularly preached to fishermen in Grimsby, Hull and other ports during the 1820s, and his

---

1. Pike, *op.cit.* (1897), pp.36-7.

Interior view of the Thames Floating Chapel, the Ark,
which was moored at London Docks in May 1818.

journals, the *Sailors' Magazine and Naval Miscellany* (1820–1827) and the *New Sailors' Magazine and Naval Chronicle* (1827–), contain numerous articles referring to this work.

'Whale fishery'[1] was also the subject of Christian missions, and Bethel flags were hoisted on board whaling ships to invite crew members to Sunday services. The Port of Hull Society cared for the whaling crews in Hull; and the Zetland, Davis Strait, Greenland Fishery, and Marine Bible Society (established at Lerwick in the Shetland Islands on 23 March 1818) looked after whaling crews and fishermen who visited the Islands.[2] Some of the captains of whaling ships kept Sunday as a day of rest and provided religious services for their men, and there is a record of a Captain Manger writing to Captain Francis Reynolds (of the Port of Hull Society) providing details of a religious service near Baffin Island.[3]

Fishermen, however, do not appear to have immediately taken to using the Bethel flag on their vessels, as Smith lamented:

> It is to be hoped that we may soon hear of Bethel Flags being hoisted in fishing vessels: their crews now, I am sorry to say, too often land on the coast, to spend the Lord's Day in drinking and quarrelling.[4]

1. Whales are not fish but mammals. The term 'whale fishery', however, is commonly used in the literature on the subject of maritime mission.
2. *The Sailors' Magazine (London)*, 1820, pp.305-8; Kverndal, *op. cit.* (1986), p.147, says this society was formed in conjunction with the *Edinburgh Bible Society*.
3. Jennifer C. Rowley, *The Hull Whale Fishery* (Lockington Publishing Co, 1982), p.22.
4. *The Sailors Magazine (London)*, 1821, p.303.

Yet earlier that same year (1821) he had referred to the establishment of
a Sailors' Children's Bethel Union at the fishing port of Newlyn with one
of its aims being, 'that a Bethel Flag be obtained for this place, to hoist on
board of vessels occasionally lying here'. Smith also credited the Methodists
with having preached to the Newlyn fishermen well before the advent of
the Bethel Movement.[1]

In the summer edition of the *Sailors' Magazine* for 1820, we read of a
concern for Sabbath observance amongst North Sea fishermen:

> Captain J.B. commanded a fishing-smack which was in the habit
> of fishing on the Dogger Bank, in the North Sea off the coast
> of Holland, (and noted for the multitude and excellent quality
> of its fish). As a servant of the Most High God, he considered
> himself bound to obey his commandments, especially that solemn
> injunction, 'Remember the Sabbath-day to keep it holy' – he had
> been accustomed also to value the Sabbath-day as a day of rest.[2]

There was also Christian work among Irish and Scottish fishermen,
especially those who visited the Thames, and Smith published an address
specifically for fishermen in February 1821, commenting that: 'The coast is
thickly peopled, and almost every port, and cove, and creek, has inhabitants
whose sole employ is to bring the produce of the sea and rivers to land.'[3]
In the spring of 1821 a Bethel Union was formed at Barking, where 600-
700 men and boys were employed in fishing. Other coastal fishing ports
soon followed in establishing similar societies, including Great Yarmouth,
Margate and Plymouth, as well as ports in Ireland, Wales, Scotland, and the
Shetland Islands. The Plymouth Bethel Union had a particularly thriving
contingent of fishermen whose influence reached along the west coast,
where other Bethel unions were soon established in fishing towns such as
Brixham and Dartmouth.[4]

Given the nature of this missionary work, it is not surprising that later
reports of the Naval and Military Bible Society (founded in 1779) explicitly
included fishermen as one of the seafaring categories to which it ministered.[5]
Nevertheless, fishermen were not ministered to in any systematic way and
in 1827 the Prayer Book and Homily Society lamented that fishermen as a

---

1. *Ibid.*, pp. 46, 161.
2. *The Sailors' Magazine (London)*, 1820, p.190.
3. *Ibid.*, pp.226, 396; *The Sailors' Magazine (London)*, 1821, p.70.
4. *The Sailors' Magazine (London)*, 1820, pp.305-8; 1821, pp.321, 323, 489, 492; 1822,
   pp.10-17. See also Kennerley, *op. cit.* (1989), pp.70ff.
5. Report of the Proceedings of the Naval and Military Bible Society, 1826, p.8ff.:
   'Laws and Regulations' (quoted in Miller, *op. cit.* (1989), p.48).

group had been neglected and river fishermen completely ignored.[1] There were, however, some organisations, such as the Port of Hull Society, which put a high priority on caring for fisherfolk.

The Port of Hull Society

As with many such societies, the roots of the Port of Hull Society were laid many years preceding its official establishment in 1821. It is quite likely, for example, that the Rev. G.C. Smith visited the port prior to 1821 and urged the local churches to begin a society and to establish a 'floating chapel'. He was certainly known well enough to the founders for them to invite him to attend the first anniversary meeting on 17 October 1822. There were also good links with Smith's Bethel Union, which provided occasional preachers such as the Rev. W.H. Angas.[2] What is known is that one important development was the establishment of the Hull Marine Bible Association, formally instituted on 13 February 1817 at a meeting with 700-800 seafarers. A prominent part was played by Captain Francis Reynolds, a Hull merchant seafarer, who acted as an agent of the British and Foreign Bible Society (BFBS) dispersing tracts and scriptures wherever he travelled in the world (which he was doing as early as 1810).[3] He wrote to the society on 24 June 1813, saying that his crew had formed a Marine Bible Association – the first of its kind.[4] We are informed by Sir James Reckitt that whaling crews were eager to attend Sunday services prior to the commencement of the whaling season in the spring, and there were also opportunities for crews of the whaling ships to attend services at sea on board vessels which carried a Bethel flag, with as many as 500-600 men attending.[5] The Hull Marine Bible Association and the Hull Religious Tract Society both appear to have given whole-hearted support to the new society, and provided scriptures and tracts at reduced prices. We are not told what event precipitated the move by several clergymen and Captain Reynolds to set up a local society on a more formal basis, although it was clearly influenced by the Port of London Society and its floating *Ark*. The group met initially in 1820 in a small chapel vestry to consider what could be done for the Hull seafarers.[6] This meeting was followed by a public meeting in St Mary's Boys' School, Salthouse Lane, on 19 April 1821, when 'The Port of Hull Society for the Religious Instruction of Seamen' was formally instituted. William Rust, a local gold and silversmith, and

---

1. *The Missionary Register*, 1827, p.236.
2. *Chart and Compass*, 1897, pp.20, 367.
3. Port of Hull Society, Fourth Annual Report, 1825, p.43.
4. British and Foreign Bible Society, Home Correspondence.
5. Sir J. Reckitt, *Lifeboat and Anchor* (Port of Hull Society & Sailors' Orphans' Home, 1907), p.9; PHS, First Annual Report, 1822, pp.15, 17-18.
6. *Ibid.*, p.15; 1866, p.24.

Congregationalist, was elected chairman, and he was supported by an Anglican layman, William H. Dikes (a local shipbuilder and manager of the Yorkshire District Bank) as treasurer and Captain Francis Reynolds (recently retired) as one of three 'gratuitous secretaries'. They were supported by a committee of twelve local clergy and twenty laymen. The constitution followed the already established form of the Port of London Society[1] and among the resolutions passed at the first meeting was the following: 'This meeting considers it highly desirable that in order to induce *Seamen* to attend to the preaching of the Gospel a *Ship* should be purchased and fitted up especially for their accommodation in public worship.'[2]

The society was to be interdenominational and services were held on board ships and in a local sail loft. Enquiries were made about the possibility of obtaining a vessel which would be suitable as a floating chapel, and during the first year funds were received from many notable people including the Rt Hon. William Wilberforce and Captain William Scoresby.[3] Captain Scoresby had been an ardent supporter of the Naval and Military Bible Society since 1794 and had given fifty guineas in 1816 to support the foundation of the Whitby Marine Bible Society. In May 1827, he was appointed Britain's first full-time Anglican seamen's chaplain with the Liverpool Mariners' Floating Church.[4]

An old merchant vessel, the *Valiant*, was obtained and fitted out with a chapel to hold 550-650 people[5] and was officially opened on 3 October 1821, when the Rev. Dr Raffles of Liverpool preached the first sermon on board. The services were popular, with 200-300 people present at each meeting, but despite this popularity it was not until 1834 that a missionary, the Rev. H. Spencer, was appointed as chaplain. Apart from arranging services on board the *Valiant*, he was responsible for visiting vessels in the harbour, talking to the seafarers in the port, preaching in the open air and caring for all the practical needs of seafarers.[6] The *Valiant* served as a floating chapel until 1849 when its work was taken over by a Sailors'

---

1. *Ibid.*, p.4; Kverndal, *op. cit.* (1986), p.229.
2. *Ibid.*, p.11.
3. Kverndal, *op. cit.* (1986), p.146.
4. *Ibid.*, pp.287-8.
5. C. Mitchell, *The Long Watch* (Sailors' Children's Society, 1961), p.17; PHS Annual Report, 1822, pp.12, 22. The *Valiant* had begun life as a Dutch merchantman named *Cornelius and Maria*, but was captured in the Channel in 1803. After repairs and a refit, she was commissioned into the English mercantile marine and renamed the *Valiant*. In 1814 she was purchased by Thompson's of Hull who sold her to the Port of Hull Society in 1821. Alterations and adaptions cost £457.6s.8d – of which £89.11s.4d was recouped from the sale of old materials.
6. Reckitt, *op.cit.* (1907); Mitchell, *op.cit.* (1961), p.23.

Institute and Chapel, which had opened in Waterhouse Lane in 1842. In the meantime, a library had been established for the use of seafarers and fishermen, an orphanage was opened for the children of seafarers and a marine school proved to be popular.

The society retained its independence and branched out in new directions. Although a certain basic education was necessary for seafarers to rise in the profession, there was little in the way of formal assessment. It was November 1850 before captains and mates in the merchant service were required to hold certificates, although skippers and second hands on fishing vessels were not included in this process until 1880,[1] thus the Port of Hull Society's establishment of the marine school met an obvious need. The PHS had been established for seafarers in general but, with the rapid development of the fishing industry along the Yorkshire coast during the 1840s, a Coast Mission was inaugurated to co-ordinate the work of the various local missions. This aspect of the work had its genesis in 1832 when the society held a meeting at Grimsby with a view to establishing a mission in that port. The work expanded and a second missionary, Mr J. Welch, 'a converted sailor', was appointed in 1843, and auxiliary groups were formed in the coastal towns and villages. By 1845 the Committee of the Port of Hull Society was able to report that the mission was active from the Humber to the Tees, with societies running in many of the smaller ports along the coast. Other missionaries were appointed to oversee the growing amount of work and by 1853 five men were employed in this task. On the eve of the international religious revival of 1858–61 a Mr Sharah was appointed as a missionary to the society and proved to be such a dynamic employee that, when he died in 1898, the society was established on a secure basis, working with fishermen and other seafarers all along the Yorkshire and Lincolnshire coasts, and provided a thriving orphanage for seafarers' children.

The Valiant *floating chapel of the Port of Hull Society.*

1. W. Mawer, *Adventures in Sympathy* (A. Brown & Sons, 1935), p.5.

The Methodists' Fishermen's Missions

The Methodists had been among the first religious groups to establish a formal response to the spiritual and practical needs of seafarers, although it was not until 1843 that the Wesleyan Seamen's Mission was founded with its base at St George's Church, Cable Street, London. (It moved to the Queen Victoria Seamen's Rest in 1902.) The work involved not only meeting with seafarers on the docks, but visiting families at home, tackling issues of social reform and caring for the sick and dying. Fishermen on their smacks at Billingsgate were also regularly visited.[1] The Wesleyan Seamen's Mission was also memorable in its appointment of the first Sailors' Bible Woman whose job was to converse with seafarers on their arrival in port, where she supplied them with details of the respectable boarding houses, provided them with literature and invited them to attend the Seamen's Chapel.

A Wesleyan 'Sailors' Bible Woman' c.1850.

The Primitive Methodists, an offshoot of the Wesleyans, had also been active, especially among fishing communities along the Cornish and Yorkshire coasts. They made a huge impact on a number of smaller communities, such as the Yorkshire town of Filey where they were responsible for a revival in 1823 with long-lasting effect on the community.

1. Wesleyan Seamen's Mission Quarterly Paper, September 1878, p.1.

Community members regularly referred to this event, and the town embraced Sabbatarianism in the 1830s. A play was recently written and produced by local people to commemorate these events.

3.2. Church of England Missions

With the growth and influence of the Port of Hull Society, the Church of England took an interest in being represented in the missionary work with seafarers in Hull. In 1828, a former independent chapel on Princes Dockside was borrowed and the Rev. John Robinson appointed minister. Later, in 1834, the Hull Mariners' Church was erected by voluntary subscription. Another group, the Sailors' Rest Society came into being in 1841 on the site of the independent chapel, and in 1873 developed links with the Missions to Seamen in London. A Seamen's Mission Hall was built in Posterngate in 1886, and in 1899 the Hull Mariners' Church Society amalgamated with the Sailors' Rest Society under the title of the Hull Mariners' Church and Sailors' Rest Society, in connexion with the Missions to Seamen. The PHS, however, remained independent, changing its name in 1917 to the Port of Hull Society's Sailors' Orphan Homes, then to the Sailors' Children's Society (SCS) in 1951, and more recently to the Sailors' Families' Society.

The Episcopal Floating Church Society

While the benevolent societies were gathering momentum in the early years of the nineteenth century, others saw the need for more innovative forms of religious contact with seafarers. The lack of welcome for seafarers in churches led to proposals for the use of modified old hulks as seamen's churches. The hulks had become redundant following the end of the Anglo-French wars and many were converted for use as training ships, prison hulks and floating hospitals – these latter being useful when epidemics of highly infectious diseases such as cholera and typhoid broke out. In 1818 the Nonconformists made their case to the Admiralty for the use of some hulks as floating churches and thus the first, the *Ark*, was established on the Thames. Leaders of the Church of England were informed of this development, in the hope that they might provide clergy and services for Anglican seafarers, but, although the Nonconformist initiative was supported by individual evangelical clergymen, the Church of England could not officially cooperate in sharing public worship with Dissenters. Kverndal has commented on this situation: 'This initiative [for a floating chapel], originating with a Dissenter, is significant as the

first in a long series of requests from different quarters through the years
for more direct Church of England involvement in seamen's mission
activity.'[1]

Encouraged by recent developments in Bristol, Dublin and Liverpool,[2] and
concerned about the influence of Dissenters, the Episcopal Floating Church
Society was inaugurated in London on 20 July 1825. The Lord Mayor of
London chaired the meeting, several members of the peerage gave their
support, and a chaplain was appointed with pastoral responsibility for seafarers
on the Thames between London Bridge and the Pool.[3] Resolutions passed
included an acknowledgement that the Church had been failing seafarers. The
EFCS looked forward to having its own floating church in due course and the
Archbishop of Canterbury, the Prime Minister and the Bishop of London gave
their support in 1827. The Admiralty allocated HMS *Brazen* in February 1828
to be refitted as a floating church, and the Rev. G.C. Smith was invited, along
with Captains George Cornish Gambier and Robert James Elliot, to examine
and advise on the vessel's suitability. After its refit, it was towed up the Thames
and moored in the Lower Pool at Rotherhithe opposite the Nonconformist
Ark. Unfortunately, further delays followed and it was not opened for services
until Good Friday, 1829. The delay in getting the vessel ready has confused
numerous writers: M. Walrond, for example, said the floating church was
opened in 1826; and Anson concurs in *The Sea Apostleship in the Port of London*,
saying that, 'the first service took place on Good Friday, 1826'.[4]

The relationship between Anglicans and Nonconformists began well,
not least because of the involvement of several of Smith's friends and
supporters on the committee of the EFCS. However, despite the initial
cooperation, Smith's relationship with his colleagues deteriorated in 1831
when Captain Elliot, apparently supported by Captain Gambier, invited
the Bishop of London to become patron of the Sailors' Home which was
being built in Well Street (now called Ensign Street). The Bishop agreed,
on condition that the chaplain would be an Anglican and the chapel
consecrated by the Church of England. This development alienated Smith
(a Baptist minister) as he feared that Dissenting clergy would be excluded.
Nevertheless, the situation eventually enabled the EFCS and the Sailors'
Home to amalgamate in the early 1840s. Close links were also forged

1. Kverndal, *op. cit.* (1986), p.182.
2. Report of the Proceedings of the Port of Dublin Society for the Religious Instruction of
   Seamen, 1824; Howley Papers (Lambeth Palace), p.213; Kverndal, *op. cit.* (1986), p.288.
3. *Ibid.*, p.186.
4. *New Sailors' Magazine (London)*, 1828, p.433. M.L. Walrond, *Launching Out Into the
   Deep* (London: SPCK, 1904), p.xiii; Kverndal, *op. cit.*, p.293; Anson concurs in his
   The Sea Apostleship in the Port of London, 1991, p.20.

with: the Destitute Sailors' Asylum, opened in 1827; St Paul's Church for Seamen, built in Dock Street in 1847;[1] and the Thames Church Mission, founded in 1844. The Sailors' Home and the Destitute Sailors' Asylum not only shared the same premises but were run by the same group of people: the Marquis of Cholmondeley, Capt. Jonathan Chapman, Joseph Meade, Capt. W.E. Farrer and the Hon. William Waldegrave; with Captain Elliott and the Rev. G.C. Smith as employees. The various Anglican societies also employed the same chaplain, each agreeing to share responsibility for his salary – prompting Alston Kennerley to suggest that these societies were now in essence a unified Anglican Mission in the Port of London.

Although the Anglican floating church was popular at first, interest quickly waned. Financial problems and some acrimony amongst members of the EFCS committee added to the difficulties and, as the situation deteriorated, so did the vessel, which sank in 1832. Nevertheless, it was repaired and two years later towed to a new site at the Admiralty Pier by the Tower where it remained until 1845. By this time, however, it had ceased to perform any church function and was finally abandoned in 1847.[2]

The Bristol Channel Mission

Despite the location of a floating church in Bristol during the early 1820s, there was a significant floating population that never saw a church visitor. This came to the attention of the Rev. Dr John Ashley in 1835, when he noted the serious lack of church involvement among the fishermen working in the Bristol Channel, and he began visiting fishermen on the islands and at sea. He appears initially to have received little practical support from existing Anglican societies and sought the advice of the Archbishop of Canterbury in 1837. Ashley was encouraged to establish the Bristol Channel Mission as an independent local society, which he did in the spring of 1839, three and a half years after his first visit to fisherfolk on the island of Steep Holm. A sailing church, the *Eirene*, was obtained in 1839, although following some delays in work on the vessel, initial visits to the Bristol Channel ports did not occur until the autumn of 1840. Dr Ashley then set out in the spring of 1841 to hold services and visit the fishing fleets.[3]

---

1. Kennerley, *op. cit.* (1989), p.63.
2. *New Sailors Magazine (London)*, 1832, p.360.
3. Report of the Bristol Channel Mission, 1842, pp.15,20. Kverndal says the vessel was built in 1841, and Kennerley (*op. cit.* (1989), p.65) says Ashley visited churches in South Wales, Devon and Somerset during 1841 to raise funds to build the vessel. This date, however, is disputable as Ashley himself says he was doing deputation work in the vessel during 1840 (BCM Report, 1842, p.15). The vessel

In 1845, the society's name changed to the Bristol Channel Seamen's Mission (BCSM) and, although Dr Ashley continued visiting for another five years – mainly self-supported – ill-health and the reduction of his personal income eventually forced him to retire. Over a period of fifteen years he visited 14,000 ships, sold 5,000 Bibles and prayer books, and provided countless services in the *Eirene*.[1] Five years of uncertainty and growing debts followed. The work, however, was taken up again in 1855 and reorganised as the Bristol Missions to Seamen (BMS) under the direction of the Rev. Thomas Cave Childs. Protracted discussions followed and the BMS eventually merged with the Missions to Seamen in 1858.

The Thames Church Mission

While Dr Ashley's work was progressing, other events were taking place in London. Several gentlemen who had been involved with the EFCS were saddened at its diminished effectiveness,[2] and a visit was arranged in 1844 to view the work of the Bristol Channel Mission. Impressed with what they saw they determined to form a society for the Thames based on similar principles, and the Thames Church Mission was inaugurated in London on 23 February 1844, with an office at the Seamen's Hospital, King William Street. The new society grew Phoenix-like from the ashes of the EFCS, with its jurisdiction being the Thames from the Pool of London to Gravesend, but modified along the lines of the Bristol Channel Mission.

The later Reports of the TCM refer to five founders, although only three of these were mentioned by name in other documents: Sir Henry Hope (1787–1863), Captain Maude (1798–1886) and the Marquis of Cholmondeley (1800–84).[3] It seems likely that the other two were Captains Robert J. Elliot and George C. Gambier – both of whom may have been the initiators of the idea for a floating church on the Thames. There were, however, seven people present at the inaugural meeting held on 23 February 1844, with apologies for absence from two others. Several had been involved with charitable work amongst seafarers for many years. Captains Elliott and Gambier had been involved with the Rev. G.C. Smith in establishing the Port of London Society (1818) and the Destitute Sailors'

---

was apparently completed by September 1839, as £450 had been paid for it on 1 June and £775.0s.9d was paid to the carpenters and joiners in September 1839 (BCM Report, 1842, Accounts).

1. BCM Report, 1842, p.20.
2. Miller, 2017, p. 48-49
3. TCM Annual Report for the years 1881–85, p.34 (copies in the British Museum Library, London. Sir Henry Hope and Captain Maude are mentioned as being founders of the TCM in M.R. Kingsford's *The Mersey Mission to Seafarers 1856–1956* (Abingdon: 1957), p.xxiii.

Asylum in 1827, among other initiatives, and all three had links with the Episcopal Floating Church Society. The Hon. William Waldegrave, RN, was a member of the EFCS Committee and the Destitute Sailors' Asylum; and Lord Cholmondeley later became Patron to Henry Cook's Portsmouth and Gosport Seamen's Mission and was a member of the British and Foreign Sailors' Society Committee.

It was agreed to send a deputation to the Bishop of London to seek his support and patronage for the Thames Church Mission. As Captain Elliot had already gained the Bishop of London's patronage for the Sailors' Home in 1831, he could therefore expect a positive welcome. The Bishop was obviously pleased with the formation of the TCM, in that he offered to write to the Archbishop of Canterbury asking whether he would be willing to become the society's Patron. A sub-committee was established to produce the society's prospectus, and its first meeting was held on 23 February 1844, at 32 Sackville Street (the home of the EFCS). The Bishop of London agreed to become a patron, and the Lord Mayor of London and Bishops of Rochester and Winchester became vice-presidents. The Bishops of these diocese are often mentioned together and apparently often supported Anglo-Catholic activities, calling for a 'mission' in late 1873.[1]

The development of Roman Catholic revivalism had its roots in 1840 when the Roman Catholic Archbishop, Nicholas Wiseman, asked Pope Gregory XVI to support the foundation of missionary priests in England. Despite initial lukewarm support, the Redemptionists, Passionists and Rosminian religious orders began parish missions in the UK during 1842–4.[2] The development of the Roman Catholic parochial missions clearly affected the Anglo-Catholics and ten years later they also began to develop parochial missions. Given the revival of Church work on the Thames, in the form of the Thames Church Mission in 1844, it seems likely that some incentive was drawn from these non-evangelical developments, although the TCM Committee encountered a number of clashes with the Anglo-Catholics.

The general aim of the TCM's work was stated as being to provide 'pastoral superintendence to the colliers and other shipping on the Thames',[3] although the aims and objectives were expanded and formalised during May of that year and various formal appointments were made. A vessel, the *Swan*, was loaned to the TCM by the Admiralty in May 1844, although it was in a poor state. Repairs were carried out and a chapel fitted to hold

1. Parsons, *op. cit.*, Vol. I (1988), p.228.
2. *Ibid.*, p.223.
3. TCM Minutes, 1844, p.1.

100 people, and a flag, pennant and code of signals were adopted after the manner of the Bristol Channel Mission.[1] Operations at first centred on the main body of the river, but in 1846 the chaplain was instructed to include visits to outward-bound vessels and fishing craft lying off Gravesend. This included a wide range of craft such as convict ships, troop ships, emigrant vessels, as well as colliers and fishing vessels. Later, during the 1860s and 1870s, the TCM chaplain was appointed 'ship's chaplain' to training ships such as HMS *Cornwall, Worcester, Goliath, Arethusa* and *Chichester*, which proved useful to the TCM as it received a regular fee from the training ships for the chaplain's services. Nevertheless, a constant supply of funds was necessary if the TCM was to maintain the work of the *Swan* up and down the Thames and, after the early success of its mission was over, it became necessary to explore other ways of ensuring a regular income. It was proposed that a lay assistant to the chaplain be appointed to release the chaplain for deputation work on behalf of the society, and this was implemented in early 1850. Nevertheless, it soon became obvious that the work on the Thames was far more than could be adequately covered by one or two men. The river was therefore divided into three districts ([1] upriver work, the Pool *etc.*, [2] Victoria Dock area and [3] Gravesend Reach), with missionaries to be employed for each district as soon as funds allowed. Problems with staff inevitably arose from time to time, but a certain degree of stability was achieved eventually and the TCM Committee was pleased with the developments.

The Missions to Seamen

Despite the consolidation of the various Anglican seafarers' missions in London, it was not until 1856 that a truly national Anglican society, the Missions to Seamen, was formed, under the direction of the Rev. W.H.G. Kingston – although the TCM refused to join. The objects and regulations of the Missions to Seamen make its sphere of influence and church affiliation clear:

1. The object of the Society is the spiritual welfare of the seafaring classes at home and abroad.
2. In pursuance of this object the Society will use every means consistent with the principles and received practice of the Church of England.
3. The operations of the Society shall for the most part be carried on afloat, and for this purpose its Chaplains and Scripture

---

1. See the typed history of the TCM (unsigned) in the Missions to Seamen's Archives at the Hull History Centre.

readers shall, as far as possible, be provided with vessels and boats for visiting the ships in roadsteads, rivers, and harbours.[1]

At the first public meeting, held on 10 March 1857, the first resolution drew attention to the Church of England's lethargic response to the needs of seafarers, and its slowness in committing itself to further this obligation:

That this meeting, fully sensible how little has been done by the Church of England for the evangelisation of its seafaring population, recognises its obligations to care for the souls of British sailors, and pledges itself to use the most strenuous exertions to provide them with that spiritual instruction of which they are so much in need.[2]

By the late 1850s many of the country's seafarers' missions were drawn under the umbrella of the three national organisations, the British and Foreign Sailors' Society, Seamen's Christian Friend Society and the Missions to Seamen, but by this time the rapid development of the fishing industry was taking place and new areas for mission were opening up.

---

1. TCM Minutes, January 1852.
2. *Ibid.*, pp.74-5.

Chapter 4
Fishing for Souls
1856–1880

4.1 Nonconformist Missions

The British and Foreign Sailors' Society

During the 1840s and 1850s the British and Foreign Sailors' Society (a non-denominational society first founded in 1818 under the name, the Port of London Society, and renamed the BFSS in 1833) experienced a protracted period of lethargy. However, it was kept alive by a few dynamic lay missionaries, such as Captain Benjamin Prynn, a pioneer of the Temperance movement who served with the BFSS from 1834 to 1856, having succeeded W.H. Angas.[1] The mid-nineteenth century brought with it a period of economic prosperity in which the fishing industry, along with others, fared well. In 1856 the BFSS experienced a new lease of life with the opening of the Sailors' Institute close to the Ratcliffe Highway and, with the expansion of the fishing fleets during the 1850s and 1860s, the society's missionaries began to concern themselves with the growing number of fishermen.[2] Many skippers were supplied with Bethel flags – 443 being handed out between 1860 and 1883, and 938 skippers joined the Bethel Union Register and received small burgee flags between 1866 and 1883.[3] But, despite this increased activity amongst fishermen, few of the BFSS missionaries appear to have regularly visited the fleets at sea until the late 1870s.[4]

Among the lay missionaries serving in fishing ports, one of the most well-known, William Johnson, was appointed by the BFSS as a missionary to sailors and fishermen at Lowestoft in 1850. The society paid half his

---

1. Pike, *op. cit.* (1897), pp.72-3.
2. The BFSS opened the first comprehensive Sailors' Institute in 1856; F.T. Bullen, *The Palace of Poor Jack* (London: James Nisbet & Co., 1900), pp.25ff; T. Wilkinson Riddle, *For Flag and Empire* (Marshall Brothers, 1915), p.23; *Chart and Compass*, 1883, p.179.
3. *Ibid.*
4. *Chart and Compass*, 1888, pp.187-188, records some visits that took place during the 1860s.

salary, and the rest came from Sir Morton Peto, civil engineer and railway developer, who is perhaps best remembered for the construction of Nelson's Column and the new Houses of Parliament. He also remodelled old Lowestoft harbour and built railway links connecting Norwich and Yarmouth, and he engaged in a number of philanthropic works. Johnson had previously worked with Peto who in 1850 had just finished building the new Lowestoft harbour. A room, which could hold about 130 people, was loaned by the Great Eastern Railway Company and was fitted out for meetings, although it eventually proved too small and meetings were moved to a large goods shed. During the period 1850 to 1864 Johnson held 14,000 meetings in these venues, with occasional congregations of 700 in the goods shed – especially when famous preachers such as C.H. Spurgeon paid a visit:

> During this time there were three companies of beachmen in Lowestoft. To these we turned our attention. Three meetings were held each Lord's Day: one in the Old Company's Shed at 9.30am, the Young Company's at 10.30, and the North Roads Shed at 11.30. Also two meetings in the week. The Bethel services were then held afternoon and evening. Once in the year we gave a free tea to about three hundred beachmen, subscribed for by various friends of the mission. Addresses were afterwards given, and at the close each man presented with a pair of woollen muffetees and a New Testament. In 1864 the present Bethel was opened.[1]

A second missionary, Edward Leather, joined Johnson and the two served together until Leather's death in 1870. Johnson continued for another twenty years and was throughout this time a popular and highly regarded local figure.[2] Noting Johnson's success, during the 1860s the BFSS appointed missionaries at many ports, such as Bristol, Ramsgate and Great Yarmouth, although at least one missioner, Mr H.V. Bailey, was appointed at Falmouth as early as 1848.[3]

Two other important developments were the initiatives of Henry Cook at Gosport and Thomas Rosie in Scotland. Both obtained vessels to visit various ports and men at sea, and both were given practical support and encouragement by the BFSS, although their organisations remained independent during the lifetimes of their founders.[4]

---

1. *Ibid.*, pp. 117-118; also Paul Davies, *The Beach and Harbour Mission: the Beachmen's Church and St John's Church, Great Yarmouth* (2011).
2. *Ibid.*, pp.117-120.
3. *Ibid.*, 1888, pp.171-178.
4. The details about Thomas Rosie are to be found in his biography by the Rev. J.

Henry Cook and the Portsmouth and Gosport Seamen's Mission

Henry Cook (1824–1893).

Born at Portsmouth in 1824, Henry Cook was the son of a prosperous Portsmouth publican. Against his father's wishes, he refused to follow the same trade and chose a life in the navy. In 1839, aged fifteen years, he obtained a berth on the HMS *Rodney* but his naval career was short-lived. During the autumn of 1840, whilst sailing in the Mediterranean from Gibraltar to Malta, the ship ran into a violent storm and, convinced that he would lose his life, Cook knelt and prayed to be spared. He survived and when the ship returned home, on 16 October 1843, he began an apprenticeship in Gosport as an improver and house decorator. He soon established himself in business on his own, and became a prosperous and respected businessman.[1] He also joined the Wesleyans and held various positions, such as Sunday School teacher, librarian and superintendent.

Dodds, *Coast Missions: a Memoir of the Rev. Thomas Rosie* (James Nisbet & Co., 1862), and in the *Chart and Compass*. Details about Henry Cook are more diverse: *Chart and Compass, The Christian, Word and Work*, newspaper articles and a scrapbook in the possession of Mr M. Criddle who runs Mr Cook's Mission at Gosport.

1. A.P. Isaacs, 'A Gosport Man of Faith and the Sea' (article in possession of the present Mission in Gosport), *Gosport Evening News*, 9 February 1968; Heasman, *op.cit.*, p.252.

In May 1853 Cook met a group of ragged children in the poor part of Gosport where he had his business stores and invited them to join his Sunday School.[1] The children's parents were also invited to attend evening services, and Cook soon found himself responsible for a lively and growing church family. The building where they initially met proved to be unsuitable so, in order to provide a more appropriate location for his school and Mission Hall, he appealed for funds He was able to purchase a plot of land in South Street, Gosport, where he had built the Gosport Ragged Day and Sunday School, which would provide a free day school for the local children, and an Industrial Home for destitute boys.[2] As an aid for the boys at the Industrial Home a small sailing vessel was obtained, and, when they became proficient sailors, the ship was used for missionary work along the coast and amongst the local fishing fleets. Of this initiative, A.P. Isaacs observed:

> Henry bought an old, lug-sailed wherry, just retired from the Portsea-Porchester ferry service, which he manned with eight poor destitute boys from the Ragged School and began mission work upon the waters. As the boys gained experience, Henry was able to sail out to ships in Spithead with bundles of tracts, then later across Spithead to St Helens on the Isle of Wight and eventually out to the Nab and Warner Lightships.[3]

The sequence of events here suggests that the vessel was at first obtained simply as a means of giving the boys an opportunity to learn seafaring. With their growing competence, it would be natural to sail along the coast to visit other ports. Cook may well have been encouraged in this innovation by Lord Cholmondeley who, with Lady Cholmondeley, was patron of the Ragged School. Lord Cholmondeley was also President of the BFSS, and involved with the TCM and numerous other charitable enterprises.[4] It is also possible that Lord Cholmondeley spoke to Cook of the work in sailing chapels by Carl von Bülow, Dr John Ashley and the more recent work of Thomas Rosie. But, wherever the idea came from, the combination of educational work, social reform and religious activity won Cook many admirers. It seems to have been the success of this work that convinced Cook the time had come to give up his painting and decorating business and to take up a full-time role as a missionary. Once the move was made, he

---

1. *The Christian*, 14 September 1893, p.17.
2. A P Isaacs, *op.cit.*
3. *Ibid.*
4. *Chart and Compass*, 1879, p.3; Lord Cholmondeley acted in a similar capacity as Admiral Lord Gambier who had presided over several of the societies established by the Rev. G.C. Smith in the 1820s.

branched out into a range of social enterprises. Cook's link between social and spiritual welfare was somewhat ahead of its time – anticipating the work of the Mission to Deep Sea Fishermen.

The Portsmouth and Gosport Seamen's Mission came into being in February 1869 with the opening of a Bethel at Gosport.[1] Other Bethels followed at Portsmouth and Rudmore, all with sleeping accommodation for visiting soldiers, sailors and fishermen.[2] By the early 1880s the PGSM was very actively engaged in work with fishermen and other seafarers along the south coast of England. Cook appears to have been an eloquent speaker and his ideas impressed many people. He also inspired loyalty, several people staying with him for many years (one of his captains, for example, remained with him for eighteen years).[3] A journalist gave the following short account of one meeting: 'Several speakers gave addresses, and some were moved to tears as they listened to Mr Cook's thrilling description of the conversion of seamen, and of the marvellous work done in various ports and roadsteads in England and France.'[4]

The wherry visited numerous ports along the south coast but was caught in a storm off Cornwall and wrecked in 1880. A new vessel, the *Annie* took up her predecessor's role.[5] Meetings, especially on board the Bethel ships, appear to have been well attended and much admired:

> I have had an opportunity of personally seeing Mr Cook, his helper, and great work. At Yarmouth (Isle of Wight) we had a good service on board of the Bethel Ship. Preached in his Mission Hall, at Gosport, and on the following day visited in his steam launch the Warner lightship, and Berrybridge Harbour. On the lightship the captain and crew received us cordially, and a meeting was held in the cabin. I saw that Mr Cook's visits were not only appreciated here, but everywhere.[6]

In 1880 Cook was invited to preach at Trouville on the French coast:

> The Protestant Society of France begged him to make the Seine his 'Parish'. The Protestant seamen and bargemen passing along that river seldom saw a priest of their faith, the Society pointed out, and they were becoming a disastrously godless lot.[7]

---

1. *Ibid.*; Isaacs, *op. cit.*
2. *Chart and Compass*, 1880, p.343; Heasman, *op. cit.*, p.252.
3. *Word and Work*, 1888, p.923.
4. *Ibid.*, p.66.
5. Isaacs, *op. cit.*
6. *Chart and Compass*, 1879, p.343.
7. *Portsmouth Evening News*, 9 February 1968.

He was accompanied on this his first visit by several friends including the Hon. Elizabeth Waldegrave, who was involved in work amongst seafarers at Southsea, and other Christian charitable enterprises, and the Russian Count Brobinsky who was especially helpful in acting as interpreter at the services on board the *Annie*.[1] Services were held nightly at 8pm, and twice on Sundays, with as many as 200 people attending each service. Occasionally two services were held on weekdays – one at 7.30pm for soldiers and seafarers and a second at 8.30pm for civilians.[2]

With the expanding work in England and along the coast of France, the *Annie* was replaced by two other vessels. The first, the *Mystery* (a schooner of 54 tons and a seating capacity for 175 worshippers), was the initiative of a Devon lady who in September 1883 invited Cook to hold a drawing-room meeting at her home. Impressed with his work, she offered a gift of £350 towards the purchase of a vessel for work along the French coast – if he could raise an equivalent amount. By 1887 funds allowed the purchase of another vessel, which was renamed the *Herald of Mercy*. This was larger than the *Mystery*, being a ketch of 80 tons and capable of seating 200 people at a service.[3] The *Mystery* was used exclusively for work along the French coast, but was from time to time supported by the presence of the *Herald of Mercy*. In 1887 Cook reported:

> The past year has been one of blessing. Our first port visited early in the spring was Cherbourg, where many resorted to the meeting, night after night, to hear the Word of God. Our object in going here first was to strengthen the hands of the workers labouring there. The vessel is a great attraction, and draws in hundreds to hear the Word. The Bible, and Gospel papers, &c., were freely distributed among the French sailors, soldiers and civilians, also among the workmen.[4]

There was a huge demand for the written word – 2,500 tracts and papers being distributed from the *Mystery* during her seven-week stay in Nantes. Bibles, testaments, gospel books, letters, cards and illustrated papers were supplied to those who attended services on board the vessels. Much of this literature was supplied by funds raised especially by many women supporters. (A certain Miss Kersham was adept at letter writing and distributed thousands of illuminated letters.) Many of these books and tracts were distributed in small library bags made by an army of female supporters. The bags, made to a standard design, eight inches by seven

---

1. *Word and Work*, 15 June 1888, p.487; also Isaacs, *op.cit.* (1969), p.2.
2. *Word and Work*, 3 August 1888, p.608.
3. Isaacs, *op.cit.* (1969).
4. *Word and Work*, 27 January 1888, p.66.

inches, were in great demand, as an appeal was made for 10,000 in 1888. The band of women helpers also knitted comforters, overalls and muffs, which were given to those in need, especially seafarers.[1]

There was, however, constant worry over payment of bills and not everyone was sympathetic to the mission work. In particular, there appears to have been a fair amount of persecution in France.[2] During one of his visits to Paris, Cook and his family came face to face with the rougher side of Paris nightlife:

> Mr Cook with his wife and three children, Annie, Henry and May were sleeping below decks when a gang of men, armed with knives, boarded the vessel, intent (as it was afterwards learned) on murdering as many of the occupants as they could, but fortunately the crew had decided to sleep under the canvas awnings on deck owing to the heat and, quickly arming themselves with boat-hooks and ropes, beat off the intruders with a sharp struggle.[3]

Nevertheless, despite such opposition, Cook spent two months in Paris and preached to 25,000 people on board the *Annie*.[4]

The work along the French coast proved to be so successful that a Sailors' Bethel and Rest was established at the small port of Deauville in Normandy, with the foundation stone being laid on 3 June 1889. Facilities were provided for seamen of all nationalities until 1897 when it was taken over by the *Société Centrale d'Evangelisation* which based a pastor there to look after the local Protestant community.[5]

The *Mystery* served only a short time; in June 1890 she was found to have extensive rot and was pronounced unseaworthy and disposed of. With funds raised by his home mission, Cook placed an order for a new vessel with a firm in Paignton, a screw steamer of ninety tons with a cabin large enough to accommodate 300 people for services. An appeal was launched for the £2,000 needed to build and fit out the vessel. Named *The Good News*, the ship was ready in the spring of 1893 and a service of dedication was held on board on 12 April.[6]

This new Mission ship was to be Cook's last enterprise. He fell ill on her first visit to France and was taken to the Mission house at Deauville where he died on 7 July 1893.[7] Following his death, the work was carried

---

1. *Ibid.*, p.770.
2. *Ibid.*, p.608; Isaacs, *op.cit.* (1969), p.2.
3. Isaacs, *op.cit.* (1969), p.2.
4. *Portsmouth Evening News*, 9 February 1968.
5. Isaacs, *op.cit.* (1969), p.3.
6. *Portsmouth Evening News*, 9 February 1968.
7. *Ibid.*; *The Christian*, 14 September 1883, p.17; *The Hampshire Telegraph*, 15 July 1893.

The screw steamer, The Good News, *1893.*

on for two years by his wife, although she eventually found the strain too much and sold the vessels, replacing them with a steam launch for visiting ships in the Solent.

In 1906 the PGSM Committee handed over the work to the keeping of the British and Foreign Sailors' Society. Then in 1912 the work was handed back to Henry Cook's son, Mr H.G. Cook, who, with a Board of Trustees, took over the responsibility for running the society. The Sunday School thrived and work continued at the Mission Hall until 1938 when it was demolished during slum clearances in that area of Gosport. The work, however, still survives as a mission.

4.2. Church Missions

4.2.1. Thomas Rosie and the Scottish Coast Missions

Thomas Rosie (1826–1860).

The Scottish coast missions were among the first organised missions to concern themselves with the welfare of Scotland's fishing communities. The work was initiated by a Mrs Simpson, the wife of a retired Royal Naval lieutenant, who, when resident in Dunbar, considered establishing a seafarers' mission which would be an auxiliary of the seafarers' society at Newcastle. Several similarly-minded friends were gathered and together they set about establishing an independent society. A meeting was held at Dunbar on 30 April 1850, with the Rev. Alexander Jack of the

United Presbyterian Church as chairman. Forty pounds had been collected with a promise of more, and the assembled group confidently established the society, naming it the Union Coast Mission (UCM). An advertisement was placed in the Edinburgh newspapers for a suitable missionary, and Thomas Rosie, aged 24 years, was appointed.[1]

Rosie was eminently qualified for the work. He grew up on South Ronaldsay in the Orkney Islands, the son of a boat-builder and shipwright, where he became familiar with the life of the fishermen and developed a strong attachment to the sea. His biographer has recorded that:

> his great delight was to sail in fishing-boats, and take part in their management. Often when he came home from school he would jump into a boat, and amuse himself with hoisting the sail or handling an oar. [. . .] He took a great interest [. . .] in the pursuits of the fishermen among whom he lived; and nothing delighted him more than permission to go out with them in their boats and share in their exciting labours.[2]

When his family later moved to Edinburgh, and he visited fishing communities along the coast, Rosie became acutely aware of the lack of an organised mission amongst these communities. Following his appointment by the UCM, he commenced work in Dunbar during the first week of June 1850, and over the next few years established a number of similar organisations: the Scottish Coast Mission (SCM), the West Coast Mission (WCM) and the North East Coast Mission (NECM). After much debate with his committees he obtained a mission yacht in 1856, and, like Dr Ashley (in the Bristol Channel) and Carl von Bülow (along the Scandinavian coasts), Rosie began an intense period of visiting seafaring communities around the Scottish coast.

Unlike other coast missionaries, Rosie's work was performed while he was still a student and, on completion of his studies at Edinburgh in 1858, he was licensed as a minister of the Presbyterian Church. Like other coast missionaries in other parts of the country, such as William Sharrah in Yorkshire with the Port of Hull Society, Rosie's work benefitted greatly from the effects of the 1858–61 international religious revival. The missions advocated Sabbatarianism and temperance, and rejoiced in seeing 'dancing and singing clubs [. . .] broken up' – but there was also a very practical concern to establish schools and to educate people.[3] In due course, Rosie was appointed chaplain to the Bombay Harbour Mission, and he sailed for India, although sadly his work there was cut short when acute diarrhoea and dysentery led to his death in 1860.

---

1. Dodds, *op. cit.*, 1862, p.24.
2. *Ibid.*, p.4.
3. *Ibid.*, p.198.

The coast missions at home had been so well organised by Rosie that they went from strength to strength. By 1861 the Scottish Coast Mission employed ten missionaries, had twenty-nine stations stretching from Cockenzie to Arbroath, and income for the year amounting to £1,567. The committee was so encouraged by these developments that it extended its sphere of work to the coast of Caithness, and hoped to establish missionaries at Thurso and Wick. In 1880, the *Chart and Compass* (the monthly magazine of the BFSS) gave the following report:

> (*The Scottish Coast Mission*) [. . .] employs [. . .] fourteen missionaries. From Berwick on Tweed to the North of Arbroath, they visit the fishermen and their families, and sailors, both British and foreign. Their last year's income was £1,458 19s 10d. [. . .] The agents of the Scottish Coast Mission visit more than twenty fishing stations and almost as many harbours for ships along the East and South Coast of Scotland. [. . .] About one half of the missionaries are thus labouring among a fishing population of nearly 20,000 souls. The others are stationed at harbours which are frequented by seven or eight thousand ships, manned by not fewer than 50,000 sailors.[1]

The West Coast Mission also flourished so well that in March 1860 the local committee formed the Girvan Town and District Mission as an independent society, supported by the Christian Instruction Society. By 1861 there were ten missionaries working on the west coast. Taking the Scottish coast missions altogether, there were thirty missionaries employed by 1861, several hundred voluntary agents working in local auxiliaries, and countless women who supported the work beavering away as 'collectors, district visitors and tract distributers'.[2]

4.2.2. The Missions to Seamen

The Church in East Anglia

With the rise of the North Sea fishing industry during the second half of the nineteenth century, the ports along the East Anglian coast expanded at a remarkable rate, with visiting fishermen adding considerably to the population. In the face of this rapid growth, East Anglia became a natural focus for organised Christian missions to fisherfolk. The Church of England was somewhat slow to respond to its responsibilities to seafarers, and the Church congresses only began to tackle the issue after 1869 (although the Missions to Seaman began its work in 1856). Even so, there was already a long history of Christian involvement in the area.

---

1. *Chart and Compass*, 1880, pp.150-151.
2. *Ibid.*, p.204.

At Great Yarmouth, as at other fishing ports, the medieval period saw the institution of a 'blessing of the fleet', festivals, guilds and confraternities; and Peter Anson mentions that an early shrine in memory of 'Our Lady of Arnsburgh' stood in the Parish Church of St Nicholas.[1] Adherence to the Church calendar, however, was mingled with superstition in that it was believed fishing on certain saints' days would bring bad luck.[2]

During a later period, charitable institutions for the care of fishermen were established: for example, the Fishermen's Hospital, erected by Great Yarmouth Corporation in 1702 as an almshouse for 'old and decayed fishermen' (and still in use for the same purpose today), and the Cottage Hospital at Gorleston, opened in 1889.[3] The early years of the nineteenth century saw some mission activity, for example, the cleaning, painting and fitting out of an ark (to hold 170 people) on the Thames in the autumn of 1821.[4] Ports around the country copied, for example, the establishment of the *Valiant* at Hull. Later years saw numerous other developments along the East Anglian coast such as the opening of a Fishermen's Reading Room at Southwold in 1864.

Before the seventeenth century the fishing industry had been dominated by the Dutch who also established a small community at Great Yarmouth, but legislation, and the effect of the Dutch Wars, eventually restricted this trade. British fishermen were encouraged to develop associations and companies to capitalise on new opportunities – but were slow to do so. When the rapid expansion of the British fishing industry began in the mid-nineteenth century much of the impetus, which centred on East Anglia, came from visiting fishermen. Each season brought a new influx; during the spring there was work as mackerel fishermen, then, after returning home for a few weeks in the summer, they returned to engage in the lucrative herring fishery. Nevertheless, despite the long history of Christian concern in East Anglia, the organised missions of the Established Church were minimal until the founding of the Beach and Harbour Mission in 1856.

The Beach and Harbour Mission

Faced with the explosion of labour in the fishing industry during the mid-nineteenth century, Dr Hills, the vicar of Great Yarmouth, established the Beach and Harbour Mission (BHM) in 1856 with the aim of serving the

1. P. Anson, 'A Plea for Catholic Seamen', *The Catholic Federalist*, August 1920; and *The Church and the Sailor* (1948), p.32.
2. P. Anson, *Fishermen and Fishing Ways* (G.G. Harrap, 1932), p.82.
3. *Yarmouth's Maritime Trail*, pamphlet published by the Maritime Museum of East Anglia.
4. *The Sailors' Magazine (London)*, 1821, pp.323-4, 489; *ibid.*, 1882, p.168.

various classes of seafarer in the port.[1] Even in a port like Great Yarmouth, the beachmen (seafarers and fishermen who worked during the winter months collecting salvage and watching for vessels in distress) did not always feel at home in local churches and, seeing the need, Mr Johnson, the newly appointed MS Honorary Chaplain, set about building a church specifically for the beachmen. In the meantime, he borrowed a warehouse, hoisted a specially designed flag and invited people to attend meetings:

> At a large warehouse opposite the north entrance to Yarmouth Roads, meetings of beachmen were held, addressed by the Curate on Wednesday mornings. We had for their use three dozen copies of the Litany, and two dozen hymn-books, and supplied them with other books and tracts. Every man of them would lay aside whatever he had in hand, and, with hats off, would stand up to sing and kneel down to pray, most of them joining heartily in the singing, and responding to the Litany.[2]

Support for the new endeavour came from a wide range of people, and St John's Church was opened for the beachmen on 14 February 1858.[3] Mary L. Walrond tells us that a keen supporter and collector for the erection of this church building was a sister of the Christian Socialist F.D. Maurice, and it was in her name that the church was enlarged after her death.[4] The church was popular from its opening, the only complaint being that it was on occasions too small – one sailor remarking to the vicar: 'You must have the ship lengthened, sir.'[5] Mr Johnson lived just long enough to see his building thrive, and died in December 1859.

The boatmen and their families working on the wherries and canal boats were so numerous and specialised in their work that a separate endeavour, the Wherrymen's Mission, was formed by one of Dr Hill's curates, the Rev. John Gott, and the MS appointed a reader specifically for this work.[6] Taking the lead from the opening of St John's Church for the beachmen, the wherry workers were accorded a chapel of their own, and St Andrew's was opened at the north end of the town in October 1860.[7]

---

1. Walrond, *op.cit.* (1904), pp.107-122.
2. *Ibid.*, pp.109-10.
3. St John's Church is now the Church of St John and St James.
4. Walrond, *op.cit.* (1904), p.110.
5. *Ibid.*, p.111. The beachmen found one corner of the church particularly comfortable and warm, and nicknamed it 'Blanket Corner'.
6. Walrond, *op.cit.* (1904), pp.108-11; Gott was later appointed Vicar of Leeds and then Bishop of Truro.
7. Anson, *op.cit.* (1874).

The Sailors' Home

Unlike the majority of seafarers' organisations and 'homes', the initiative for the Yarmouth Sailors' Home appears to have come from local fishermen and seafarers who were members of the well-organised beach companies. With the support of the Missions to Seamen and local churches, following a series of meetings in the early summer of 1858, it was proposed that a small institute be opened as a meeting-place and reading room for the local fishing community. The Great Yarmouth Beachmen's, Fishermen's Institute and British and Foreign Sailors' Home was duly opened on 23 July 1858, in temporary premises, and, although it could not offer accommodation, shelter was provided at night for stranded and shipwrecked seafarers.[1]

Chart 2
Great Yarmouth Shipwrecked Sailors' Home.
Annual Usage Data, 1859 to 1864[2]

	1859	1860	1861	1862	1863	1865
Institute						
Members		224	220	227	223	201
Reading Room	8120	7668	7502	8490		
Pupils	738	711	342	339		
Visitors	2382	1577	3312	2922	3131	1078
Refuge						
Coffee Room	6928	7832	6885	8139		
Inmates	441	705	376	421	459	551
Shipwrecked			209	240	336	412

The need for more permanent accommodation soon became obvious and the temporary home was replaced with a purpose-built Sailors' Home, erected on the site of the old Coastguard Station at a cost of £2,000. The Mayor and other dignitaries joined the Board of Directors, and this undoubtedly ensured the success of the institute.[3] Bedrooms, bathrooms

1. Details were kindly provided by the staff at the Maritime Museum of East Anglia, which was based in the old Walrond Institute.
2. Kennerley, *op.cit.* (1989), p.85 (source: daily log of the Sailors' Home, Norfolk Record Office, SO4/5, SO4/6). During the 20th century the need for such a home declined and in 1964 the building was converted for use as the Maritime Museum of East Anglia. The museum has now been transferred to new premises and is called the *Time and Tide Museum*.
3. Kennerley, *op.cit.* (1989), p.85.

and drying-rooms were among the facilities available to shipwrecked sailors. The building also contained a small museum, school, library and refreshment facilities, all of which were supported by members, who subscribed one penny a week. This was financed by public subscription with the assistance and support of the Great Yarmouth Authority, which also provided the site on a long lease.

The Church at Sea

The visiting fishermen in ever increasing numbers worked for many months without attending their churches at home. The Great Yarmouth clergy looked for an upright captain who would be willing and able to host services on board his vessel. They consulted with the captains of the fishing vessels but found to their dismay that not one was a committed Christian.[1] When a suitable person was eventually found, the clergy drew up a set of rules stating that the master of a vessel acting in the capacity of a clergyman at sea, should:

1. be a communicant of the Church of England;
2. begin each service with the Litany or some collects, that he migh take the passage of Scripture and explain it;
3. then conduct the rest of the meeting as he thought best, for it is desirable not to be too much tied down, but to conduct the service in accordance with the feelings of those assembled.[2]

A signal was required, to function in the same manner as the Bethel flag and it was agreed with Mr Walrond, the Honorary Secretary of the Missions to Seamen, that a flag resembling that on the mission's publications should be used:

> Flags are presented publicly at the South Mission Room. We have printed rules for the guidance of those entrusted with flags, and a printed form of presentation. Every man entrusted with a flag must bear the character of a devout man, and desirous to benefit his fellow-fishermen. At the time of presenting the flag, he says publicly, 'I am a Communicant of the Church of England, and intend to remain so. I will abide by these rules, God being my Helper, and will return the flag to the minister of the parish whenever requested by him to do so.' In the year 1866 no less than eleven flags were flying to call to worship the fishermen of the North Sea.[3]

---

1. Walrond, *op.cit.* (1904), p.112.
2. *Ibid.*, p.113.
3. *Ibid.*, pp.113-14; Presumably this flag replaced the Beach and Harbour Mission's

In 1862 the Scripture Reader, Mr Vallins, paid a visit to the North Sea fishing fleets:

> We left Yarmouth between four and five in the afternoon, and found the fleet between ten and eleven o'clock the same night. The sea was bespangled with lights at the mast-heads of the smacks as far as the eye could reach. There were eight men in the cutter besides the master, who was a pious man. All seemed willing to listen to me; so I took my seat near the helm and discoursed with them very freely on spiritual things during the whole passage. [. . .] When the daylight appeared, it turned out to be a splendid Sabbath morning, and the smacks everywhere began hauling their nets and bringing their fish on board. It was soon seen that I had come to spend the day with them, and some came on board to shake me by the hand, while others greeted me from the distance.[1]

Following breakfast, Vallins was invited to hold a service on the largest vessel in the fleet, and forty-two men, twenty-one of whom were masters of fishing vessels, gathered for worship. Other services followed during the day, and it was well into the evening before he could return to his own vessel – where he joined in hauling the nets, and discovered the back-breaking labour of the work and the small returns.

Similar visits were made by other Missions to Seamen readers and local clergy, but these visits were sporadic. On shore the Sailors' Home found itself called upon to meet rapidly expanding needs, not least in caring for the increasing number of fishing apprentices. The Scripture Reader set about educating the boys, and on the first evening attempted to conclude with a thirty-minute session on religious instruction and prayer, but the boys reacted against this, turned out the lights and overturned the forms. The Reader persevered, and the Vicar of Great Yarmouth, George Venables, later recorded that, since that first session, 'the improvement has been very marked and encouraging, and once or twice the young lads have asked that there might be prayer'.[2]

The Walrond Institute

By 1874 the Beach and Harbour Mission had an annual income of £600 and was able to employ two full-time clergy and one lay agent; three parishes also licensed clergy for the work.[3] Nevertheless, there were pressing

---

earlier flag.

1. Walrond, *op.cit.* (1904), p.117; also *The Word on the Waters*, 1962, pp.226, 119-20; and 1873, 115-16.
2. *The Word on the Waters*, 1874, p.102.
3. *Church Congress Report*, 1874 (Brighton), App. A, p.546 – by Canon Scarth.

needs: 'Two additions are greatly wanted here, *viz.* a clergyman whose work shall be done exclusively, or almost exclusively, afloat, and a Smacks' Boys' Home.'[1] The first objective does not appear to have been realised, as in 1882 the MS reports still show the work as being predominantly shore-based. The sea-going smacks were provided with bags of books and the men were visited by the reader, but the number of fishermen now working in the port, especially in the autumn, was too vast for the few Christian workers, and unlike many of the local fishermen who worked in the fleets, the Scottish herring fishermen came ashore for Sunday worship:

> During the herring season, which lasts from September to Christmas, a great many vessels are employed, which are laid up the rest of the year; these carry about ten men and boys. Besides our own boats, this year we had over 250 boats belonging to the fishing villages on the east coast of Scotland, each manned by seven hands; these stayed about six weeks so that in all we had over 3,000 strange fishermen here, most of them being in harbour on Sunday. During that time a minister was sent here from Scotland, who held services on the quay. A special service was held for them in the Parish Church, but most of the boats were at sea on the night appointed. I visited among them daily, giving tracts, speaking to them on deck and holding Bible readings in the cabins.[2]

The second objective met with a more-ready response. Following the death of the Missions to Seamen Secretary, the Rev. Theodore A. Walrond, in 1873, friends and supporters set about raising the necessary £2,315 to build the Walrond Memorial Home for Smacks' Boys. This was opened on 15 February 1876 by Earl Nelson. The Ms Reader, Mr Goldswain, was appointed manager of the Home, which, apart from providing accommodation for over 100 smacks' boys, had a large reading room for sailors and fishermen on the first floor, which became a focal meeting point for the local seafarers.[3]

A small cutter, the *Dove*, was provided for the Reader in 1876 by the Vicar of Great Yarmouth, in order to visit and hold services on the vessels and lightships.[4] With the growing number of vessels visiting and working from the port two scripture readers were appointed and a new Mission boat, the *Anna Ross*, was given to the society for its work at Yarmouth.[5]

1. *The Word on the Waters*, 1874, p.100.
2. *Missions to Seamen Annual Report*, 1882 (published 10 May 1883), pp.68-69.
3. *The Word on the Waters*, 1876, p.113.
4. *Church Work Among Sailors in 64 Home Ports* (at the Convocation of the Lower House of Canterbury, February 1878), p.27.
5. Built in 1889 and launched in February 1890, it served until 1905 when it was

During the early years of the twentieth century, the fishing industry experienced another recession and by 1906 there were no longer any smack boys using the building. Therefore, the Walrond Institute was sold. By 1920, however, an upturn in the herring fishery led to the re-letting of the building for use by visiting Scottish fishergirls. The Institute did not survive the Second World War; in 1941 it was destroyed in an air raid. After the war, the fishing industry never recovered its prewar status, although the Missions to Seamen continued to employ a locally appointed reader. The literature of the Walrond Institute says little about its relationship with the Sailors' Home thus, with no evidence to the contrary, we can assume that the two institutes worked harmoniously for the benefit of the local fishing community.

4.2.3. The St Andrew's Waterside Mission

In the wake of the international evangelical revival of 1858–61 and the establishment of the English Church Union in 1859, the foundation of the St Andrew's Waterside Mission in 1864 was partly a response to the evangelical seafarers' missions, and partly a reinforcement of the parochial system. At the same time, the growing influence of Anglo-Catholics (especially since 1833 following the success of the Oxford movement and the missions in the 1840s and 1850s, led by Fr Luigi Gentile and Fr Dominic Barbari) was eagerly embraced by the second generation, with Anglo-Catholics making a significant impact on Victorian Christianity.

The rediscovery of the tradition of mission priests and parish missions (following the example of St Vincent de Paul), and the growing number of second-generation Anglo-Catholic clergy working in urban parishes during the second half of the nineteenth century, attacked head on the alienation from the churches felt by the working classes. The influence of priests, such as Charles Lowder, Arthur Stanton and Stewart Headlam in London, and Robert R. Dolling in Portsmouth, must have given impetus to the Nonconformists working with fishermen and other seafarers in London and the country's ports. Indeed, the Moody and Sankey meetings in 1875 were partly a response to the Anglo-Catholic missions to London of 1869 and 1874.[1] Gerald Parsons tells us that Anglo-Catholic revivalism reached its peak with the London missions of 1869–74. Hence, the subjective and emotional experience of the evangelicals was paralleled by the objective and all-encompassing beliefs and practices of the Anglo-Catholics.

---

replaced with a new motor launch, the *Dorothy* (Notes on Great Yarmouth held in the MS Archives, Hull History Centre).

1. Parsons, *op.cit.*, Vol. I (1988), pp.226-30.

The foundation of the St Andrew's Waterside Mission in 1864, therefore, came at a time of significance for the Anglo-Catholic clergy in fishing ports around the country, who would provide the backbone. While the work of the Beach and Harbour Mission was developing in Great Yarmouth, the new Anglo-Catholic society was emerging further south. Founded in 1864 by the Rev. C.E.R. Robinson, the Saint Andrew's Waterside Mission[1] worked as an independent society for 75 years and had as its stated object:

> To encourage the worship of God at sea, and to advance the influence and teaching of the Church of England among sailors, fishermen and emigrants on board ship or elsewhere, through the agency of the Parochial clergy at home, and the responsible clergy abroad.[2]

The SAWM began as a society concerned with the fishing and seafaring community of Gravesend but quickly expanded to have agents in seaports all over the world. As an organisation inclined to High Church principles, riding on the wave of Anglo-Catholic revivalism, it hoped to establish a balance against the predominantly evangelical presence amongst seafarers. This position, however, caused some problems because the different beliefs and practices of the various missions sometimes gave rise to confusion. For example, the Rev. Forbes A. Phillips of the North Sea Church Mission, a SAWM offshoot founded in 1896, had no qualms about drinking a few pints with fishermen in their local pubs and was not averse to occasional rough and tumble. The evangelical groups, on the other hand, tended to be strictly teetotal and encouraged all with whom they came into contact to 'sign the pledge'. Not surprisingly, perhaps, when approaches were made by the SAWM to the Thames Church Mission and the Missions to Seamen with a view to amalgamation the offer was rejected.[3]

Origins and Development

During the years 1855–7 the Rev. C.E.R. Robinson was a curate at St Thomas' Church, Ryde, Isle of Wight, although he already had pastoral experience as a chaplain to Price's Patent Candle Company.[4] A fellow

1. SAWM was renamed the St Andrew's Waterside Church Mission in 1892. I have used the term SAWM up to the point when the name was changed, and thereafter used SAWCM. The Minutes of the SAWCM are kept in the MS Archives at the Hull History Centre.
2. Quoted in H.G.F. Hicks, *The Bishop of the North Sea* (published privately, 1930), pp.29ff. (copy in Great Yarmouth Reference Library).
3. From a paper in the MS Archives that gives a brief history of the TCM; see also MS Minutes, 1873, Minute no. 1154. (Minute no. 16325 says: 'Commander Dawson read a memorandum which he had prepared of our relations for many years with the SAWCM. It is to be kept as a record.' (This 'record', however, is missing.)
4. *Crockford's Clerical Directory* (1880); the Rev. R.J. Boggis, *History of St John's Torquay*

clergyman on the Isle of Wight, the Rev. Thomas Cave Childs, worked as chaplain to the Bristol Missions to Seamen, with responsibility for the English Channel. He appears to have greatly impressed Robinson (as he had earlier impressed W.H.G. Kingston) with his commitment and endeavour in that he

> worked day and night, through fair weather and foul, at first in a small open boat with his Devonport boatmen, and afterwards in a cutter (named, like her Bristol sister-ship, the *Eirene*) among sailors and nationalities, holding brief services afloat, sometimes as many as ten a day and distributing Bibles, *etc.*, to seamen in their own languages.[1]

Following another curacy in Therfield, Hertfordshire, during the years 1859–61, Robinson was appointed Vicar of Holy Trinity, Milton-next-Gravesend, and almost immediately followed Childs' example by visiting, with his curate, the Rev. John Scarth, the many vessels that called at Gravesend. Scarth later wrote a history of the SAWM and made the following comments on the beginnings of the society:

> In the first instance, it was an effort on the part of the parochial clergy to do something for the amphibious part of the population, fishermen, watermen, and others, who gained a precarious livelihood on the river, but who dwelt on shore. The work next went out on to the emigrant ships, with their motley assortment of passengers; but it soon extended to all classes of vessels that remained for a time at Gravesend, and it became more interesting and effective as, in course of time, the same officers and men came frequently within the influence of the clergy.[2]

Rev. Robinson gave his own account of SAWM's beginnings. The work, he said, was of three kinds:

1. Visits to ships outward bound, carrying passengers, either emigrants or troops;
2. Visiting ships of all kinds, carrying cargo only, and therefore having only sailors on board;
3. Ministering to all sorts of amphibious people, who live like water-fowl almost more on the water than on the land.[3]

(Devonshire Press, 1930), p.133.
1. Walrond, *op.cit.* (1904), p.47.
2. Scarth, *op.cit.* (1890), p.22.
3. *The Monthly Packet*, October 1868. Reprinted in the SAWM Report, 1868, p.3; also in Scarth, *op. cit.* (1890), p.12.

Determined to have the Anglo-Catholics represented in missionary work amongst seafarers, Robinson nevertheless acknowledged that 'the rough work hitherto [had been] done only [. . .] by Nonconformists'.[1] But this was not strictly true; as has already been seen the TCM, MS, BMS and EFCS represented a good deal of Anglican involvement – although no group thus far had exclusively represented the Anglo-Catholic movement. There was also the continuing aversion of the Anglican clergy to this kind of work – a situation which did not escape the notice of the seamen, relayed by Mr Robinson in the following anecdote:

> 'Why, you've taken up with a Methodist parson!' said a pilot to a dock agent, who had kindly given me a lift in his little screw steamer, just after we parted at the pier head. 'No!' he said, 'That's the Rev. Mr [Robinson] of [St Andrew's] Church!' I have found this sort of thing in every direction.

Prior to the foundation of the SAWM, Robinson contacted the Missions to Seamen:

> In 1863 it was reported that a letter had been received from a gentleman in Gravesend making some enquiries as to what Society was in operation to promote the spiritual welfare of seamen at Gravesend. The Rev. Robinson, Incumbent of a church in Gravesend, had visited the *Swan* subsequently in order, if practicable, to establish some place, or to obtain some vessels that the watermen and seamen might assemble for Divine Service.[2]

The work had at first been based in a rented house which was formerly the Spread Eagle Tavern. The lower story was fitted out as a chapel, and the upper rooms used as a mission house, incorporating storage space, an office, a school for poor children, a reading room, night school and lending library.[3] A nameplate bore the legend, Waterside Mission, a committee was formed to oversee the work in January 1864, and the Bishop of Rochester was elected as Patron. Mr (now Canon) Robinson took on the responsibility of Honorary Chairman, and his curate, the Rev. John Scarth, became the Honorary Secretary and Honorary Treasurer. A regular visitor and teacher in the weekday evening school was Charles George Gordon (later General Gordon of Khartoum), who was a friend of Scarth, and was at that time engaged in building fortifications at Tilbury.[4]

---

1. Recorded in *ibid.*, p.18.
2. SAWM Report, 1868, pp.2-3.
3. *The Penny Post*, 1 April 1870, p.102.
4. Scarth, *op. cit.*, pp.8-9.

Expansion

When the lease on the property came up for renewal in 1869, the Committee looked at the possibility of erecting a memorial church for the work, based at Gravesend in the parish of Holy Trinity. Part of the Waterside Mission (the old Spread Eagle Tavern) was demolished and the church built as an adjunct to the building. When an appeal was launched, a lady donated £1,000 to erect the building as a memorial to her father, stating that the gift was given on condition that other funds be raised to purchase the freehold of the mission house and wharf. She also asked to remain anonymous, but she was later revealed to be the daughter of Rear-Admiral Sir Francis Beaufort, KCB, Hydrographer of the Royal Navy, and the inventor of the Beaufort Wind Scale.[1]

With £200 in the bank, and £1,300 still to raise, Canon Robinson instituted a Building Committee, and set off around the country, at his own expense, to raise funds – returning with £800. Building work commenced with the first stone being laid on St Peter's Day, 29 June 1870, and Rear-Admiral Ingleford presented a Communion plate and a peal of four bells to mark the occasion. A year later the church was completed with all outstanding debts paid, the new building was consecrated on St Andrew's Day, 30 November 1871, and dedicated to St Andrew by Bishop Claughton, Archdeacon of London, acting on behalf of the Bishop of Rochester. A memorial plate was placed in the chancel which recorded the church's dedication to the memory of Rear-Admiral Sir Francis Beaufort, KCB, and three memorial windows were placed and a brass memorial plate.[2]

The Waterside Mission was renamed Saint Andrew's Waterside Mission (SAWM), and a new chapter in the work began.[3] In the meantime, Canon Robinson, had taken up a new post as the incumbent of St John's Church, Torquay, leaving Mr Scarth, now vicar of Holy Trinity Church, to take over responsibility for running SAWM.[4] Under Scarth's leadership five members of staff were soon employed. The work of the mission continued to expand and in 1872 a day school was begun for the children of fisherfolk, while overseas clergy offered to act on behalf of SAWM for the benefit of seafarers in their ports. In 1873 operations were extended into Victoria Docks by arranging for the local vicar to act on SAWM's behalf, and in 1875 part of the parish of Tilbury, the fort, and the coastguard station, were placed in the care of the mission under the authority of the Rev. A.E. Clementi-Smith, Rector of Chadwell St Mary at Grays. Other clergy were appointed to similar positions.[5]

1. Boggis, *op. cit.*, p.135.
2. SAWM Report, 1871.
3. *Ibid.*, 1875, p.47.
4. Boggis, *op. cit.* (1930), p.135.
5. SAWM Report, 1875.

This system of providing grants to enable clergy to work specifically with seafarers proved effective, and SAWM adopted the general principle in its relationship with waterside parishes. The work was formalised in 1876 when a Council was established in London, and a constitution drawn up and presented to SAWM's General Meeting in June.[1] Premises were secured in the City Chambers, close to Fenchurch Street Station, for offices and a book depot with a librarian in charge. A salaried Assistant Secretary was appointed in 1877, based at the depot in London, to ease the growing burden of work on Scarth; and a steam launch was obtained, called the *Messenger*, to work in the vicinity of Gravesend.

The St Andrew's Waterside Mission.

Then in 1881 news came of the death of Canon Robinson, who, at the age of 51, suffered a heart attack at his home in Torquay, and died on 4 January.[2] During the same year, Canon Scarth began to suffer from ill health. He retired from his post as Honorary Treasurer to the mission, although he continued as Honorary Secretary. Two years later he resigned his charge of the parish of Holy Trinity and was appointed incumbent of Bearstead, though he stayed in position as Honorary Secretary to SAWM.

1. *Ibid.*, 1876, pp.69-70.
2. Boggis, *op. cit.* (1930), p.164.

A Church Ship

The idea of a church ship was mooted at the Brighton Church Congress in 1874 when the Rev. E.L. Salisbury argued that such a vessel should be sent to work amongst the fishing fleets. Despite the growth of the Church's work among seafarers and fishermen during the 1850s and 1860s, it was not until 1869 at the Liverpool Church Congress that any mention was made of the idea that a vessel should be sent out to the fishing fleets.[1]

The annual church congresses commenced in 1861 and provided a forum for debate on a range of issues. The seafarers' missions took advantage of this forum and from 1869 to 1902 there were regular contributions from the representatives of maritime missions. Canon Scarth mentioned on several occasions that the churches lacked involvement with seafarers, and at the Swansea Church Congress, in 1879, he pointed out that there were precedents:

> At the mouth of the Thames, not far from my parish one of the best works among seafaring people, both afloat and ashore, has been carried on for twenty years, with God's blessing, and with great success. The rector had a boat of his own with which he occasionally went out with the fleet, and it was not unappropriately named the *Kingfisher*. Not a boat of that fleet goes out on Sundays.[2]

Regular reports were given in *Our Own Magazine*, about a vessel called the *Kingfisher*, which visited ports along the west coasts of England and Scotland. This may have been the same vessel mentioned by Scarth, although it was said to be based at Ramsey on the Isle of Man, not at the mouth of the Thames. It is of course possible that the clergyman in question had earlier been an incumbent at the mouth of the Thames, and later continued his maritime mission work on the Isle of Man.[3]

In 1875 SAWM had also advertised for help in transporting clergy to and from the fishing fleets:

NORTH SEA FISHING FLEET

The frequent opportunities of supplying the 700 or 1,000 men constantly at work in their hazardous employ have not been lost sight of. The men are very grateful and if we could but be sure of the weather at sea being propitious for Mission work, one of the clergy would occasionally go out as the fleet is seldom visited. Any yacht sailing in that direction and willing to make a Mission trip

---

1. Church Congress Report (Liverpool), 1869, pp.183-7.
2. The Swansea Church Congress, 1879, p.141; also Scarth, *op. cit.* (1889), p.28.
3. *Our Own Magazine*, The Children's Special Mission, London, Vol. VI, 1885.

among the different fleets would be doing a great kindness to the Fishermen if it would take one of the Clergy of the Mission there and back.[1]

A year later visits appear to have been made on a fairly regular basis, and magazines *etc.*, were taken out to the fleets on the 'fish steamers'.[2] The idea of clergy regularly visiting the fleets, and of a 'sailing church ship' specifically for fishermen, was therefore 'in the air' by the early 1880s.

The topics of the talks included the Royal Navy, merchant marine and canal workers, as well as seamen and fishermen.

Chart 3
Speakers at the Church Congresses

1869 Liverpool	Earl Nelson	Rt Rev. Dr Ryan	Henry Duckworth	Rev. C.E.R. Robinson Contributor to the discussion
1874 Brighton	Commander W. Dawson (Ms)	Rev. E.L. Salisbury	J. Scarth (SAWM)	Rev. E.A. Williams
1875 Stoke-upon-Trent	Dawson	Rev. Canon Barclay	/	Discussion – several speakers incl. Rev. J. Gott
1876 Plymouth	Dawson	Rev. J.B. Harbord	Scarth	Robinson (SAWM). A wide-ranging discussion
1879 Swansea	Dawson	The Rt Rev. E. Trollope	Scarth	Admiral A.P. Ryder. A wide-ranging discussion
1881 Newcastle	Dawson	Mather (TCM/MDSF)	Scarth	Agnes Weston
1885 Portsmouth	Weston	Rev. J.B. Harbord	Scarth	A wide-ranging discussion, including Rev. T. Stanley Treanor
1888 Manchester	Dawson	Rt Rev. E.R. Wilberforce	/	A wide-ranging discussion
1889 Cardiff	Dawson	Rev. C. Griffiths		Wide-ranging addresses and discussion
1890 Hull	There were several addresses and a wide-ranging discussion, including a discussion paper by Rev. R. Meddings of Grimsby.			
1895 Norwich	Dawson	Ven. C.M. Woosnam	Scarth	Sir G. Baden-Powell & Rev. Forbes A. Phillips
1902 Northampton	Papers given on the Royal Navy and the Mercantile Marine. Speakers include Rev. E. Lambert and Agnes Weston.			

1. SAWM Report, 1875, p.59.
2. *Ibid.*, 1876, pp.17-18.

4.2.4. The Thames Church Mission (1856–1904)

Developments and Difficulties

W.H.G. Kingston of the MS approached the Thames Church Mission in 1856 suggesting an amalgamation:

> William H. G. Kingston Esq., one of the Hon. Secretaries to the Central Society for Missions to British Seamen Afloat and Ashore, being in attendance from the above Society stated that he was deputed by his Committee to ascertain whether the Thames Church Mission Society would unite with their Society (now in course of formation) – the members of the TCM to become members of the Central Society for Missions to British Seamen – thus forming a part of one great scheme without losing in any way its individual character which its early supporters may wish to retain.[1]

The offer was rejected. Another approach was made in 1865 but this, too, was rejected although both organisations agreed to work more closely together. The Missions to Seamen responded with an offer to provide a scripture reader for work in the upper part of the river, and with the TCM's agreement a Captain Gummer was appointed at a salary of £80 per annum. Unfortunately, the joint experiment did not work and the MS reader was withdrawn.[2]

While relations between the TCM and MS remained amicable, this was not the case with the SAWM. When the SAWM commenced work at Gravesend in 1864, there was bound to be some conflict with the TCM which had an agent stationed in the same locality. A dispute arose over the baptism of a child in 1865 although the SAWM was on this occasion conciliatory, but other incidents arose from time to time. When Robinson wrote to the TCM Committee in 1867 suggesting an amalgamation of the two organisations the TCM, not surprisingly, rejected the offer.[3]

The early 1860s were a difficult period financially for the TCM, but by 1866 finances were in a healthy state and the Committee felt confident enough to appoint a lay Secretary, an assistant chaplain, three Scripture Readers, and a clerical secretary, the Rev. C. Gordon. Larger premises were now required and the TCM moved to new offices at 10 Poultry. But this period of prosperity did not last and by 1869 changes in the nature of shipping necessitated changes in the type of ministry offered. Finances were

---

1. MS Minutes, 7 March 1856.
2. TCM Minutes, October 1865.
3. *Ibid.*, 1867.

also running low and it became necessary to dismiss at least one member of staff, Rev. C.R. de Haviland. This seems a rather odd choice and suggests that the Committee was not entirely satisfied with the chaplain's work.[1] The TCM then moved back to King William Street where it remained until the lease ran out in 1876, then rented two rooms at 30 New Bridge Street, Blackfriars, with partial use of another office.[2] Throughout this turbulent period the *Swan* had served the TCM well, but by 1874 it was found to have decaying woodwork and was returned to the Admiralty – to be replaced in 1882 with another vessel, also named the *Swan*.[3]

The late 1870s saw regular changes of secretary, culminating in 1880 with the appointment of Ebenezer Joseph Mather.[4] He settled in quickly, began reorganising the structure of the TCM, and made a favourable impression. The next two years, however, told a familiar story. The chaplain, Rev. Anton Tien, who had been with the TCM for twelve months, was dismissed following the receipt of a letter by Captain Littlehales complaining that Mr Tien had 'professed Mahomedanism and his conversion to Islam' while working in Constantinople. Although Mr Tien strongly denied the charge, he was dismissed because, seemingly, the Committee was not entirely happy with his work.[5] Two other employees followed: a long-serving collector for having embezzled funds; and Mr J.F. Burnes, Missionary, for being absent without permission and for appropriating money from the mission.[6]

In 1881 Mr Mather visited the Short Blue fishing fleet, which was owned by Samuel Hewett, and in 1882 purchased, with Mr Hewett's help, a vessel for mission work among the North Sea fishing fleets. During the same period, he also initiated work amongst the navvies employed on the extension of Tilbury Docks and opened a Mission Hall there to be used as a day school for local children, the school being run by the contractors, who employed a schoolteacher on behalf of their employees' children.[7] Two rooms were also taken in High Street, Poplar, and used as a Sailors' Rest and Reading Room. These rapid changes made several enemies for the Thames Church Mission – with much of the venom directed at Mather. There was, for example, conflict with Ritualist clergy linked to the SAWM, in particular with Rev. A.R. Clementi-Smith, rector of Chadwell

---

1. *Ibid.*, January 1869.
2. *Ibid.*, 16 June 1876.
3. The *Swan* was replaced in 1888 by a steam launch, the *Edward Auriel*.
4. A brief biography can be found in the New Dictionary of National Biography.
5. TCM Minutes, June 1876.
6. *Ibid.*, 1 July 1880.
7. *Ibid.*, 16 July 1880, 14 April 1881, 28 July 1882 and 17 November 1882.

St Mary, who wrote to the Archbishop of Canterbury objecting to the
TCM's work amongst navvies – a work in which he was also engaged.
The correspondence was particularly vituperative, and Mr Clementi-Smith
drew the Archbishop's attention to the fact that Mather was a member
of the Plymouth Brethren. It may well have been partly as a result of this
that Mr Mather became a member of the Church of England in 1883.
Staff problems also continued to plague the TCM. James McDiarmid was
dismissed for 'gross ill-treatment of his wife, and general misconduct', and
was thought to have been 'deranged'.[1] And in April 1883, Rev. J.F. Guthrie
was dismissed for planning to elope to America with the niece of the master
of the TCM's steam launch. Mr Guthrie refused to inform his wife of the
reasons for his dismissal, and during the next year she regularly petitioned
the TCM committee to reconsider her husband's case.[2]

Despite these personnel difficulties, the TCM's work amongst the
North Sea fishing fleets, known as the Mission to Deep Sea Fishermen,
was prospering. In December 1883, the TCM Committee agreed to rent
two further rooms on the ground floor, mainly for use by the MDSF
aspect of the work, and funds were kept in a separate bank account known
as the 'Fishermen's Fund'. The workload, however, became a strain on the
TCM, and agreement was finally reached in 1884 for the two sides of the
work to separate. The MDSF became an organisation in its own right and
the TCM reverted to its original role of serving seafarers on the Thames
– although Mather remained Secretary of the TCM for a while following
the separation.

Apart from the financial strain, the separation of TCM and MDSF also
seems to have come about as the result of differences in church affiliation.
Under Mather's influence, and although he had joined the Church of
England, the MDSF claimed to be un-denominational. However, the
statistics available cast some light on the ideology of the staff. It can be
seen, for example, that the sale of prayer books diminished, and the giving
away of tracts increased quite markedly under Mr Mather's secretaryship.
Conversely, prayer book sales increased dramatically when Mr Mather's
association with the TCM ceased in 1886. Following the separation of
the TCM and the MDSF in 1884, the MS again approached the TCM in
1885 with a view to amalgamation, but the Committee again rejected the
offer.[3] Despite the Missions to Seamen's wish to consolidate the various
societies concerned with maritime mission, during the 1890s a spate
of new organisations came into being, several of which were primarily

---

1. TCM Minutes, 28 July 1882.
2. *Ibid.*, 20 April 1883.
3. *Ibid.*, 20 November 1885.

concerned with ministering to fishermen, such as the North Sea Church Mission, and the Salvation Army's Salvation Navy. The TCM felt the pressure, especially in terms of increased competition for fund-raising. Debts accrued in the early 1900s, and by 1903 the bishops supporting the TCM urged the mission to amalgamate with the MS. The TCM Committee bowed to the inevitable and its last meeting took place on 31 March 1904.[1]

1. *Ibid.*, 31 March 1904.

Chapter 5
Fishing for Souls
1880–1900

5.1. Nonconformist Missions

Late Victorian Britain saw a period of economic decline beginning in the mid-1870s. Among Christians there was a growing recognition that evangelicalism was not sufficient alone to improve the condition of the poor, and there was a gradual rejection of the belief that economic laws were immutable (aided by the effects of controversies in science, geology, history and theology). State intervention was therefore seen as necessary to ensure positive change. Theological changes, too, from an emphasis on the Atonement to that on the Incarnation, along with the impact of Christian Socialism, had an important influence. John Kent has argued that it was Moody's campaigns in Britain (1873–5 and 1881–4 and 1891–2) that motivated the Anglican evangelicals to identify more clearly and closely with their Nonconformist contemporaries in responding to people's practical needs.[1] As a result, the country's fishing ports gradually saw a growing emphasis on the work of institutes, especially in the larger ports such as Grimsby, Hull, Lowestoft, Aberdeen and Fleetwood.

The Emergence of the Mission to Deep Sea Fishermen
Given the nature of the development of the Mission to Deep Sea Fishermen, the problems the society faced, and the relationship of the founder and director with his committee, it will be helpful to examine the issues in a little more detail here. It should not, however, be assumed that the issues were unique to the MDSF. The initiator of organised seafarers' missions, the Rev. George Charles Smith, encountered his share of difficulties, including periods of imprisonment, the loss of some of his innovations, and public distain. Other leaders of maritime missions, such as Rev. Dr John Ashley and Ebenezer Joseph Mather, also encountered problems as they struggled

---

1. Kent, *op. cit.* (1978), p.299.

to make headway with their work and visions. The fruits and failings of the founder of the Fishermen's Mission should therefore be seen within this wider context. There were also precedents for practically all aspects of the work of the MDSF – the use of sailing churches, the distribution of literature, woollens, services at sea, and medical aid, although some aspects were new, such as the opportunity for leisure activities at sea (viewing lantern-slides, interesting talks on a variety of subjects, boxing matches, tea and so on).

The Formative Years

The Mission to Deep Sea Fishermen began as an aspect of the Thames Church Mission's work in 1881, with the secretary, E.J. Mather, mainly responsible for the day-to-day running of both – but the rapid growth of the MDSF led to clashes of interest and strains upon the finances of the TCM. By November 1884 the situation had become so difficult for everyone involved that the TCM Council sought to distinguish the two aspects of the work. A Board was formed to oversee the running of the MDSF, which in turn gave way to a new Council. A 'Deed of Covenant' was drawn up in June 1886 and the MDSF was established as an independent society.[1] Despite the underlying difficulties, the eventual separation of the MDSF and TCM was fairly amicable and many people associated with the TCM became long-standing supporters of the MDSF. Unfortunately, the TCM never really recovered from the shock and amalgamated with the Missions to Seamen in 1904. In contrast to the decline of the TCM, the MDSF, apart from some difficulties over 1889–90, went from strength to strength, becoming the Royal National Mission to Deep Sea Fishermen in December 1896, and, now known as the Fishermen's Mission, continues its work to the present day.

Little physical evidence remains of the TCM's sixty years of work (1844–1904), although the TCM Minute Books are located at Hull History Centre. Extant materials of the early MDSF (1881–6) are also sparse: the Minute Books are with the RNMDSF, a few notes kept by the Missions to Seamen (also held at Hull History Centre), half-a-dozen journals in the British Museum, a few personal letters, references to the TCM/MDSF's work in national newspapers, and a few passing comments in books by E.J. Mather and Alexander Gordon, and novels such as those by R.M. Ballantyne and James Runciman. Many documents were destroyed by the RNMDSF staff when additional space was needed, others were lost during the Second World War when the Mission was relocated to Padstow, and yet

---

1. TCM Minutes, 21 November 1884; MDSF Minutes, 18 June 1886; A. Gordon, *What Cheer O?* (James Nisbet & Co., 1890), p.72; E.J. Mather, *Nor'ard of the Dogger* (James Nisbet & Co.,1887), pp.189-90.

other materials fell victim to floods.[1] Given this situation, no comprehensive and objective account has ever been produced outlining the Mission to Deep Sea Fishermen's early development, although a number of popular books about the work have been published.

Ebenezer Joseph Mather

Ebenezer Joseph Mather in 1884.

Sadly, Mather's books are lacking in some important aspects of the MDSF's work, and some recent popular books (such as Stanley Pritchard's *Fish and Ships*) contain many errors. The following account therefore makes use of the accessible extant material, and corrects many of the errors and idealisations that have crept into publications about the Society's origins.

In February 1880, Ebenezer Joseph Mather, a young man of 30 years, applied for the post of Secretary to the *Thames Church Mission*.[2] The Society had experienced some difficulty in finding a suitable person, and had terminated the previous Secretary's employment on completion of his three-month probationary period. A sub-committee met on 9 February to interview Mather and, although he was a member of the Plymouth Brethren,

---

1. *Toilers of the Deep*, Autumn 1957, no. 760, p.4.
2. Known as 'Ebb' or 'E.J. Mather' to his friends (letter to the RNMDSF from Miss Gladys Mather, his daughter, dated 8 December 1970).

this does not seem to have deterred the Committee (Appendix 8). Even so, the situation here is far from clear. Mather's wife appears to have been a devout Anglican, and Mather himself had several Anglican friends.

It also appears that some members of the TCM had Plymouth Brethren sympathies. Nevertheless, given the anti-clerical stance of the Brethren, it comes as no surprise to hear that Mather formally became a member of the Church of England about 1883.[1] Kverndal says of this situation: 'The alleged Irvingite leanings of certain leaders in the Episcopal Floating Church Society resulted in the disaffection of others.' Admiral Gambier, for example, had Irvingite sympathies.[2] Nevertheless, the TCM Committee was impressed with Mather, and he

> was engaged on three months' probation (subject to approval of the General Committee) at a salary of one hundred guineas a year, on the understanding that he is to receive 10% Commission on Subscriptions obtained through his instrumentality, and to have full liberty to continue his private business, provided it does not interfere with the work of the Society.[3]

We are not told what Mather's 'private business' was although the TCM Minutes for 25 July 1884 say that he wrote and edited articles for the Religious Tract Society. Other notes refer to his obtaining £1,000 for the first Mission ship, and suggest that he personally benefited from the fishing activities of the Mission vessels. With experience as an auditor (the profession recorded on his marriage certificate), and as a market gardener, he presumably had some private business in these areas; he also later became a director of the 'Pure Water Company'.[4] He refers to his various means of income in his book *Nor'ard of the Dogger*, where he said that, when faced with the increasing demands upon his time by the MDSF in 1884, 'It now became necessary for me to relinquish one or two other occupations and sources of private income.'[5] He seems, also, to have engaged in a fair amount of buying and selling, obtaining, for example, literature from the Bible Society at a 50 per cent discount,[6] plus a general discount for Mission

---

1. Kverndal, *op. cit.* (1986), pp.294, 335-40. See also the *New Sailors' Magazine*, 1831, pp.289-93; 1832, p.360; 1834, pp.259-60; and 1838, pp.281-85.
2. The Irvingites were a religious sect formed by Edward Irving (1792-1834). The group broke away from the Presbyterians and advocated very strict ritualistic beliefs and practices.
3. TCM Minutes, 9 February 1880.
4. MDSF Minutes, 7 June 1889.
5. Mather, *op. cit.* (1887), p.190.
6. He did, however, mention this to the MDSF Council, MDSF Minutes, 3 December 1886.

societies which worked with seafaring people. This was in stark contrast to the usual ten per cent (in some cases 20 per cent) obtained by other societies. It is possible that he was profiting personally from this, as he was accused, in 1889, by the MDSF Council, of dishonesty with regard to his connection with the Bible Society.[1] He also obtained two old hulks at Yarmouth for £10, and later sold them to the TCM Committee for a total of £50.

Not a great deal is known of Mather's private life prior to his appointment with the TCM, although a useful summary is given in an anonymous article in the *Chart and Compass*, the journal of the British and Foreign Sailors' Society, in December 1889:

> He [Mather] was the son of poor but respected and religious parents. When quite a boy he manifested a shrewd business-like turn for making money. He became a junior clerk in a bank at Worcester (or a boy there), but instead of trusting to ordinary banking methods of making money, young Mather was found buying Manchester and other goods wholesale, and selling retail to the clerks, &c. From the first his head was screwed on right, he was all there. Then came market gardening, but that was too tame, or not sufficient scope for budding genius. He then travelled with a government official who was a real Plymouth,[2] and so got introduced to a circle which he afterwards most successfully bled for his great schemes. It is a pleasure to meet with a sharp boy! The 'Thames Church Mission' was without a secretary, he applied for the post, and being strongly recommended secured the position.[3]

The essence of this is verified by one of Mather's daughters in a letter to the RNMDSF,[4] and in a letter written by Mather to the TCM Finance Committee dated 21 October 1884:

> The Secretary further wishes to say that [. . .] he came to the Mission not as a novice, but as an expert who had for ten years held the position of Auditor under Government and in relinquishing his licence as a Broker of the City of London and throwing his services into the work of the TCM he lost pecuniarily – while thankful

---

1. MDSF Minutes, 2 August 1889.
2. The Plymouth Brethren are a conservative evangelical group. There are, however, two main branches: the Open Brethren and the Exclusive Brethren. I assume Mather had been a member of the Open Brethren as some branches here were more liberal and willing to work with non-Brethren people.
3. *Chart and Compass*, December 1889, p.369.
4. Letter from G. Mather to the RNMDSF dated 18 November 1970 (RNMDSF Archives).

to be engaged in the service of Christ. He has always desired and does still to act with thorough loyalty to this committee. He wishes it to be understood that the large increase in the income is to a considerable extent owing to the kindness of his personal friends – and that whenever the Mission is in temporary difficulty – he can (as at present) command the loan of funds free of interest.[1]

The details of Mather's first 30 years can be filled out a little from a small number of sources, such as his autobiography, *Memories of Christian Service*, Dr A.T. Schofield's *Behind the Brass Plate*, the TCM Minutes and a few letters written in later years to the RNMDSF by his children. Official sources such as registers help a little, but the material is sparse.

Following the successful completion of his three-month probation, his position as Secretary to the TCM was confirmed as from 11 May 1880, 'on the existing terms'.[2] He proved to be astute and competent. In November he reorganised some of the TCM's activities at a saving of '£52 a year, without diminishing the efficiency of the Society's staff'. The Committee was delighted with the changes, and raised his salary to £250 per annum from 1 February 1881.[3] Encouraged by this support Mather suggested a complete reorganisation of missionary districts in July 1881, which was approved, put into operation and resulted in much saving of labour and a greatly improved efficiency of service.[4] One aspect of this reorganisation is particularly significant: an important part of the TCM's work involved the distribution of Christian literature to emigrants, but was a task shared by missionaries and chaplains. Mather reorganised the distribution so that the missionaries travelled on board the emigrant ships as far as Gravesend, using the opportunity to distribute literature supplied by the Religious Tract Society and the British and Foreign Bible Society, and to talk with the emigrants – thereby leaving the chaplains free to concentrate on holding services for the emigrants.

Although effective, this rationalised approach must have annoyed the staff of the Anglo-Catholic St Andrew's Waterside Church Mission, who found themselves repeating work already done by the TCM. Throughout his time with the TCM, Mather sought ways of making the work more efficient, which inevitably meant dismissing some employees when their jobs became superfluous. At the same time, he recognised the need to adequately reward those who worked well – for example, in January 1882, he requested and obtained a salary increase for the colporteurs – and must

1. TCM Finance Committee Minutes (volume dated 31 July 1884-1 October 1896).
2. TCM Minutes, 21 May 1880.
3. *Ibid.*, 28 January 1881.
4. *Ibid.*, 15 July 1881, 18 November 1881.

thereby have won the respect and support of his staff, several of whom joined Mather when he set up the MDSF as an independent society.[1] In all, Mather spent six years with the TCM, yet he says remarkably little about this period in his writings, and the TCM receives no mention by name in either *Nor'ard of the Dogger* or in his autobiography.[2]

The Founding of the MDSF (1881-82)

In the summer of 1881 Samuel Hewett, owner of the Short Blue fishing fleet, which worked in the North Sea, invited the TCM to 'do something during the summer months for the spiritual benefit of his employees'.[3] Mather seized the opportunity, reflecting that, 'An occasional visit from a missionary might do good.'[4] He visited the fleet himself during the period Saturday, 27 August to Friday, 2 September 1881,[5] accompanied by the TCM's assistant chaplain, Rev. R.B. Thompson. They sailed from Billingsgate on the steamer *Supply* and spent five days on the Dogger Bank. Hewett's request, and Mather's visit to the Short Blue fleet, was in essence the beginning of the work of the Mission to Deep Sea Fishermen. Hewett had not only made the request, but offered to 'convey and feed free of charge any Missionary or Scripture Reader who may be sent out from time to time'.[6] As a mark of good faith Hewett and Co. also increased their annual subscription and offered to supply coal for the TCM's steam launch, the *Swan*, at a saving of nine shillings and six pence per ton upon the retail price.[7] The visit had a profound effect on Mather and the TCM Minutes for November 1881 record his impressions:

---

1. *Ibid.*, 20 January 1882.
2. Mather's autobiography was published anonymously around 1922. Nevertheless, with some knowledge of his life, it is not too difficult to identify the situations, events and people.
3. TCM Minutes, 18 November 1881.
4. *Toilers of the Deep*, 1886, p.66.
5. The actual dates of Mather's visit to sea are never clearly stated, some references being to August 1881 (*Toilers of the Deep*, June 1887, vol. 2, p.51) and others to September 1881 (TCM Minutes, 23 June 1882; *Toilers of the Deep*, Jan 1888, vol. 3, p.28). This apparent inconsistency dissipates when we discover that the final week in August 1881 runs over into September. If he departed on Saturday, 27 August 1881 and returned on Friday, 2 September 1881, and we allow the first and last days as travelling time to and from the fleet, this would enable him to have spent five days among the fleet, one of which would be a Sunday. This tallies with Mather's account in the TCM Minutes for 18 November 1881. However, Mather's diary notes (Appendix 5) says that he left London on a Tuesday and returned home the following Monday. This would still provide dates straddling August and September, but this raises the question whether he is talking about the same voyage in both his diary notes and his later reflections!
6. TCM Minutes, 18 November 1881.
7. *Ibid.*, 8 November 1881.

The Secretary took with him 1,000 portions of illustrated tracts, and 500 sheets of hymns as gifts to the smacksmen by whom they were received with deep gratitude. The men as a whole are wild and godless, but amongst them are some very earnest Christians who are most anxious for the conversion of their fellows, and heartily thanked God for the prospect of Gospel Services during the summer months. On his return he sent out George Clark, Scripture Reader, who returned greatly encouraged by his visitations from vessel to vessel, and confident that God's blessing had attended his labours.[1]

In later reflections upon this first visit, Mather said:

Our arrival was the signal for a wild scramble for the empty fish-boxes we had taken out. Boats manned by fellows as rough, unkempt, and boisterous in manners as appearance, put off from all the smacks, and our deck soon swarmed with 400 of the wildest men I had ever encountered. Amongst the 1,500 hands in the fleet there were perhaps 50 or 60 professing Christians, but the great majority were utterly careless and godless, and on that afternoon appeared to indulge in language more coarse, profane, and disgusting than usual. When all the boxes were out, then came the delivery of the fish, and with it an opportunity for dispensing the store of books. These were thankfully – even greedily – accepted, and the few words spoken for the Master were in most cases respectfully listened to.[2]

The visit was successful, and 'after his return Mather sent out four suitable men for a fortnight each'.[3] Following this nine-week experiment, he was able to assess the development, report back to the TCM Committee, and put forward Hewett's request that 'the Society should during the summer months do something for the spiritual benefit of [the company's] employees'.[4] The Committee members listened to the account favourably but postponed any final decision, although they did agree to give an extra two week's leave of absence to any member of staff who wished to spend this time 'in spiritual work with the North Sea fishing fleet on the Dogger Bank'. Members of staff took up the offer and on their return all talked of their warm reception.[5] Services were held, tracts distributed, woollen cuffs and comforters handed out, and copies of the Bible sold.

1. *Ibid.*, 18 November 1881.
2. *Toilers of the Deep*, vol. I, May 1886, p.65.
3. *Ibid.*, 1886, p.66.
4. TCM Minutes, 18 November 1881.
5. *Ibid.*, 20 January 1882, 19 May 1882, 16 June 1882.

The TCM Minutes for 18 November 1881 referred to the employment of Mr George Dixon as a Colporteur. He had previously been employed by Henry Cook's Portsmouth and Gosport Mission to Seamen, and Mather was presumably aware of Cook's work – especially his use of Bethel ships. Lord Cholmondeley (a member of the TCM Committee) was also a patron of Cook's Mission, and may have discussed this work with Mather. All this will have helped shape Mather's ideas for a Mission ship among the North Sea fishermen.

The Ensign

The idea of a Church of England Mission ship for the fishing fleets was not new. Speakers at the Church Congresses for 1874 and 1879 had made just such a plea. As Mather was a speaker at the Newcastle Church Congress in October 1881, he had most likely read the earlier Congress reports, which dealt with the question of 'the Church and the Sailor', and he perhaps had also pointed them out to members of the TCM Committee. With the Anglican and Nonconformist precedents of John Ashley, Carl von Bülow, Thomas Rosie, Henry Cook and the Thames vicar referred to by John Scarth, plus the support of Lord Cholmondeley, Mather had every reason to be optimistic. That he had for some time been thinking of the possibility of launching a Mission ship is borne out by his own comments in *Nor'ard of the Dogger* where he says that, when he first visited the fishing fleet, 'there flashed upon me for the first time the thought, "If the devil has his own mission-ship [the coper], [. . .] shall not God [. . .] have His mission-ship?"'[1] On Saturday, 10 June 1882, a Skipper Budd visited Mather in his office to talk about a Bethel ship (the two first met when Mather visited the Short Blue fleet in June 1881 and had apparently discussed the idea then).[2] Budd had injured his hand and Mather sent him for medical treatment but invited him to call again the following Monday. He returned with a Mr Barnes, captain of the carrier ship *Supply*, which had transported Mather to the Short Blue fleet a year earlier. In the meantime, Mather had discussed the plan with several friends and had been told that the cost of a second-hand vessel would be in the region of £1,000. The following Friday, 16 June, at the TCM Committee meeting, Mather 'mentioned that there was a great desire for a specially equipped Mission ship, and requested the prayers of the Committee upon the matter'.[3] But this request appears to have been a ruse. In *Toilers of the Deep* for June 1887, Mather said:

---

1. E.J. Mather, *op. cit.* (1887), p.44.
2. *Toilers of the Deep*, May 1886, p.11.
3. TCM Minutes, 16 June 1882.

It was on the 12th June 1882, that two smacksmen read with me the text upon the wall, 'He that cometh to God must believe that He is, and that He is a rewarder of them that diligently seek Him', and then we asked Him to look down from heaven upon the Deep Sea fishermen and send them 'the means of grace', in order that their hearts might possess 'the hope of glory'. Within three days of that prayer meeting the first Mission vessel was provided. Sunday, the 12th June 1887, will be the fifth anniversary of that memorable prayer meeting. The 12th June 1882, was my birthday.[1]

As the vessel was 'provided' (he presumably means that the purchase money had been offered) by the 15 June 1882, the minutes of the Committee meetings on 16 and 23 June would seem to demonstrate Mather's astuteness; he had put the members of the Committee in a position whereby they could not deny that God appeared to have answered their prayers. Returning to the Committee on 23 June, he reported that £1,000 had been donated 'after constant prayer' for the purchase of a vessel suitable for work in the North Sea. The £1,000 had been offered with the request that Mather become the managing owner, it being the case that the TCM could not itself own a fishing smack.[2] After telling the Committee members about the financial gift, they were of opinion that 'the offer was so distinctly an interposition of the Divine hand in answer to prayer that it would be wrong not to accept it'.[3] The Committee, however, must have had some warning (perhaps a few days') of this development, and had taken the opportunity to discuss the issue before the meeting, because Mather had arranged for Daniel H. Budd, a 'Master Fisherman', to be present.[4] Having gained the formal consent of his Committee, Mather brought Skipper Budd into the room and he was appointed 'Honorary Agent' of the Society with the intention that he be skipper of the new Mission ship, which would carry a large lending library, medicine chest and harmonium. At a later meeting, he was also appointed an agent for the Shipwrecked Mariners' Society, the Bible Society and the Church of England Temperance Society.[5] Had the Committee not been aware of the developments before

1. *Toilers of the Deep*, June 1887, vol. 2, p.151.
2. Letter in the RNMDSF Archives to Dr Gilbert Smith, 7 April 1888.
3. TCM Minutes, 23 June 1882.
4. More recent letters and articles refer to 'David' Budd. This mistake may have arisen as the result of misreading the name 'Daniel', which at first glance does indeed look like 'David', in the TCM Minutes of 28 June 1882. There was, however, another mission skipper called 'David Budd', Daniel's son, which has no doubt added to the confusion.
5. TCM Minutes, 28 July 1882.

the meeting on 23 June, they would, no doubt, have been annoyed at
Mather's presumption in bringing this potential Mission skipper before
them, hence they may well have had some sort of interview with him to
determine his suitability. As Mather was to be the managing owner of
the vessel, the Committee gave him permission to 'transact any private
business provided it was not detrimental to the Society'.[1] He had been
assured by several smack owners that the Mission ship would be able to
maintain itself by trawling, and the prospects at that time did indeed
look good. The Committee was convinced.

The *Ensign*, a 56-ton, yawl-rigged fishing smack, was originally built
by Hewett & Co. in 1877 at Southtown, Great Yarmouth. Hewett sold
it to Mather and offered him free access to his stores, workshops and dry
dock, which was located in the rear of Dock Tavern Lane.[2] On Friday, 14
July 1882, three weeks after its acquisition by Mather, it was ready to put
to sea.

It has been suggested that the anonymous gift of £1,000 came
from Samuel Hewett, the owner of Hewett and Co.[3] Although never
mentioned by name, the evidence points to Hewett being the person
who gave the donation; in *Nor'ard of the Dogger* Mather says that the
person who originally asked what he could do to help the fishermen was
a friend with an interest 'in the fleet known as the Short Blue', which was
owned by Hewett. This friend also talked about 'our men in the North
Sea'. Later, when the 'friend' offered to help Mather in his enterprise,
he said, 'I can't afford to give you a vessel', from which we may infer
that he owned some, but he was prepared to give a loan. A later aside
by Lionel Dashwood, in his correspondence in *The Record* (6 January
1890, p.27, published by Morgan and Scott, London) stated: 'Surely,
he [Mather] cannot have forgotten that the original owner of the *Ensign*
was more than vexed at the change of name of that vessel' (which was
changed to the *Thomas Gray* in 1886). Mr Hewett would obviously have
been vexed, as such an action implies a desire to cut all threads linking
the MDSF with its original benefactor. Gordon says: 'the first vessel had
been lent by a Nonconformist'.[4] It would be interesting to know whether
Hewett was a member of the Brethren and attended the same meetings as
Mather. This would give credence to Mather's remark that a 'friend' lent
the money. This is indeed a most likely possibility. Hewett was an astute
businessman and a personal gift would be a necessity as it would have

1. *Ibid.*, 23 June 1882.
2. *Yarmouth Mercury*, 25 November 1956.
3. J.L. Kerr, *Wilfred Grenfell: His Life and Work* (G.G. Harrap & Co. Ltd, 1959), p.41.
4. Gordon, *op. cit.* (1890), p.79.

been difficult to convince his Board of Directors to part with such a sum
or to loan a smack, with no security and for such a risky venture. Mather
was only too aware of this, as he said of a donation which Hewett's Board
gave the TCM nine months after the *Ensign* sailed: 'It was given, not
by private philanthropists, but by a Board of Directors sitting round
their table voting away the monies of the company in aid of a Mission.'[1]
Hewett and Co. became annual subscribers, along with several of the
company's directors.[2] If the donor was indeed Hewett, this would explain
his reticence to be named – he would not want to be seen to be wholly
responsible for sending out a fully equipped Mission ship. Far better
to use an existing society that had a good record of evangelistic work
amongst seafarers – and the TCM worked with the fishermen at Barking,
which had for many years been the centre of Hewett's operations. If the
scheme failed, Hewett would lose nothing (the £1,000 was after all only
a loan – and this at 4 per cent interest)[3] and, if it succeeded, the company
would benefit from hard-working and faithful employees. The risk was
all Mather's, who, as managing owner, would be fully responsible for the
scheme's success – or failure. The donor had said to Mather: 'Now, if you
are willing, for the sake of the object you have in view, to undertake the
entire responsibility and risk of managing a fishing-smack, I don't mind
finding the money.'[4]

During the 1880s Hewett was busy replacing all his smaller vessels (*i.e.*
those of approximately 50 feet and less) with newer and larger ones of 75
feet in length, in order to work in more distant fishing grounds such as
the Horn Reef off Jutland.[5] Even though the *Ensign* was not an old vessel,
it was small and quickly becoming obsolete. With hindsight, therefore,
Hewett's 'gift' was astutely made. The cost of a brand-new sailing smack
in 1881 was approximately £1,500.[6] Thus, Hewett managed to dispose of
an old vessel at no cost to himself. If the scheme worked, Hewett stood
to gain from his hard-working fishermen employees – if it failed, the
money would be repaid, plus 4 per cent interest, by Mather, who took
all the personal risks. As an auditor, Mather must have been aware of the
implications, although he probably thought that by using the *Ensign* as a
fishing smack, as well as a mission vessel, he could more than cover these
costs.

---

1. TCM Minutes, 15 December 1882.
2. *Ibid.*
3. E.J. Mather, *op. cit.* (1887), p.190.
4. *Ibid.*, pp.61-2.
5. Personal letter from Derek Farman, 30 November 1989.
6. Robinson, *op. cit.* (1996), p.89.

The Maiden Voyage (July 1882)

The *Ensign* sailed from Gorleston on Friday, 14 July 1882, and Mather joined her at sea nine days later. The only newspaper reference to the sailing of the *Ensign* appeared in the *Yarmouth and Gorleston Times* on Saturday, 15 July 1882:

> Messrs Hewett and Co. have just disposed of their cutter *Ensign*, a craft of 70 tons (Captain Budd, master) to the Thames Church Mission, on board which, when out fishing with the fleet on Saturdays and Sundays, religious services will be held. It is expected during the summer that several clergymen from London will occasionally proceed to sea, and hold services at the fleet. She is to be refitted.

By the time of the newspaper report, the vessel had already sailed, the reporter perhaps having misunderstood the nature of the information he had been given – which may account for the absence of reporters on the quayside. Nevertheless, the vessel made a great show of sailing on a Friday, a day universally regarded by fishermen as bringing bad luck to any who set sail. The only extant account of this event comes from a 'Mission hand' of the *Ensign*, whose words were recorded by Alexander Gordon in his book *What Cheer, O?*:

> I well remember the sneering remarks made by many who heard of the new Mission that had been started. 'Well', says one, 'I'll give 'em one voyage, and that'll clue 'em up.' 'What's the use of sendin' that thing out to them smacksmen?' said another; 'they don't care a lot for missions or anythink besides; better by half let 'em alone.' The day came for us to set sail; up went our big blue flag, with 'Thames Church Mission' written across it. Then up followed the mainsail, and away came the tug to tow our little vessel out of the river Yare. Off we went; many cheered but more sneered and laughed at us. But on we glided with the steam tug ahead of us, and we were soon out of hearing of all voices, whether raised for or against. Outside the harbour we made sail, and got clear of all danger of sandbanks, and then shaped our course for Messrs Leleu and Morgan's fleet, being well stocked with books and magazines of various kinds, and many warm woollens. We had plenty to do. The next morning we joined the said fleet, but we had rather a strange reception; many bore up round us, and spoke to us, and asked us what we meant by that big flag that floated in the breeze at our topmost head. This being Saturday we had no time to lose, for we were commissioned from the head office to proceed direct to Messrs Hewett and Co.'s

fleet. So our skipper, after distributing among those that came on board, tracts, magazines, and cosy wraps, made sail for the 'Short Blues'. About six or seven in the evening we joined them, our flag still flying at our topmost head. This being Saturday night, we lay to, and our little craft was made ready for the men to come on board the next morning for praise and prayer. Unfortunately, there were not many among this largest fleet of smacks in all the North Sea that were religious men. However, Sunday morning came; out went our little boat, ready to fetch any one on board that we thought we could manage to get. The morning was very fine, and our first meeting was after all held on board of the steamship *Frost*, the fish-carrier belonging to Messrs Hewett and Co., the steamer being much larger than the *Ensign*. There was a great number of fishermen on board, and the Word was preached to them with power, and I heard many say, 'This Mission means us good'; but at the same time there were many very indifferent to us, and these showed us no kindness. Sunday being over, we began our toil as the rest of the smacksmen did. Down went our trawl, and so we went on during the week, boarding the steamer sending our fish to market, holding meetings where we could, and speaking a word in season. Now this is the very thing that tells home with the fishermen – personal contact with them, putting the things that make for their peace before them.[1]

Lines eight to eleven suggest that the cheering (and sneering) took place on the quayside where the *Ensign* was relaunched. This is rather different from the idealised picture, drawn as a frontispiece to *Nor'ard of the Dogger*, to commemorate the event that shows the crowd at the entrance to the harbour. Despite the ridicule preceding the launch, the work proved effective and in succeeding months was received with warm support by the various fishing fleet owners. Nine months after the first voyage, Mather received a letter from Hewett praising the work: 'Our men have been completely revolutionised; we believe great good has been done, and we gladly become annual subscribers of ten pounds and ten shillings to the funds of the Mission.'[2] This was accompanied with a donation of £50.

The Mission ship was called a Bethel ship by the fishermen and owners, and Mather and others at the TCM took up the name,[3] but this had unfortunate repercussions. The BFSS, MS and other seafarers' Missions

---

1. Gordon, *op. cit.* (1890), pp.61-3.
2. Mather, *op. cit.* (1887), p.96.
3. TCM Minutes, 28 July 1882.

The somewhat idealised picture of the Ensign *sailing from Gorleston, 14 July 1882.*

had been using the Bethel flag since it was pioneered during the early years of the nineteenth century. Numerous smacks in the fishing fleets now carried Bethel flags, and missionaries had been visiting the North Sea fleets since the 1860s. Mather was familiar with this earlier work (as his address to the Newcastle Church Congress in 1881 shows), and by not crediting these earlier efforts he caused great offence.[1]

Despite the problems, 1882 was a propitious time during which to launch a new evangelical mission. Moody and Sankey were in the middle of their second tour of Britain (1881–4). Those who attended the meetings were mainly drawn from the middle classes, and it was from this group that support was gained for the new missionary enterprise. Mather was also able to make good use of publicity material that highlighted the poor social conditions at sea: for example, two young Hull fishing apprentices had recently been murdered, and death was all too common from drink supplied by the copers.

Expansion (1883–84)

It soon became obvious that one Bethel ship was inadequate for the work in the North Sea, let alone further afield, and Mather began to moot the idea of a similar vessel 'for every fleet' – a cry that received added support in March 1883, when the newspapers announced that 360 fishermen had

---

1. *Chart and Compass*, Sept 1886, p.281.

been lost in the 'Great March Gale'.[1] However, the developments during 1882 were becoming a strain on the resources of the TCM and towards the end of the year the Committee voted the sum of £110 as a salary for a competent clerk to relieve Mather of correspondence, in order that he might give his attention 'to the extension of the Society's influence and work'.[2] In January 1883, Mather employed Alexander Gordon, formerly a tutor, as Shorthand Clerk and Accountant. Following these developments, Mather encouraged the TCM to expand its sphere of operations to the south of the River Thames, and sought the cooperation of various clergy in work amongst the navvies. One of these correspondents, however, was not too happy at the idea. The Rev. A.R. Clementi-Smith, a Ritualist, had close links with the SAWM, which was already engaged in navvy work there, and was highly critical of the evangelical influence of the Thames Church Mission, linking it with Mather's membership of the Brethren.[3]

The *Ensign* appears to have been a great success during its first six months, and this led to a proposal by several others who were willing to provide funds for the purchase of similar vessels:

> One Christian man, in particular, a banker, had been watching with special concern. The outcome of the brief negotiations between these two men (Mather and Dashwood) was, that they managed to form a partnership consisting of four persons, of whom the new helper was one.[4]

A 'Special Committee Meeting' was convened for Wednesday, 21 February 1883, to discuss the situation, and Mather read out a letter from the Rev. Cecil M. Bevan in which he and Mr George Lionel Dashwood offered:

> to purchase in concert with other gentlemen at least two more smacks suitable for similar service to that so successfully achieved by the *Ensign*, the vessels to be managed on behalf of the owners by Mr Mather and placed at the disposal of the TCM for spiritual work amongst the deep sea fishermen.[5]

The Committee approved the offer and a special fund was established to meet other expenses, such as crews' wages, ship's fittings and maintenance. Bevan and Dashwood were subsequently elected members of the TCM

---

1. Mather, *op. cit.* (1887), p.145.
2. TCM Minutes, 17 November 1882.
3. TCM Minutes, 18 January 1884, p.326, refers to objects made by the navvies and sold on behalf of the TCM.
4. Gordon, *op. cit.* (1890), pp.63-4.
5. TCM Minutes, 21 February 1883.

Committee. With the Society's support, Mather negotiated the loan of three more vessels: the *Salem* (later renamed *Temple Tate*); the *Cholmondeley*; and the *Edward Auriel* (later renamed *Clulow*).[1]

This burst of activity illustrated practical Christian concern for the working classes, which reflected a more general concern, expressed this same year, 1883, in Andrew Mearns' pamphlet, *The Bitter Cry of Outcast London*, although Mearns argued that voluntary action alone would not bring about the necessary changes. For a brief time the TCM's apparently effective response appealed to the sensitivities of those conservative evangelicals who had little sympathy with urging state intervention. But financial support on the scale required was short-lived and depended mainly on the philanthropy of a few individuals. As the national economic situation worsened, so the MDSF moved into a period of crisis. The vessels were owned by Dashwood *et al.*, who had contributed a total of £4,800 to their purchase. But Mather tended to take all the credit for the Society's expansion, and this generated a good deal of animosity between the various parties.

The *Salem* was purchased in May 1883 and, after undergoing structural alterations, left Grimsby dock on her first cruise as a Mission ship.[2] It had been bought from Mr H. Mudd, a smack owner at Grimsby and supporter of the *Port of Hull Society*.[3] This vessel, like the *Ensign*, was second-hand and refitted for work as a Mission ship. The *Cholmondeley*, however, was specifically built for the work, as was the next vessel, the *Edward Auriel*. Both vessels were of 70 tons burden, and therefore larger than the *Ensign*, and more appropriate for work at greater distances.

Events were now moving fast, leaving the TCM Committee concerned about public support for its work. In an attempt to resolve its difficulties, the Committee agreed to submit a special resolution to the 1883 Annual Public Meeting:

> That this Meeting, in resolving that the Report now read be adopted, and that the existing Committee be reappointed, with power to add to their number, expresses its most hearty sympathy with the effort to win for Christ the thousands of Seamen, Emigrants, Fishermen, and others within the Society's extended sphere of operations, and hereby sanctions such extension.[4]

1. Mather, *op. cit.* (1887), pp.186-7.
2. Gordon, *op. cit.* (1890), p.64.
3. *Toilers of the Deep*, 1887, p.140.
4. TCM Minutes, 20 April 1883.

Partnership

The 'Partnership Agreement',[1] drawn up on 31 October 1883, stated that four gentlemen (George Lionel Dashwood, James Morton Bell, the Rev. Cecil Maitland Bevan and William Frederick Alphonse Archibald) purchased two trawling smacks (*Salem* and *Cholmondeley*) and became the joint owners and proprietors of these vessels. The two smacks were bought for £2,800, which had been shared equally between the purchasers, plus other expenses to cover the cost of refitting. The vessels were to work as fishing smacks, with the profits going to the four partners plus Mather. When not engaged in fishing, the smacks were at the disposal of the TCM to minister to the 'spiritual necessity and welfare' of the North Sea smacksmen. The vessels were, however, advertised as being 'Mission ships' working for the TCM and, as such, there must have been considerable confusion as to who was responsible for what, even though the Mission ships were to be self-financing. The extension of the MDSF's work inevitably brought with it a number of other costs and the TCM Annual Report for 1883 took up this point:

> Although the Society incurs no responsibility with regard to [the vessels'] maintenance, it has been found absolutely necessary to create a special 'Fishermen's Fund' to cover the expenses of missionaries who may from time to time be sent out from London, besides other incidental expenses.[2]

By the end of 1883 the MDSF/TCM had three Mission ships working amongst the North Sea fishing fleets. It must be remembered, however, that the Mission work was engaged in after the day's fishing had been completed and that the profits from the *Salem* and *Cholmondeley* went to the owners and Mather. It appears likely that Mather also received some of the profits from the *Ensign*, although the amount cannot have been great, as he later stated that the income for the first year was just £90.[3] The details regarding the receipt of profits from the vessels owned by Dashwood *et al.*, were spelt out by Dashwood in a letter to Mather, dated 17 July 1884:

> Mr Wilde remains with me, and next week I propose to send you the £1,000 to repay the others. Shall I lunch with you on Monday? What do you say to have as remuneration 1/5 and GLD 1/5, and his friend 2/5 of the profits.[4]

---

1. A copy of the 'Partnership Agreement' is in the RNMDSF Archives.
2. TCM Annual Report, 1882 (in the British Museum Library).
3. *Toilers of the Deep*, 6 February 1884, p.330.
4. Letter in RNMDSF Archives.

Fortunately, 1883 appears to have been a good year financially, both for the fishing industry and for the TCM, and support for the work was growing:

> The Secretary having pointed out that very great benefit had accrued to the Mission during the year 1883 from the kind and energetic efforts of various Clergy in the towns he had visited as the Society's Deputation; as also through the influence of several incumbents of Waterside Parishes.[1]

'Going to Church' in the North Sea.

All these developments inevitably meant more administration and, in November 1883, Mather was given permission to negotiate for two rooms on the ground floor of the building, and to make up for the extra cost by sub-letting the boardroom to other societies.

News of the economic success of the fishing industry during 1883 was widely disseminated via the International Fisheries Exhibition of that same year. This encouraged many businessmen and women (such as Baroness Burdett-Coutts) to put their money into fishing fleets. The number of vessels grew rapidly but, unfortunately, resulted in over-fishing. A recession set in during 1884–5 and many of these business ventures failed. The situation worried Mather and his colleagues, and a chain of events began that quickly led to the separation of the MDSF and the TCM. With the benefit of hindsight, Mather concluded that the recession had set in during 1883:

---

1. TCM Minutes, 6 February 1884.

whereas it was possible in 1882 to reckon upon the payment of working expenses by fishing, this ceased to be the case in the following year, and the records alike of the great fishing companies and of the smaller owners, from that date down to the present (1888), shows a most lamentable falling off of earnings; two large fleets have practically been suspended, after working for some time at a loss, and others have been most severely tried. Allowing, therefore, that it is pleasant to see on the receipts side of the Annual Statement a sum of £2,000 figuring under the heading 'Sales of Fish', we must not delude ourselves by the supposition that this represents profit.[1]

Towards Independence (1884–85)

A new vessel, the *Edward Auriel*, was added to the MDSF fleet in January 1884. It was provided by Dashwood, who dedicated it to the memory of a clergyman. The Bishop of London performed the Dedication Service, and sanctioned the holding of Holy Communion services on board the MDSF vessels.[2]

While this suggested proactive development in the work of the Society, Mather said that he found 'the strain [. . .] at times was almost unbearable, and the labour overwhelming',[3] and in March there is the first mention of an illness that recurred periodically during the next five years.[4] His physical condition was not helped by the TCM's financial worries, but at the same time his illness continued to keep him away from important Committee meetings and, while the TCM Minutes do not specifically refer to any unease among the Committee about their Secretary, there does appear to have been increasing anxiety about the way things were developing. In order to cope with the increasingly complex finances, the Committee agreed (on 15 February 1884) to transfer the 'Fishermen's Fund' to a separate account. The TCM Minutes for early 1884 give the impression that Mather was taking on more and more responsibility for developments within the TCM. By May the financial situation was so serious that the Committee was only too relieved to take up Mather's suggestions for a reorganisation of Committee structures, especially the establishment of a 'Finance Committee', with responsibility to meet on the day prior to the General Committee meeting if possible, to vouch the cash statement to be

1. Wood, *op. cit.* (1911), pp.203-4.
2. TCM Minutes, 2 January 1887.
3. Mather, *op. cit.* (1887), p.190.
4. Mather, *Memories of Christian Service* (Marshall Brothers, c.1922), says that the problem was rheumatism.

submitted by the Secretary to the General Committee, and to inspect the Journal, Petty Cash Accounts, General Cash Book and Bank Pass book. The bank also expressed concern during May at the TCM's overdraft of £456. Mather said this was largely due to five months of illness on his part and he promised to reduce the financial burden. Gifts reduced the overdraft to £113 but, in the meantime, the Committee felt it necessary to request a loan of £300 for two months, with Midland Railway Stock as security.[1] The situation continued to deteriorate, however, and Mather was forced to consider alternative approaches; 'It speedily became evident to me that those who had invested money in the three vessels [. . .] would do well to realise their capital without delay.' Once this procedure had been completed Mather was left as 'the sole registered owner of the *Ensign*, *Temple Tate, Clulow, Cholomondeley* and shortly afterwards of the *Edward Birkbeck*'.[2]

With regard to the relationship (and burden) of the MDSF to the TCM, Mather offered a number of suggestions in November 1884: withdrawal of the loan of the four vessels from the Committee of the TCM; separation of the funds (TCM and MDSF); and Mather to continue as Secretary to the TCM. He pointed out that the overall saving would be £355.12s.0d plus five members of staff who would be transferred to the new Society. The TCM Committee met again a week later and agreed to Mather's proposal. The MDSF was allocated the basement, and the TCM would move back to its original offices on the first floor (vacated in November 1883). A 'Declaration of Trust' was issued, the 'Fishermen's Fund' closed and a Board formed of four people, one of whom was Mather.[3] The second member of the Board was Mr Charles S. Read (a member of the Stock Exchange),[4] the third appears to have been Mr Samuel Hoare MP, but the fourth is unknown. Under the agreement, Mather retained his post as paid Secretary to the TCM, remained a member of the General Finance Committee, and continued as editor of the TCM's magazine, *Light from Aloft*. Alexander Gordon worked part-time for both the TCM and the MDSF. The TCM Committee asked Mather and Gordon to place a security with them, and Gordon duly handed over the requested £200. But Mather may have been experiencing some personal financial difficulty in that, on 30 January 1885, the requirement for his security was waived.[5] The pressures on him must have been enormous. In the event, he suffered from illness, was unable to attend TCM meetings, and gradually abandoned

1. TCM Minutes, 16 May 1884, 30 May 1884.
2. Gordon, *op. cit.* (1890), pp.71-3.
3. TCM Minutes, 21 November 1884.
4. Gordon, *op. cit.* (1890), p.73.
5. TCM Minutes, 30 January 1885.

his involvement with the TCM altogether. Concerned about this situation, the TCM Committee asked that 'the books and accounts of the TCM be kept entirely distinct from those of the MDSF, and [. . .] be audited every month for the Finance Committee'.[1] Unfortunately, no Minutes or other records appear to have survived for the period 20 November 1884 to June 1886. Only inferences, therefore, can be drawn from documents in various publications as to developments within the MDSF during this period. The extant Minutes of the MDSF begin on Friday, 18 June 1886, when the new MDSF Council met for the first time.

In retrospect, Mather took an enormous risk but he could not possibly have known how long the recession would last and he was in any case faced with a fairly stark choice: he could either sell the MDSF vessels for what he could get or establish the MDSF as a separate organisation and try to raise funds from the public. He had little to lose by pursuing the latter, but his health suffered during the process and the worry and difficulties appear to have had a long-lasting detrimental effect on his marriage.

On 19 June 1885, Mather took an important step in the direction of his complete severance with the TCM, when he resigned his position as Secretary and suggested a modification of his role:

> The Committee discussed a scheme which had been placed before the Sub-Committee on the previous day and recommended by them after careful consideration –
>
> The Secretary pointed out the impossibility of his continuing to spend so much time as he had hitherto done in conducting drawing-room and Public Meetings after the conclusion of the ordinary duties of the day in the office, and strongly urged the desirability of appointing a Clergyman to canvas, conduct meetings, and preach Sermons for the Society in London and its vicinity. The Missions to Seamen Society he explained obtain the major portion of their income of £26,000 per annum from the successful efforts of travelling Church Agents.
>
> The Secretary asked the Committee to give him carte blanche to test for one month the possibility of the Rev. Mr Bloomer carrying out this scheme, [. . .] the Committee, after receiving from Mr Bloomer the assurance of his willingness to accept such employment, unanimously resolved to agree to the Secretary's proposal in order that if successful Mr Bloomer might at the July Committee Meeting be confirmed in his duties.[2]

1. *Ibid.*, 28 November 1884.
2. *Ibid.*, 19 June 1885.

Rev. Bloomer was duly appointed at a salary of £300 per annum; and on 20 November 1885, Mr Mather resigned as paid Secretary to the TCM:

> Pursuant to notice privately given to all Members of the Committee, Capt Maude moved the following Resolution, which was Seconded by Admiral Fishbourne, that Mr Mather's resignation of the office of paid Secretary of this Society, and his offer to act as Honorary Secretary be accepted, and that he be elected a member of the General Committee, and of the Finance Committee.[1]

A decision was deferred until the next TCM Committee meeting, to be held on 1 December 1885. At this meeting several members expressed concern that 'there should be a paid Secretary wholly in the employ of and responsible to the Thames Church Mission Committee'.[2] With one of the clerks also employed by both societies, the Committee was concerned not to make too hasty a decision, and referred the matter to the Finance Committee. An emergency 'General Committee Meeting' appears to have been held under the chairmanship of Admiral Beamish, and a number of important decisions reached that were detailed at the Committee meeting held on 18 December. Reading between the lines there would seem to have been great dissatisfaction with the way Mather had handled events, and there is a marked change of tone which suggests the Committee was determined to put its house in order. At the December Committee meeting doubts were raised about the November proposal. Nevertheless, Mather does appear to have been allowed to act as 'Honorary Secretary', because in the Minutes for 18 February the following year, we read of his resignation from that post.

Independence (1886)

Towards the end of 1885 the MDSF moved from the premises shared with the TCM in New Bridge Street to Bridge House, 181 Queen Victoria St, which had nine spacious rooms.[3] Of this period, Mather later said: '[the MDSF] started in 1885 with a mortgage on the vessels of about £10,000.'[4] The first edition of the monthly magazine, *Toilers of the Deep,* appeared in January 1886. The style and format was popular and full of lively stories and illustrations, and popular authors were brought onto the MDSF Council. These included George A. Hutchinson, the editor of *The Boy's Own Paper* (also editor of *Toilers of the Deep*), and R.M. Ballantyne, who subsequently contributed regular features in *Toilers of the Deep* and published two

---

1. *Ibid.*, 20 June 1885.
2. *Ibid.*, 1 December 1885.
3. Gordon, *op. cit.* (1890), p.76.
4. *Toilers of the Deep*, Jan 1888, vol. 3, p.29.

novels about the work of the MDSF.[1] That the early magazines still make interesting reading today says a great deal for the publicity skills of Mather and his team.

In February 1886, it became obvious to Mather that he had to give up some of his commitments: 'It now became necessary for me to relinquish one or two other occupations and sources of private income, as the increasing demands of the Mission necessitated close personal attention.'[2] He resigned his Honorary Secretaryship with the TCM. At a meeting on 18 February, after the Chairman had called attention to Mather's resignation, the following resolution was passed:

> Mr Mather having formally notified his retirement from the Honorary Secretaryship in consequence of the appointment of the Rev, H. Bloomer as paid Secretary, the Committee think it proper that his resignation should be entered on the Minutes of the General Committee and that the Bankers be informed that henceforth Mr Mather's signature to cheques will be only that of a Member of the Committee.[3]

Mather followed this move in March by resigning his editorship of the TCM magazine, *Light from Aloft*, and in June he resigned from the TCM Finance Committee.[4] But (perhaps in order to keep an eye on developments) he retained his seat on the TCM General Committee.

The work of the MDSF came to the notice of the Duchess of Grafton who, during March 1886, donated £2,150 for the purchase and equipping of a Mission vessel, to be called the *Euston* in memory of her husband. This was the first fully paid-for vessel and was built at Great Yarmouth where it was dedicated on 29 May 1886. Thomas Gray, head of the Board of Trade Marine Department, had hoped to be present at the *Euston's* launch but, in his absence, sent a warm letter of approval. This letter, however, has given rise to some distortion of the history of the RNMDSF in its present-day literature in that it is assumed that the letter was written on the launch of the *Ensign!*[5]

The MDSF began to move into a new phase, and Mather set about establishing a new team. On 18 June 1886 he met with his new Council, and the MDSF was formally instituted.[6] Dr Alfred T. Schofield, an old

---

1. R.M. Ballantyne, *The Young Trawler* and *The Lively Poll* (both published London: James Nisbet & Co., 1886).
2. Mather, *op. cit.* (1887), p.190.
3. TCM Minutes, 18 February 1886.
4. *Ibid.*, 18 June 1886.
5. Stanley Pritchard, *Fish and Ships* (Mowbray, 1980), p.21.
6. MDSF Minutes begin on this date.

school-friend of Mather, saw himself as 'being one of the six founders of
the DSF', and 'took an active part in the proceedings'.[1] The new Board
consisted of:

R.M. Ballantyne
G.A. Hutchinson
Thomas B. Miller
The Rev. D. Wise
Dr Alfred T. Schofield
E.J. Mather (Founder and Director)
(James Curtis, Honorary Solicitor)

Samuel Hoare MP, took over as Treasurer and at some point during the early
weeks Frederick Treves, the eminent Victorian surgeon, became associated
with the work.[2] This was a formidable team, and the Council had oversight
of six Mission vessels:

Ensign
Salem
Cholmondeley
Edward Auriel
Edward Birkbeck
Euston

The crews, shore-workers and office staff totalled approximately sixty
employees, and there were numerous other individuals and groups involved
with the work such as fundraisers, people making garments and collecting
books and magazines, and a constant stream of people wishing to visit
the fleets on board the Mission vessels to see the work in action. In the
meantime, a donation of £2,300 had been received from Mr Henry A.
Campbell JP, in July 1886, for the purchase of a new Mission ship, the
Ashton. The letter accompanying this gift spelt out the request that the
vessel be used ecumenically:

> I also especially desire that *Christians*, lay and clerical, of all
> denominations, may be free to preach the gospel in this vessel, so
> long as they do so without putting forward any views which may
> be called distinctly 'sectarian', and avoid proselytising. The main
> object of the Mission being to win souls to *Christ*, and not merely
> to a section of His Church.[3]

---

1. A.T. Schofield, *Behind the Brass Plate* (Sampson Low, c.1915), p.146.
2. The first reference to Mr Treves appears at the Council Meeting of 22 June 1886,
   where it is recorded that he sent his apologies for not being present. Even so,
   Mather said that Treves joined the MDSF in September 1886, so this date was
   probably the first meeting he attended.
3. Gordon, *op. cit.* (1890), p.80.

But other expenses also had to be met. The loan of £1,000 for the *Ensign* was repaid at four per cent interest by 23 July 1886,[1] and the vessel was lengthened, refitted and renamed the *Thomas Gray* – a move which, according to Dashwood, irked the original benefactor.[2] The *Salem* also had to be refitted – and within a few months the MDSF found itself with a heavy debt.[3] An appeal for funds was made in order to pay off the mortgages on the vessels and to help maintain the work.

Over the next few months Mather's relationship with the TCM deteriorated further and, on 17 December 1886, he was formally requested to resign his seat on the General Committee, which he duly did. The reasons for this request were given as: first, because he had not been present at any meeting of the General Committee since his election (*i.e.* since 20 November 1885); and, second, because the confusion that had arisen in the minds of contributors to the TCM with regard to it and the MDSF made this course necessary.[4] One factor in the deteriorating relationship may have been the MDSF Council's decision to explicitly identify the society as an 'undenominational' rather than a 'Church' organisation – partly brought about by the request of Henry Campbell that the society be non-sectarian.[5] Mather's resignation from the TCM Committee in December 1886 ended the final chapter in a difficult, and sometimes painful, relationship.

The MDSF Council had a 'Deed of Covenant' drawn up in June 1886 specifying that the responsibility for the ships, stores, belongings *etc.*, now lay with the Society: with regard to Mather,

1. [he was to] receive back all the money he had personally spent;
2. the Council was to indemnify him against all debts and liabilities now due and existing on account or in respect of the said ships or smacks *etc.*;
3. [he was] to receive a yearly stipend of not less than £800 per annum, and to receive £1,000 per annum as soon as the annual income of the MDSF shall amount to £20,000 per annum;
4. [he was given] an entirely full and free discretion in arranging and carrying out all meetings in relation to the said Mission – whether such meetings shall be public or private;
5. [he was given] the fullest liberty to conduct and complete as heretofore all arrangements for literary work, and for visitors to enter into and stay on board of any of either of the Mission vessels;

1. Mather, *op. cit.* (1887), p.190.
2. *The Record*, 6 January 1888.
3. MDSF Minutes, 12 November 1886.
4. TCM Minutes, 12 November 1886.
5. *Ibid.*

6. [he] shall from time to time have full power, and is hereby
   authorised to sign, make and give Bankers' cheques and to
   accept, draw or endorse Bills of exchange or Promissory notes
   on account and in respect of the Mission;
7. [he was given] responsibility for staff;
8. [and] the power of veto on any proposed new Council members
   (and similarly of such members of the Council);
9. [and he was permitted] to conduct 'private business'.[1]

The MDSF Council was now responsible for all the employees. The
salaries of the staff and skippers alone came to over £1,000 annually and,
on top of this, there were crews' wages, administration, maintenance of
ships and Mather's salary.

The various changes, and the enthusiasm of the new Council, had an
effect. The income for the first six months of 1886, according to Alexander
Gordon, was £12,363 and for the year, £24,784. For the first time since
1882/83 the MDSF appeared to be doing well financially.[2] By the end of
1886 Thomas B. Miller and Dr Gilbert-Smith had joined the Council, and
they were followed in the new year by three others, Henry A. Campbell,
Thomas Gray CB and R. Scott Moncrieff.[3] With the financial situation
more secure, some important new initiatives were undertaken: Dr Schofield
began training the Mission skippers in first aid and Frederick Treves and
Mather began to explore the possibility of providing floating hospitals to
work amongst the North Sea fleets.

5.1.1. Late Nineteenth- and
Early Twentieth-Century Fishermen's Missions

The late nineteenth and early twentieth centuries saw the advent of several
maritime mission initiatives among fishing communities. The town of
Folkestone provides an example. In 1890 the Folkestone fishing community
suffered economically, as did many others – although Henry Cook visited in
his vessel *The Herald of Mercy* and provided practical and spiritual help for
the fisherfolk. In the same year a Fishermen's Club was opened to provide
recreational diversions. But all this was clearly just scratching the surface.
Recognising the scale of the problem, Mr Charles Barclay (a member of the
Barclay banking family) responded by funding the erection of a Bethel that
was opened in 1894 and provided a range of facilities to help meet local
needs. After Barclay's death in 1901, the building was bought by the Royal

---

1. The 'Deed of Covenant' is kept in the RNMDSF Archives.
2. This figure rose to £30,000 in 1887: *Toilers of the Deep*, 188, p.104.
3. MDSF Minutes, 12 November 1886 and 29 January 1887.

National Mission to Deep Sea Fishermen, which continued for many years the work begun by the Bethel's founder.[1] Such initiatives were common in fishing communities, many being influenced by organisations such as the RNMDSF, St Andrew's Waterside Church Mission, the Salvation Navy and W.F. Stewart's *Albatross* Yacht Mission.

The Salvation Navy

The experience of conversions among the late nineteenth-century Grimsby fishing fleet led the Salvation Army in January 1880 to open a corps in Grimsby, where some of fishermen had advertised their meetings at sea by hoisting the Salvation Army flag. The Salvation Army newspaper, *The War Cry*, of 29 July 1885, told of 'thirteen fishing vessels flying the Army flag, lashed together so that their crews could take part in [religious] meetings'.

In 1885 the Army received the loan of a vessel, the *Iole*, from John Cory who suggested that Mrs Booth could cruise in it for her health. Army members nevertheless used the vessel to visit seaside towns along the coast in a programme of evangelism during the summer months, and the success of this work led to the establishment of the Salvation Navy. Unfortunately, in June 1886 the *Iole* ran aground on a sandbank in the Humber and sank. It was quickly replaced by another vessel, the *Vestal*.

Robert Miller says of this work: 'The Salvation Navy was part of [a] wider [maritime mission] movement, although it seems to have fallen victim to the 1914–18 War. Its title was revived briefly in the 1950s as a local ministry to canal people.'[2] Miller's assumption that the work closed down (based on the documents available to him) is, however, misleading. Motor vessels were obtained in the twentieth century, including the *Catherine Booth*, bought in Norway in 1900 and used for thirty years, and the *William Booth*, purchased in 1947, which played an important role for 15 years in the Army's work in Alaska.[3]

The Salvation Army archive contains two files of documents on the Salvation Navy but the details are sparse – although *The War Cry Supplement* for 18 March 1978 shows that, with the expansion of the Salvation Army's international work, the Salvation Navy also featured in the society's plans. In 1884 the steamship *Parade* worked among the islands and fishing centres in Sweden. Following the success of this work other vessels were bought, including the *Vestal*, *Glory*, *Victory*, *Hanna Ouchterlony* and the

---

1. www.warrenpress.net/FolkstoneThenNow/FishermensBethel.html, accessed 4 May 2015.
2. Robert Miller, 'The Salvation Navy', an article published in the IASMM Newsletter, Spring 1996, p.12; also *The War Cry, Supplement II*, 18 March 1978.
3. *Ibid.*

Commissioner Ögrim launched in 1953. A Viking fleet was established in Norway to take the gospel to isolated villages. In Canada, in 1894, the *Glad Tidings* worked off the coasts of Labrador and Newfoundland; and in the same year the *Salvationist* set sail from St John's, while the *William Booth* worked among the fishing communities of the Great Lakes. Work was also established in Japan during the 1930s and later, following the Second World War, a series of ships (*Noah Maru* – 'Noah's Arks') acted as free shelters for homeless people. Other vessels were employed in France and Australia. Back in England the *Salvo*, a converted barge launched in 1950, worked on the 2,000 miles of inland waterways, as did the *Pilgrim* which was launched in 1973. In 1975 the Army's chartered steam launch, the *Hope*, was transported in sections from the Netherlands to Bangladesh where it worked with relief operations.[1] Among the various organisations influenced by the RNMDSF, the Salvation Navy must rank among the most extensive and influential in its use of vessels as Bethel ships worldwide.

Scotland

Religious revivals in fishing communities appear to have been especially common during the nineteenth century. During the 1820s, for example, Primitive Methodism made quite an impact along the north-east coast, especially in Yorkshire and Lincolnshire. The wider-ranging revival was that of 1859–60 which began in the United States, before moving to Scotland, England and Wales via Ulster. This revival had long-term effects on many communities and led to a spate of church-building, for example, in the Suffolk fishing village of Lowestoft where the Fishermen's Bethel was opened in 1862 and Christ Church in 1868. In 1921, the Scottish fisherfolk's revival began in Lowestoft, centering on the two churches built almost sixty years earlier, and quickly embraced other East Anglian communities, such as Great Yarmouth and Gorleston. This revival quickly moved north as the Scottish fishers returned to their homes.

Scotland has a long history of mission work among fishing communities, where, as in mining and agricultural communities, religious revivals fell on fertile ground, offering as they did an escape from the immediacy of despair, generated by economic decline, via the promise of better times either from improved economic conditions or the hope of salvation and millenarianism. With reference to the emergence of revivals among Scottish fisherfolk, Anson remarked: 'Within the past hundred years the fisherfolk of the east coast of Scotland have been greatly affected by more than one religious revival movement which has swept over them like a prairie fire.'[2]

1. *The War Cry, op. cit.*
2. P.F. Anson, *Fishing Boats and Fisher Folk on the East Coast of Scotland* (London: J.M.

Lynn Abrams has also noted the eagerness for religion among the women of the Shetland Islands. She provides examples from the early 1800s but points out that, given the preponderance of women on the island, the religious meetings offered an opportunity for social gatherings. She goes on to suggest an explanation for the appeal of visiting evangelical preachers:

> One explanation of the popularity amongst women of visiting evangelical preachers, particularly in the early part of the century, was the contrast they posed with the moral stance and disciplinary stance adopted by ministers of the Church of Scotland and the Free Church (after 1843). It seems likely that the women were alienated by the harsh attitudes towards sexual offences displayed by these churches and their lay members through the kirk sessions, particularly when it was the women who took the full brunt of their moral punishment. Another reason was the disapprobation heaped upon women who consumed alcohol at a time when male culture amongst the labouring classes was, to a significant degree, lubricated by alcohol.[1]

In the 1850s when Thomas Rosie established the Scottish Coast Missions, he set the scene for later developments. The international revival of 1859–60 especially affected Scotland where it focused on Peterhead before spreading throughout north-east Scotland. The main evangelist of this movement appears to have been James Turner, a Peterhead cooper and herring-curer, who was responsible for converting 8,000 people during a two-month period along the north-east of Scotland. Further revivals followed, especially those orchestrated by the Salvation Navy and the Baptists.[2] Moody and Sankey also had an important impact on the Scottish fishing communities in 1874 and enthused the fisherfolk with their rousing hymns and sermons.

W.F. Stewart and the Albatross Yacht Mission

In 1903, the Scottish evangelist, William (Willie) F. Stewart of Edinburgh, like Thomas Rosie, obtained a vessel, the *Albatross*, which was dedicated in Leith Docks. Stewart's own account of the work tells us that the 'idea of a Yacht Mission was the direct outcome of a special effort held in Fraserburgh, from January to March 1902'. The Mission yacht was obtained and launched a year later:

Dent, 1930), pp.44-6.
1. Lynn Abrams, *Myth and Materiality in a Woman's World: Shetland 1800–2000* (Manchester: Manchester University Press, 2005), p.143.
2. Anson, *Scots Fisherfolk* (Banff: The Saltire Society, Banffshire, 1950), pp.46-7.

The Mission yacht Albatross I.

On Monday, May 12, 1903, the Mission yacht *Albatross* slipped quietly
out of Granton Harbour on her way to the fishing ports in the North of
Scotland. Their Royal Majesties, King Edward VII and Queen Alexandra,
were in the city that day, but a little company of interested friends were on
the shore to wave farewell to the crew.

In his edited collection of articles about the work of the *Albatross*
Mission, the author said:

> My brother, W.F. Stewart, was the leader, the 'Chief' they called him,
> of the Yacht Mission crew. His interest in Christian work began when
> he was a young man, learning manufacturing in a Borrder town.
> One morning, in the summer of 1893, my father handed me a letter.

The letter told of W.F. Stewart's religious conversion and his intention to
dedicate his life to the work of mission. William was joined by his brother
and sister in preaching and singing in neighbouring towns, and the work
flourished as the *Albatross* mission was formed in 1903. Among the many
letters received from those influenced by the work, the following came
from a supporter in Thurso:

Well do I remember a letter which came from the Rev. Alexander
Soutar, Thurso. It related so impressively the remarkable movement
associated with the visit of the *Albatross* Mission party. Hundreds
had been influenced in Thurso. The letter overflowed with gladness.
It was a spontaneous testimony, and coming from one so jealous
of everything which savoured of mere emotion or sensationalism it
made a deep impression on my mind.[1]

The Stewart family owned a textile business which they began in Leith in
the late nineteenth century. This later moved to Galashiels, although W.F.
Stewart remained in Edinburgh and commuted each day to the mill by train.
With the advent of the *Albatross* Mission, Stewart spent time both running
missions during the summer and working at the Mill. The vessel (funded

partly by his family's textile business and
partly from gifts and collections at religious
meetings) was fitted out as a Bethel ship, and
Stewart and his crew visited fishermen in the
fishing fleets and the fishing communities
along the coast, where they held religious
services, especially for the herring workers.
Thenceforth, Stewart acted as an evangelist
on behalf of the Home Mission Committee of
the United Free Church, and crew members
were selected for their eager Christian faith
and musical gifts, especially their singing,
in order to perform as a group at the many
meetings they led.

W.F. Stewart (The Albatross
*singers can be seen in the photo
inside the lifebelt).*

The work continued for a quarter of a
century around the Scottish coast 'from the
extreme north of Shetland to Berwick-on-
Tweed and Campbeltown, from Peterhead
and Fraserburgh on the east to Stornoway
on the west'. This work must have acted as preparation for the 1921–2
revival and sustained spiritual life in the Scottish fishing communities once
revival enthusiasm had waned.

Over time four different vessels in turn were obtained, allowing the
work to continue for over thirty years. With the sale of *Albatross IV* in
the late 1930s, the Mission work came to an end and Stewart returned to
running the family business until his son took over responsibility around

1. Alan Stewart (ed.), *The ALBATROSS Yacht Mission*, published privately.

1947.[1] Stewart's evangelistic work would appear to have been influenced by: the British campaigns of Moody and Sankey; the RNMDSF (especially Wilfred Grenfell); and perhaps also the work of Thomas Rosie.[2] He is also likely to have drawn on the work of the Salvation Navy.

While Stewart's mission preceded (and overlapped) with the 1921–2 fishermen's revival, he tended to concentrate on evangelisation along the Scottish coast. His work, nevertheless, helped prepare the ground for the revival, although this latter event had a wider impact among the herring fishers, taking in fishing communities from East Anglia to the far north of Scotland. Unfortunately, there appear to be few accounts or reciprocal references to Stewart's work and the revival in Scotland, although the various maritime missionaries cannot but have been aware of each other's work. Indeed, the RNMDSF provides a helpful example of this. In the society's magazine, *Toilers of the Deep*, for June 1921, Captain Cowe of the Aberdeen Mission, while visiting Lerwick, commented:

> Reference has been made to Sunday fishing when your English fishermen came down to catch herring, of course herring was not cured on Sunday, so they had time on shore. I was on the *Albatross*, and we would draw out the platform and sing and preach the Gospel.[3]

The Fishermen's Revival of 1921–22

The revival began in East Anglia in the spring of 1921, under the preaching of the Rev. A. Douglas Brown. At that time there were over 1,000 fishing vessels at Great Yarmouth and 600 at Lowestoft. As each herring drifter carried a crew of nine or ten men and boys the total male workforce on the vessels was about 16,000. On shore there were about 3,000 Scots lasses curing herring in Yarmouth and Lowestoft – not to mention the coopers and other men associated with shore work.

Among the popular preachers who conducted meetings during the 1921–22 revival were Rev. Douglas Brown, Jock Troup (a cooper by trade who found a calling to preaching, much like the Peterhead cooper, James Turner, in 1859–60), Dave Cordiner and Willie Bruce. As the revival centred on the herring fishery, it has tended to be overlooked, and thus Stanley C. Griffin, in his 1992 book on this work, called it 'A Forgotten Revival'. A more recent book by George Mitchell, entitled 'Revival Man – the Jock Troup Story', published in 2002 and a DVD about Jock Troup's

---

1. Details provided by W.F. Stewart's grandson, Alan Stewart, 1 June 2015.
2. Stewart, *op. cit.*, p.3.
3. *Toilers of the Deep*, June 1921, p.74.

Some of the significant preachers in the Scottish Revival Movement:
Mr Bill Bruce (standing) with Jock Troup, and the Rev. A. Douglas Brown (circled).

role in the Revival provides further details about the man and his mission.[1] Clearly these men were significant preachers. What is surprising is that there appear to have been no female leaders of the revival. Mitchell has offered a helpful definition of the term 'revival':

> Revival is a largely unheralded, contrived eruption of God's presence and power among His people, which results in a significant, large-scale disturbance of their present state, a deepening of their spirituality, and a partially measurable, long-term impact of the Gospel upon the surrounding community of unbelievers. It occurs within the evangelical communities of believers, and there is often an individual or a small group of individuals at the heart of the action.[2]

By the autumn of 1921 the revival had gathered momentum and moved through East Anglia, taking hold of the town of Lowestoft, involving many of the fisherfolk who had arrived there for the annual herring fishery. The

1. George Mitchell (Christian Focus Publications, 2002); Gary Wilkinson, Jock Troup & the Fishermen's Revival, DVD, 2012.
2. Mitchell, *op. cit.*, 2002.

impetus for this revival was perhaps largely due to the work of Rev. Douglas Brown. With the influx of the herring fisherfolk in the autumn, the revival spread along the East Anglian coast and eastern Scotland, with much of the inspiration coming from the preaching of Jock Troup. Newspaper reports for December 1921 suggest that over 10,000 people had been affected.

Peter Anson was present in Great Yarmouth and Lowestoft during October and November 1921 and later visited the Scottish towns and villages in the summer of 1922 where the revival took hold. Anson has provided an eyewitness account of events. He recorded his impressions in an article published in *The Month* in November 1922. He was generally sympathetic to the development and commented on the revival's effects:

> A good number of these zealous 'converts' of Yarmouth, 1921, are now 'backsliders', and have drifted into apathy and indifference. [. . .] Taken as a whole, however, those who persevere seem to predominate over those who fall away. Their 'conversions' are something more than mere emotional crises. In fact, they bear every sign of a real spiritual movement, accompanied by the action of grace.[1]

Anson also pointed out the economic difficulties faced by the fishing communities in 1921, and the atmosphere of expectancy and belief among evangelical Protestants provided a good 'harvest time' for the subsequent revival.

More recently, John Lowe Duthie explored the history of this movement in an article in *History Today*, entitled 'The Fishermen's Revival', and offered a number of explanations for its impact. After the brief period of economic boom following the First World War, the fishing industry encountered a period of economic decline accompanied by anxiety and hopeless despair (similar to the experience of many one hundred years earlier, following the Anglo-French wars), along with strikes and stoppages during the years 1919–21. Within this context, the evangelists, some of whom placed an emphasis on preaching about an imminent religious millennium, helped to build hope and provide comfort for members of the fishing communities. Duthie concluded his article by saying: 'The interplay of economic circumstances, group psychology and local culture provides the most convincing explanation of events in north-east Scotland in late 1921.'[2]

Overall, therefore, there would appear to have been a number of factors, which influenced the 1921–22 revival, including the aftermath of the First World War and the high loss of life, the Influenza pandemic of 1918, the

---

1. Richard F. Anson, 'The Recent Religious Revival among the Scottish Fisher-folk', *The Month*, November 1922, pp.414-24.
2. John Lowe Duthie, 'The Fishermen's Revival', *History Today*, December 1983, p.27.

economic problems of the post-war period, the failure of the herring fishery and the influence of millenarianism in the preaching of the revival's leaders. While it is not suggested that these factors were the necessary cause of the revival, they would together have provided a helpful mixing-pot in which the revival occurred. It was also not uncommon for local churches to be involved in providing practical and spiritual support for the herring girls – such as the club provided by the North Sea Church Mission in Gorleston in 1909, and a woman employed by St Andrew's Church in Grimsby to work with the visiting herring girls.[1] Other support came from several national societies, including the Missions to Seamen and the Royal National Mission to Deep Sea Fishermen.

5.2. Church Missions (1891–1900)

5.2.1. Scotland

Introduction

As the numbers of fishermen and herring lasses increased during the late nineteenth and early twentieth centuries the need for medical and spiritual care became more acute. Support came from a range of individuals and churches. The clergy of churches in Grimsby, Great Yarmouth, Gorleston and Lowestoft, among others, all sought to provide staff to meet these needs. And the Church of Scotland provided clergy and lay workers.

There were also some individuals, such as Margaret Harker of Blofield, Norfolk, who provided medical support for the fishergirls working in East Anglia. Margaret had joined the Red Cross in 1910 and set up a detachment at her home. She was subsequently appointed their commandant. Having later gained experience during the war years, she set about doing what she could for the herring fishers when they visited the local ports. Margaret worked from a dressing station on the ground floor of a building in St Peter's Road, Great Yarmouth (the Church of Scotland used the upstairs rooms), providing as many as 300 dressings for the girls each day, and treatment for boils and other complaints for the men. Clearly the work was too much for Margaret alone and she arranged for a trained nurse to be in charge at each session, overseeing the work of some VADs (Voluntary Aid Detachment Nurses). She also responded to the herring girls' moral welfare in the fishing ports by helping them obtain suitable lodgings.[2] Margaret's work has since been commemorated

---

1. SAWCM Report, 1890, pp.60-3; and 1909, p.69.
2. Barbara Pilch, *Windows on a Life: the Story of Margaret Harker* (Blofield, Norfolk: Images Publications, 2006), p.51.

in the memorial windows installed in Blofield Church. There were no
doubt other women around the coast who also worked selflessly with the
visiting herring fleets, although few have received the kind of recognition
that Margaret Harker did. But there were some appointed by the Scottish
churches. Of this work, Peter Anson has observed that: 'In normal times
a staff of about thirty ladies and eight ministers were engaged in working
in the chief centres of the herring fisheries, supplying spiritual, social and
medical aid to men and women.'

Commemorative windows in Blofield Church, Norfolk,
in memory of Margaret Gordon Harker JP.

The Church of Scotland

The Church of Scotland established its Mission to the Workers in the
Herring Industry (commonly known as Work Among the Fisherfolk).
Anson commented on this work: 'The [Church of Scotland] Mission
to Fisherfolk has been ministering devotedly to the spiritual, social and
medical needs of the Scottish fishing community for over seventy years.'[1]
The society would therefore have started about 1880. Rest Huts and
Dressing Stations were established in Scottish and East Anglian ports,
and in Buckie there was a flourishing club for fishermen and boys where
popular concerts and parties were held. More information about this work
is provided in an article by Ella Ross; writing in the journal *World Dominion*
in 1953, Miss Ross tells us that during the herring season at Lerwick (from
June until the end of August), 'the Church of Scotland had the only Rest
Centre and Dressing Station in operation'. But in the autumn, when the
herring fishing was concentrated on East Anglia, the work in Lowestoft was
'shared by the Missions to Seamen, the Royal National Mission to Deep

1. Anson, 'Seamen's Welfare in Scottish Ports', *op. cit.*, c.1949, p.12.

Sea Fishermen, and the Scottish Episcopal Church'.[1] Church of Scotland ministers relieved from their parish duties worked among the fisherfolk as they moved around the coast. It soon became obvious, however, that the large number of women working at gutting and packing the fish needed more specialised help than the ministers could provide.

Ella Ross (centre) was Superintendent of Fishing Stations under the Church of Scotland's Home Board. Here she is having her morning chat with fishergirls on the quay at Yarmouth.

Apart from their spiritual needs, there were the social and medical needs of the Scottish fishermen and fishworkers. Rest Huts and Dressing Stations were established around the Scottish coast, in Orkney and the Shetland Islands, as well as along the English coast especially in East Anglia at Great Yarmouth and Lowestoft. This work was largely overseen by Miss Davidson who was appointed by the Church of Scotland to work among the herring fishers.[2] Miss Ross has also provided us with some information about the working week for the fishergirls during the early 1950s:

> Evening by evening Scots folk stream into St Andrew's House (Great Yarmouth) to visit friends in the Sick-Bay, to have dressings done, to join in the games and enjoy the music, or just to sit in a chair by the fireside and exchange news of the day; their fellowship takes on a deeper significance as we join in our evening worship. [. . .]

1. *Ibid.*
2. Ella Ross, 'The Church and the Herring-Fishers', *World Dominion*, July-August 1953, pp.197-202.

Monday evening is the women's night. The fishermen have gone out to start a new week, there have been no herring in the yards, for Scots fishermen do not go to sea on Sundays, so the women come to St Andrew's House; but we have found that we have no place large enough to contain them, and this meeting had to be held in the Congregational Church. [. . .] Saturday is the fishermen's day, for then they come in to write letters home, make up week-end parcels, and in the evening enjoy the games or listen to the choir-practice, which usually finishes as community hymn-singing. A group is generally found in a corner playing Lexicon, apparently unmoved by the crowd milling round, but noise means nothing to this group of fishermen, who are deaf and dumb yet one in the fellowship. [. . .] On Sundays the services provide the opportunity beloved of the fisherfolk, for praise and worship. Our choir lead the singing.[1]

A little more detail about Miss Ross can be gleaned from an article in the *Weekly Scotsman*. Prior to working with the Church of Scotland's Work Among the Fisherfolk, she gave up a business career and spent twelve years working with down-and-outs in Glasgow's East End. Then, in 1948, the Church's Home Board appointed her to the position of Superintendent of Fishing Stations, the only full-time worker with this mission. In Great Yarmouth she had a staff of twelve, mostly volunteers, along with a highly qualified nurse and a number of VADs, at St Andrew's House on the South Quay, with its auxiliary canteen, dressing station and social and religious centre, which was active throughout the herring season. When the herring season was over, Miss Ross worked as the Church's deputation officer visiting churches to speak at meetings about her work. The work was well-supported by the herring girls who met regularly in the canteen to sing well-known songs. Some of the fishermen also formed themselves into a choir and performed regularly at meetings in fishing ports.[2] The work, therefore, provided an active and much needed resource for the herring fishermen and their families.

The Scottish Episcopal Church

Anson tells us that the Flying Angel Missions (Missions to Seamen) began their Scottish work in 1914, and that all the clerical and lay workers there were licensed by the Scottish Episcopal Church. The Scottish Episcopal Mission to Fisherfolk (SEMF) appears to have been founded to care for the spiritual, social and medical needs of Scottish fishermen and fishworkers. Mirroring the work of the Church of Scotland Mission, during the herring

1. *Ibid.,* p.201.
2. 'With Scots Fisher Folk at Yarmouth', *Weekly Scotsman*, 3 November 1949, pp.1, 3.

season the SEMF established Rest Huts and Dressing Stations around the Scottish coast, in Orkney and the Shetland Islands, as well as along the English coast especially in East Anglia at Great Yarmouth and Lowestoft. At Grimsby, too, at St Andrew's Church in 1889, a woman was employed to work with the fishergirls, and in 1906 a Deaconess, Miss James, along with a nurse was employed to work with the girls and to attend to medical problems. With the increase in Scottish herring fishers visiting Grimsby in the early 1900s, the workload of St Andrew's staff increased dramatically, although a clergyman from Stornoway travelled with and ministered to the herring fishermen, thereby relieving the staff at the East Coast ports to some extent.[1]

The Missions to Seamen 'began work in Scotland, working under the Scottish Episcopalian Bishops, all its clerical and lay workers being licensed by the Episcopal Church'.[2] The Scottish Episcopal Mission to Fisherfolk stated its objective as being to care for the spiritual, social and medical needs of Scottish fishermen and fishworkers.

It seems that at times both organisations (the Church of Scotland's Mission to Fisherfolk and the SEMF) worked together. For example, in 1920 the Episcopalian Church in Scotland arranged for a Miss Mary Graham to travel to Lerwick to work with the herring girls. A booklet about the history of St Magnus' Church, Lerwick, offers the following comment:

On arrival [Miss Graham] sought out premises to be used exclusively for the girls and soon after she secured a hut which had been in storage. It has been brought to Lerwick in 1918 by the Church Army and erected at Alexandra Wharf as a recreation hut for the Naval personnel stationed there [. . .] within a short time a considerable number of girls used the hut, mainly to have their hands dressed, and this was much appreciated. The District Nurse treated over 200 cases of cut or poisoned hands during the season. The canteen was managed by a Mrs Donald and several ladies provided much help. Games, concerts and knitting formed a pleasant change for girls who worked long and tiring days over the gutting farlins or in the curing sheds. [. . .] During the 1920 season a total of 2,748 girls used the facilities.

The spiritual side of the work was hampered by the lack of a chaplain dedicated to the care of the girls. [. . .] However, Miss Graham frequently took Prayers with the girls in the hut.[3]

1. SAWCM Reports for 1899 and 1905.
2. Anson, *op. cit.*, c.1949.
3. *A Brief History, 1864–2014, St Magnus' Church, Lerwick*, published by St Magnus Church, June 2014, pp.19-20.

The SEMF was also very active in the East Anglian ports during the 1940s, and the author of a letter in the Missions to Seamen archives, dated 21 June 1944, stated: '[of the] work at Lowestoft [. . .] the Scottish Episcopal Fisherfolk Mission have a particular and long interest'.[1] A second letter (25 June 1946) states: 'We would like to send to you [to Antwerp] a Miss Gellatly, a Scottish lady, who during the war was loaned to us by the Scottish Fisher Girls Mission.'

The relationship between the two Scottish societies is somewhat confusing and Anson was not particularly clear on the distinction. Unfortunately, a search for more information about the two societies has proved unproductive and this does seem odd given Anson's suggestion that the work of the Church of Scotland began c.1880.

5.2.2. The Thames Church Mission and the Mission to Deep Sea Fishermen

With the separation of the TCM and MDSF in 1886, and the latter's stand as an 'un-denominational' (in modern terms non-denominational) society, the Church of England again found itself without any sustained presence among the fishermen at sea, although the MDSF retained good links with the established Church. The Missions to Seamen had developed a range of activities and facilities in the fishing ports and used some small craft to visit vessels in the harbours, but visits to the fleets were sporadic.

A more direct response to the work of the MDSF came from representatives of the Anglo-Catholics. The Saint Andrews' Waterside Mission was urged by clergy in the ports to purchase and equip Church ships for work at sea and, when these were obtained, they worked mainly from Grimsby, Brixham and Gorleston, under the care of the parochial clergy. While the clergy at Grimsby and Brixham remained firmly under the wing of the SAWM, the vicar of Gorleston took the opportunity to develop an independent organisation, the North Sea Church Mission. This society was successful for a few years but had to sell its vessels by the end of the century.

5.2.3 The St Andrew's Waterside Church Mission

Introduction

In 1887 the Rev. J. Spawforth of Grimsby made an eloquent plea:

> It will readily be seen that fishermen have but little opportunity for religious worship when ashore, and for a time it was thought that nothing could be done for the men afloat. The Mission to Deep

---

1. Letters of 21 June 1944 and 25 June 1946, signed G.F.T., in the MS Archives.

Sea Fishermen, conducted by Mr Mather, has developed both the opportunities and the possibilities of work among the men at sea, and while a generous recognition should be given to Mr Mather for what the MDSF has been enabled to do, his success ought to be an incentive to Churchmen to equip every fishing port of the kingdom with a Church Ship, which should go with the men to their labours, and which should seek to serve both their temporal and spiritual welfare.[1]

When the SAWM made an appeal a year later to replace its steam launch, *Messenger*, three vessels were subsequently provided: the *Kestrel* (a steam launch), the *Sapper* (a large yacht) and the *Water Kelpie* (a smack).[2] A donation of £500 was also given to be put towards the purchase of another vessel. This provided the opportunity to develop the Church Mission at sea. The *Sapper* was used for work between Gorleston and the Isle of Wight, 'taking in Ports on the Dutch, Belgian, and French coasts'. The *Sapper*, therefore, had its work cut out trying to cover such a wide range of ministries. In 1893 a new vessel, the *Goshawk*, was donated by a member of the Royal Yacht Squadron to sail as a Church ship in the North Sea. A clergyman was based permanently on board and a doctor appointed to sail with her. By 1899, however, the expense of maintaining the seagoing vessels became prohibitive and the North Sea work was curtailed. The *Sapper* and the *Goshawk* were sold.[3]

Other changes followed, notably the revision of the Constitution, Rules and Regulations in 1892, and a change of name. Wanting to emphasise its Church and international character, the society became known as the St Andrew's Church of England Mission to Sailors, Emigrants, and Fishermen, at Home and Abroad,[4] shortened to St Andrew's Waterside Church Mission.

The end of an era came with the death of Canon Scarth, the SAWCM's Director, on 22 September 1909, at the age of 83 years. The work of the SAWCM, however, continued to develop in new directions, especially during the 1914–18 war years when it provided a supportive service for seafarers engaged in action – many of whom were fishermen. By the 1920s, however, the society found itself having to run down some of its British work. The offices at Liverpool were closed in 1922, the steam launch was sold and replaced by a motor boat, now placed under the control of the incumbent

1. SAWM Reports, 1887, p.52; and 1888, p.15.
2. *Ibid.*, 1888, p.15; and 1889, p.10.
3. *Ibid.*, 1897, pp.9-10; 1890, pp.10-12; 1893, p.17. The *Goshawk* was 141 tons register and could accommodate a congregation of 150.
4. *Ibid.*, 1892, p.18.

at Tilbury. In the meantime, the property at Gravesend was in a poor state of repair and in 1924 the Gravesend Municipal Council demanded that drainage and repairs be attended to promptly. The building was offered to the Parochial Church Council of Holy Trinity Church, along with a grant of £50 to help with the necessary repairs, but the members of the Parochial Church Council were unwilling to take on what they saw as a liability. The building was put up for sale in 1926 and eventually sold to a Mr J.C. Quirk who hoped to use it as a college to train boys of poor parents for a merchant navy career. The £500 received for the property was then put into the ordinary income account of the SAWCM. During the 1930s it became increasingly obvious that the SAWCM was duplicating the work of the Missions to Seamen, a situation eventually perceived as pointless, and the two Societies merged in May 1939.[1]

Given the parochial nature of the SAWCM's work it may be helpful to examine the impact of the work in the two fishing communities of Grimsby and Brixham.

Grimsby

Work in Grimsby commenced at the end of 1876[2] under the general direction of the vicar of St Andrew's, the Rev. W. Marples. His arrival in 1870 coincided with the beginning of the dramatic expansion of Grimsby as a fishing port, which, during the period 1876–1900, saw the number of fishing vessels registered there rise from 600 to 1,000 and the number of fishermen from 3,500 to 10,000. In light of this expanding population, Canon Scarth argued:

> It was no use attempting to reform abuses that existed chiefly at sea, unless we could gain a good influence over the fishermen and families on shore. Therefore, as Grimsby was fast taking the lead of Yarmouth and was the nearest port to the Dogger, it was arranged that the vicar of St Andrew's, Grimsby, should have a Mission curate for special work among fishermen.[3]

The 'Mission curate', the Rev. H.T. Harte, visited the docks in the mornings to talk with the fishermen, distributed books, tracts and magazines, and helped to establish a 'Mission Room' close to the docks in early 1878, which was open from 6pm to 9pm. The work quickly developed in a range of directions and, when a general strike occurred in 1880, this led to much hardship amongst the fishing community, with the St Andrew's staff being called upon for both pastoral and conciliation duties – thereby gaining the respect of all in the local community.

1. *Ibid.*, 1938, pp.8-9.
2. *Ibid.*, 1876, p.16.
3. Scarth, *op. cit.* (1890), p.69.

When Mr Marples left Grimsby in 1882 the new incumbent, the Rev. James Spawforth, took up the work with enthusiasm and by 1884 was able to record that 3,366 visits had been made by young men to the Mission Room, and 590 bags of books supplied to smacks.[1] Mr Harte had pointed to the 'considerable increase' in the number of fishermen visiting the docks Mission Room by 1884 and said that the amount of work necessitated the employment of other helpers: a Mr D.H. Lee, a lady missioner and the Rev. P.P. Goldingham. The Mission Room was becoming too small for the work and new premises were opened in 1885 in Freeman Street, the town's main shopping centre, where the extra space allowed for the inclusion of a small chapel.[2]

Mr Lee kept statistics for the visits to the Mission Rooms and the number of smacks supplied with literature. But, when he ceased to work full-time, the statistics ceased to be recorded in the Parish Magazine for a while. A summary of Mr Lee's statistics can be found in Appendix 7. These provide a helpful overview of attendances at the Mission Rooms between 1883 and 1888 and, while the figures for each month are incomplete, the general picture remains fairly consistent. There is a general increase in the use of the Mission Rooms, while the attendances dip a little during the summer months of April to August, presumably when the fleeting system was in full swing. It would have been interesting to see what happened after March 1888, although Mr Lee's partial retirement meant that such lists were no longer kept. With the opening of the *Water Kelpie* in the docks in 1891, however, a new (although incomplete) set of statistics was begun and these show a gradual increase in attendances up to 1895. As there were still attendances at the Mission Rooms, we can assume that the numbers were generally good until the late 1890s. This fits well with what is known about the subsequent development of the Grimsby Mission.

A 'Perfect Church Colony'

Mr Spawforth was succeeded by the Rev. Richard Meddings in June 1889, who set about reorganising the structure to cope with the growing work, and he increased staff numbers to eight (then ten in 1892), including two lay evangelists and a woman to work with the fishergirls and local women. A new Grimsby Mission flag was produced for use on local smacks and a white metal badge with the St Andrew's inscription upon it.

Of the work on the smacks Mr Meddings said:

> Seven hundred and eight smacks were supplied with parcels of reading [between June and December, 1890], their delivery on board giving good opportunity for personal intercourse and intimacy with

---

1. SAWM Reports, 1878, p.38; 1879, p.31; and 1882, p.44.
2. *Ibid.*, 1885, p.51.

the crews. [. . .] One of our large Day Schools has been used as a Mission Room for Sunday Evening Services, and has had a regular congregation of from 100 to 200 people; thus preparing for the new Fishermen's Church which is being built close by.[1]

A new building, incorporating Waterside Mission Rooms and Church House, was opened on the corner of Strand Street and Albion Street in 1890-92 The building operated as a parochial centre with staff available twenty-four hours a day. (The parish report for 1891 says that the building was: 'Open free from 3pm until 10.30pm and has 7,427 visitors recorded for the year, or an average of 150 a week.') Two years later the Fishermen's Church was erected a short distance from the Mission Rooms:

> the same roof gives shelter to four Clergy, and to the Lay Reader and Mission Woman. These premises, together with the Fishermen's Church and the Day Schools, all in a group, form a perfect church colony in the poorest part of the parish, with untold opportunities for wholesome influence and usefulness.3

The corner stone of the small Waterside Fisherman's Church was laid on 16 April 1891, and was dedicated to St John the Evangelist, being a Chapel of Ease to St Andrew's Church.

The work proved to be expensive, and debts, which in 1891 were thought to be simply the result of erecting new buildings, were seen in 1892 as 'a chronic state of living beyond our means'. The facilities, however, were popular and included a club room where billiards could be played, pipes smoked and ginger beer sold, although gambling and alcohol were banned. This room also incorporated an office and the 'Pure Literature Department', and was available for 'Instruction and Bible Classes'. A further room for the sole use of fisherlads was added in 1893. Open-air work was commenced during the months of March to November, as fishermen preferred to be on the pontoon looking after their smacks, meeting friends and watching to see who would arrive on the next tide. These services, initiated and run by the Lay Reader and Bible Woman (Mr and Mrs Kerr), accompanied by one of the clergy, were held between 11am and 12 midday with a congregation of several hundreds. Similar services were held during the week:

---

1. *Ibid.*, 1890, pp.60-3.
2. *Grimsby News*, 18 July 1890.
3. SAWCM Report, 1897, p.58. The Church was erected in Strand Street, the gift of the Rev. Beauchamp St John Tyrwhitt.

Some examples of SAWCM badges.

On Monday and Thursday nights an Open-Air Service has been held at different points in the parish, followed by a meeting indoors. On Saturday nights a regular Service has been held just off our leading thoroughfare, which must in the course of the year have arrested many thousands for a moment's thought. A harmonium is used to lead the singing; the clergy wear their academicals; and a banner, surmounted by a brass cross, proclaims who and whence we are.[1]

A Church Ship

In June 1885, Mr Spawforth wrote in the St Andrew's parish magazine that a smack was now necessary for visiting fishermen at sea. The Grimsby clergy had spent several seasons visiting the North Sea fleets by travelling out with a local skipper or carrier ship, and moved from boat to boat to visit and hold services. It was hoped that the Church ship would form part of the parochial machinery and visit the fleets at sea during the summer months. When the fleeting season ended, the smack would form a Dock Church for the single boaters, visiting fishermen and local fishing families. The cost of such a vessel was estimated at £2,500, but funds were slow to come in – only £239.5s.4d being raised over two years.[2]

Shortly after his arrival in Grimsby, Mr Meddings visited the Grimsby Ice Company's fleet at sea in order to become acquainted with the daily life of the local fishermen. The *Sapper* was loaned for a while and, under Meddings' authority, the vessel made the first of several trips to the North Sea, Holland and France in May 1890. But it proved unsuitable for North Sea work and at the Hull Church Congress in late 1890 Mr Meddings appealed for a larger vessel.[3] Following a tour around the coast of Britain, the *Water Kelpie* was loaned to the Grimsby Mission in October 1891,

---

1. SAWM Report, 1890, p.61.
2. *Ibid.*, 1886, p.58; and 1888, p.62.
3. Church Congress Report, Sept/Oct 1890, pp.469-70.

but was also found to be unsuitable for work at sea and was moored in the fishing docks, where it was used for services, meetings and acted as a Reading Room. However, even the relatively modest expense of £60 a year for the vessel's upkeep was a heavy burden for the Grimsby Mission, which was struggling to pay off debts. A request was made for half the cost of the upkeep to be met by the parent society, which was agreed to. The *Water Kelpie*, flying the SAWCM's flag, proved to be such an attraction to local and visiting fishermen that the skipper slept on board and was always on hand to supply tea, coffee and literature.[1]

The Water Kelpie *in Grimsby Docks.*

An appeal was made for a Church ship in 1892. A year later the *Goshawk* was donated to the SAWCM and, in June 1894, the vessel, with fishermen, clergy and a doctor on board, wound its way clockwise around the coast. On arrival at Grimsby the vessel was met with 'a perfect ovation', and handed over to the care of Mr Meddings, who used it for several trips to the fishing fleets. Unfortunately, the high cost of essential repairs and alterations before the vessel was launched at Gosport cost more than expected and, as the hoped-for funds failed to materialise, the *Goshawk* had to remain inshore during the summer months of 1895.

Frustrated with waiting for a Church ship, the vicar of Gorleston launched an appeal for funds to purchase his own vessel. The SAWCM Committee, embarrassed by two appeals for similar projects, withdrew its appeal for funds for the *Goshawk* for a time. Meddings' curate, Mr Best, joined the North Sea Church Mission, set up by Gorleston's vicar, in June 1895, and this must have added to Mr Meddings'

1. SAWM Report, 1891, p.65; SAWCM Report for 1892, pp.13, 48; and 1894, p.19.

frustration – although he wisely refrained from expressing any explicit animosity in the SAWCM Annual Reports. But his frustration could not be kept completely silent:

> We did wait – waited a long time – for a Church Ship, which came, and did some good work; and then, as if the *Goshawk* were a migratory bird, flew away, and has not returned [. . .] the absence of the Church Ship and her sailing priest from the Grimsby fleets during the past year has been a cruel disaster to our work, and a grievous disappointment to our fishermen and lads.

The Report for 1895 carried a conciliatory statement:

> The Committee regretted that the *Goshawk* was not able to visit Grimsby last year; they trust, however, that the fishermen will have an opportunity shortly of welcoming her, and that such good work as was commenced on her last visit may be repeated.

When the *Goshawk* put to sea again in the summer of 1896, it was emphasised that its purpose was to visit 'the principal fishing stations [. . .] and all our large fishing fleets'.[1] Meddings sailed with her to Aberdeen and the islands of Orkney and Shetland where he visited numerous trawlers from Hull and Grimsby, as well as the herring fleet which was in full season at Aberdeen.

Although Meddings continued to make appeals for the donation of a suitable vessel for Church work at sea, the regular loan of the *Goshawk* negated the urgency of this need. The various other requests from the vicar – £50 for a trained lay worker with local navvies, £100 for the erection of an institute for local youths and so on – must have been somewhat off-putting to potential donors. Funds were not forthcoming either through the Grimsby Mission or through the parent society and the *Goshawk* was again laid up in 1897. The SAWCM Committee acknowledged that the sought-for funding was unlikely to emerge, and decided in 1897 to return the vessel to her owner.[2]

Developments on Shore

Although the Grimsby Ice Company's fleet was disbanded in 1896, the influx of fish to the port was increasing, as was the supply of coal and other commodities. Sail was giving way to steam and the docks were faced with a constant supply of fish from steam trawlers. The docks were enlarged to meet the growing demand – and this had repercussions for the St Andrew's

---

1. SAWCM Report, 1895, p.20.
2. *Ibid.*, 1897, pp.9-10.

Grimsby Mission. The *Water Kelpie* had been berthed in a prominent position near the fish pontoon but, as this was now to be extended, the Waterside Mission had to move some distance away into Alexandra Dock – not easily found by visitors and not readily accessible to the fishermen. Another suitable site for the *Water Kelpie* could not be found and after a year of being laid aside the SAWCM sold the vessel. The memorial plate was taken from the vessel and fixed to the wall of the Fishermen's Church as a memento of the seven years' service provided for fishermen. Meanwhile, a Mission Room and depot for literature was opened close to the docks and a trained layman was employed for work amongst the navvies.

Despite all this work St Andrew's did not attract many fishermen to its services, so the vicar decided to take the Church to the people, and Sunday morning services were recommenced on the quayside. A local newspaper reported:

> Earlier in the summer this work was conducted by a layman, but for the last few months it has been conducted entirely by the Vicar of St Andrew's and his staff of curates. Some of the features of the services are novel, at least to us. For instance, it is rather striking to see the preacher in cassock and surplice and ecclesiastical headgear, standing on a pile of fish boxes, clinging with one hand to the pole of a Mission banner, or brass cross, and gesticulating violently with the other hand, as he warms to his subject, inspired by the upturned faces of a crowd of men generally to be numbered by hundreds.[1]

In 1898 the SAWCM Report announced the establishment of the Grimsby and Cleethorpes Orphanage for the Orphan Daughters of Fishermen and Sailors. Mr Meddings pointed out that it appeared to be the first of its kind, and would help any family, and take girls recommended by any part of the SAWCM. Facilities provided offered 100 separate bedrooms, officers' rooms, board rooms, a play room, cooking kitchens, and a laundry. The Orphanage, however, appears to have had a short life, as a note in the SAWCM's Minutes for 13 October 1900, states that the Grimsby Orphanage was closed, and the £700 raised from the sale of the property was handed over to St Andrew's Parish by the Trustees, to 'augment the endowment of the benefice of St Andrew's, Great Grimsby'.

By the beginning of the new century sail gave way to steam and the fleets all but disappeared. This change brought with it new attitudes. The fleeting system of the 1880s, for all its bad points, gave the men opportunities for leisure but, with the advent of steam trawlers, such opportunities decreased

---

1. *Grimsby Times*, 2 September 1898.

and Sundays became working days. The Grimsby clergy had to adapt to this situation and finding that visits to sea were no longer viable they concentrated on shore-work in the dock area. Even this was becoming more difficult, however, as the pace of worklife quickened. A second Mission Room was opened in the centre of the docks in 1900, which increased the workload on the already hard-pressed staff whose numbers had been of necessity reduced. The increasing number of Scottish fishermen and their families, following the herring round the coast, caused added pressure, although help came from a clergyman from Stornoway who travelled with and ministered to the herring fishermen. As the numbers of women workers increased, the St Andrew's vicar appealed for 'a couple of trained sisters, to work with the fishermen's families and the fish-curing girls'.[1]

When Mr Meddings left Grimsby in 1907, the new incumbent, the Rev. C.H. Lenton, responded with vigour to the rapidly changing scene. He moved the largely middle-class congregation from the Fishermen's Church to the Parish Church and put great effort into making the services and atmosphere appropriate to the needs of the local population. A large Mission Hall and house was purchased in Market Square and put to good use – although the outbreak of war in 1914 put greater pressure on Church staff and prevented the Church raising sufficient funds to pay off the outstanding debt on the premises. The local fishermen were quickly trained for minesweeping and this change of work, plus an influx of countless naval personnel to the port, again meant a heavy workload for the St Andrew's staff.

Continually changing work patterns following the end of the First World War, and the depression of the 1920s, put great pressure on St Andrew's to sell off some of its property and to reduce the number of clergy and lay workers engaged in oversight of the fishing community. Hence by the 1930s there was no longer any mention of work at Grimsby in the SAWCM Annual Reports.

Brixham

A Bethel Union was established in Brixham in 1822; and the hymn-writer Henry Francis Lyte concerned himself with the fishing community when he arrived there in 1824.[2] But by the 1870s the population had become too large for the small Christian presence in the town. When Canon C.E.R. Robinson moved to the incumbency of St John's Church, Torquay, in November 1870, he encouraged his church to meet the growing need in Brixham, and the members raised £2,200 to erect the Church of St Peter

1. SAWCM Report, 1899, p.53; and 1905, p.57.
2. *Sailors Magazine (London)*, 1822, p.1; B.G. Skinner, *Henry Francis Lyte* (University of Exeter, 1974), p.13.

the Fisherman in Sleepy Lane, Lower Brixham.[1] The SAWM also gave a
grant of £50 per year towards the stipend of a Mission Curate, the Rev.
Arthur Gordon Stallard, who was appointed in 1877. Brixham had about
150 trawling smacks working from the port in the 1880s and approximately
6,000 residents in the parish – most of whom were directly involved in the
fishing industry either at sea or on shore:[2]

> The men who are engaged in this work are obliged from almost
> their childhood to live hard, rough lives of danger and toil; and
> their life has been supposed to affect their conduct and character
> so much, that a 'Brixham Trawler' is often used as another way of
> saying a rough fellow. The Church, too, for many years did not do
> much for these her rough children.[3]

Mr Stallard, nevertheless, paid tribute to the kindness, loyalty and
the religious nature of the local fisherfolk. The Brixham fishing fleet did
not work on Sundays and as a result the church had a regular number
of fishermen attending services: ' [On] Saturdays, the beautiful bay
is full of smacks making their way to their moorings, where they lie
safely till Monday morning, and then they are off again to their fishing
grounds.'[4] A large house was used on Sunday afternoons for Sunday
School classes for fishermen aged over 17 and was attended regularly
by 100. At the same time about 70 of the older fishermen attended
Bible Instruction classes in the Church building. The Sunday evening
services were crammed full of attenders and the choir was composed of
young fishermen dressed in blue ganseys.[5] Stallard regularly invited the
fishermen to his house following services, and prior to their going out
to sea they visited their vicar in turn for a blessing. But with such erratic
periods on shore the fishermen's allegiance to the church was not always
great, as one fisherman explained:

> You see, we begin fairly well for a week or two, and feel the loss of
> the Services at church and our Communions; but after a bit, one
> day is so much like another, that we don't think about it; then we

---

1. Boggis, *op. cit.* (1930), p.163. Robinson later moved to St John's Torquay, where he
   died in 1881 (SAWM Report, 1881, pp.38-9) – the very year that E.J. Mather, in
   response to the needs of the North Sea fishermen, began the MDSF.
2. Skinner, *op. cit.*, p.48. Skinner says that the population had risen to 5,684 in
   1841; and the SAWCM Report for 1894, p.82, gives the population for that year
   as 6,500.
3. SAWM Report, 1887, p.54.
4. SAWM Report, 1887, p.54.
5. Scarth, *op. cit.* (1889), pp.71-2.

get not to care whether we are away from them or not; and then even when we come back it is an effort to us to begin to come to the Services regularly.[6]

Large companies tended to insist upon Sunday work from their employees, especially when they were working with the North Sea fleets, and by the 1890s Sunday fishing had become a normal fact of life. The Brixham church made an attempt to counteract this attitude and inaugurated a society binding its members to refrain from Sunday work. But the Brixham Trawlers Sunday League never gained much support and the vicar resigned himself to the inevitability of Sunday work.

In 1885 Stallard made a visit to the North Sea fleets in a hired local trawler to see for himself what conditions were like. The spectacle of their local vicar among them obviously impressed the men as they attended several services on the trawler. Many Nonconformists also came, and the vicar thoroughly enjoyed himself: 'We had many hymns, and went through the morning service, and then I preached to them. I never had so attentive a congregation as these men, crowded into our hold.' The earnestness of the fishermen attending services must have astonished many Christians on land. In one case ten ships were lashed together for a service in calm weather, and two fishermen rowed ten miles to collect a young lad from a vessel lying off from the fleet, in order that he should be able to attend the service.[7]

In 1886, after a discussion with the local baker who belonged to St Peter's Church, one of the fishermen remarked that he wished there was a Church ship at sea with the local fleet. The baker took up the remark and offered to help if the men would set to work on the scheme. A party of twelve fishermen and the baker met with Stallard and told him of their plans, subsequently presenting him with £60, which they had collected from local people, and urged him to establish a Church ship to sail with the Brixham fleet. This amount paid for the hire of a smack for two months, and one of the local owners offered his own vessel to be fitted out as a Church ship, placing himself at the disposal of the Mission to sail as skipper. The local fisherfolk also promised to give something each week towards the Mission's expenses. Following an appeal for funds in the *Church Times*, a smack, the *Dauntless*, was obtained in the spring of 1887, fitted out and made ready for sea.[8] She sailed from Brixham on 26 April 1887 and reached the local smacks two days later when the fishermen immediately boarded her to see the vessel and

6. SAWCM Report, 1887, pp.55, 74.
7. *Ibid.*, 1885, p.52.
8. *Church Times*, 9 March 1888.

greet the vicar. The day was very busy with services at 8am, 11am, 2.30pm and 6pm, many men remaining on board throughout the whole day. After a successful eight weeks, the Church ship returned home on 17 June. The SAWM Committee was delighted with this response and appealed for funds for Church ships at Brixham and Grimsby. Unfortunately, the funds did not materialise, and the Brixham fishermen wrote to Mr Mather of the MDSF urging him to provide a regular High Church minister on his society's vessels. The request was ironic given the poor relationship between the SAWM and the MDSF, and perhaps not surprisingly the request went unanswered.

The small number of Brixham smacks fishing off the Irish coast in 1886 quickly turned into a flood, so that by 1887 very few Brixham vessels worked in the North Sea.[1] When the smacks moved into the Irish Channel during 1888 and 1889, the aim of a Church ship for the North Sea was inevitably called into question. Rapid changes were also taking place in the fishing industry – new bye-laws, for example, of the Devon Sea Fishery Board in 1894–95 prohibited trawlers working within certain limits of Devon bays. This had a dramatic and devastating impact upon the Brixham inshore fishermen who depended upon these bays for their livelihood. After much discussion on the point, a small sloop, the *Icthus*, was hired, the hold fitted up as a chapel and the vessel sent out to visit the Brixham smacks in the Irish Channel. It sailed on Thursday, 31 May 1888, with Stallard on board, and carried medicines, literature and woollens for distribution amongst the fishermen. The Admiral of the Great Western fleet of Brixham, though not a member of St Peter's Church, wrote to Stallard to thank him for the care that had been shown to the fishermen in his fleet.

The constant hiring of vessels was not a cost-effective way of operating, and Stallard again appealed in 1889 for a permanent Church ship at sea – pointing out that local people had collected £440 towards the cost. This need was partially met in July 1890 when the SAWM sent the *Water Kelpie* to assist the local clergy – but the vessel was unsuitable for deep-sea work and another appeal was made for a larger vessel. This was not forthcoming, and the *Water Kelpie* was again used in June and July of 1891 to visit the local fishermen in the Bristol Channel.[2]

During 1890 a house was obtained on the Brixham quayside and turned into a Sailor's Rest and Reading Room. At first it proved to be very popular and had 50-60 fisherlads frequenting the premises each evening to play bagatelle and other table games. But by 1912 the premises had closed through lack of use.[3]

1. SAWM Report, 1886, p.61.
2. *Ibid.*, 1891, p.89; and 1901, p.70.
3. *Ibid*, 1890, p.66; SAWCM Report for 1892, p.13; 1894, p.81; and 1912, p.65.

Having spent thirteen years at Brixham, Mr Stallard moved to Plymouth in 1891. He was greatly loved and respected by his parishioners who gave him the affectionate title of 'Trawlers' Bishop', and when he died, 'after a lingering affliction of the heart caused by overwork and want of proper rest, [. . .] [he was] borne to his last resting place [. . .] by Brixham Trawlers'.[1]

5.2.4 . The North Sea Church Mission (c.1895–c.1917)

Introduction

The North Sea Church Mission, established by the Rev. Forbes Alexander Phillips at Gorleston, Suffolk, in June 1895, was from the outset a Church society that had close links with the St Andrew's Waterside Church Mission. The NSCM existed for approximately ten years (1895–1906) and advertised itself as: 'The only Church of England Society working summer and winter among the North Sea fishing fleets'.[2] A letter sent to the SAWCM Committee, dated 12 June 1895, suggests that the NSCM was organised around this time. Gorleston had 14,000 residents in 1894, most of whom were connected with the fishing industry – this number was greatly increased by visiting fishermen and the annual influx of Scottish fishermen and their families during the herring season.

In 1876 the SAWM Report referred to the proposed holding of an 'Eight Days' Mission' at Great Yarmouth. The Mission was held on 21– 30 April 1877 and appears to have been organised by the 'Special Local Mission Society', which worked with parishes in Great Yarmouth. This initial involvement of a Church Society Mission at Great Yarmouth was so successful that the SAWM considered trying to participate in mission work during the herring season. But this did not materialise as 'neither the Vicar nor the Mission could secure a suitable missionary in time'.[3] Good links were, however, established, particularly with the Rev. A.R. Abbott, vicar of St Andrew's Church at Gorleston. He was an enthusiastic supporter of the SAWM, and his concern that the Church be involved at a very practical level with fishermen led him to appeal in the *Church Times* for funds towards the building of a Church Mission in south Gorleston, where some 4,000 fishermen and their families lived. He pressed the SAWM to supply a Church ship for work in the North Sea but, when he died in 1892, he had seen his dream only partially realised in the local presence of SAWM's vessel, the *Sapper*.[4]

---

1. *Ibid.*, 1901, p.13.
2. Advertisement in the Great Yarmouth Printing Co. Annual for 1898, p.228.
3. SAWM Report, 1877, p.30.
4. *Church Times*, 14 February 1888; SAWCM Report, 1892, p.62.

The Rev. Forbes Phillips

The new incumbent, the Rev. Forbes Phillips, was instituted as vicar of
Gorleston in the Church of St Andrew on 17 July 1893, having moved
from All Saints Church, Newcastle-upon-Tyne, where he had been curate
since 1889. Within a short time of his induction, he established a Cycling
Club, Dramatic Society, Choral Society, and had become such a notable
character in the vicinity that the local press said of him:

> The new vicar of Gorleston seems bent on doing some practical
> social good in our midst and we hail his efforts with much
> satisfaction. With the Rev. Forbes Phillips at the wheel 'Unity,
> Harmony and Success' will be the motto.[1]

Phillips was a Churchman who disliked nonconformism and temperance
– although he admired the Salvation Army. In his younger days he had been
a member of a teetotal society but changed his views and appealed to men

The Rev. Forbes Phillips.

to give up excess rather than give up beer
altogether: 'I can take beer without getting
drunk. Are you not man enough to do the
same? This, I often found, produced the
required result, and I heartily recommend it
to my brother clergy.'

His antipathy towards the Temperance
movement was forcefully made as he regularly
visited the local public houses for a drink
with his parishioners. Yet he respected those
advocates of temperance who were sincere,
whilst abusing those who were not, saying
that 'the temperance idea is a good one but it
is ruined by intemperate advocates'.[2]

The SAWCM Committee was delighted
when Phillips displayed the same enthusiasm
as his predecessor for the purchase and
equipping of a distinctive Church ship for
work in the North Sea, and loaned him the *Sapper* – but he concurred
with the Grimsby Mission in judging the vessel too small for the work. In
response to requests from East Coast clergy for a Church ship, he obtained
the *Goshawk*, which after some initial work at Grimsby, was placed at
Phillips' service. An annual grant of £40 was also provided, and Phillips

1. *Norfolk Fair*, June 1969, p.45.
2. Athol Forbes (pseudonym for the Rev. Forbes Phillips), *Cassock and Comedy* (C.
   Arthur Pearson, 1898), pp.175,180.

wrote a report in which he praised the *Goshawk* but regretted the limited amount of time it had been able to spend with the North Sea fleets; he said he hoped 'to raise funds to sail the *Sapper* out to the fleets until such time as the work can be done by a more suitable ship.'[1]

Mr Phillips, his clergyman and a lay missionary visited the smacks and ships in port and distributed literature and notices of services. A large store was purchased and turned into an institute for the fishermen. Facilities included a coffee bar, reading room, space for religious meetings and Friday evening lectures on elementary first aid – a certificate of proficiency being awarded when the course had been completed and an examination successfully taken.[2]

A New Mission

Having experienced some success with the SAWCM's vessels, and the establishment of a self-supporting Fishermen's Institute, Phillips was keen to develop the work further and he set about forming his own Mission to North Sea fishermen, although he maintained that the initiative had been one that the fishermen had themselves asked for. The North Sea Church Mission was subsequently inaugurated, with offices based at Waterside, Gorleston. However, the SAWCM was now embarrassed by appeals going out from two societies for the same purpose, and 'withdrew appeals for the *Goshawk* for a time, lest there should be any appearance of antagonism'.[3] A number of friends were found to finance the scheme, and a vessel, the *Will Morgan*, built in 1881 (of 41 tons register, number YH830), was bought, fitted out and launched in June 1895. The Rev. E.S. Best, formerly Sailing Curate at Grimsby attached to the *Sapper* and *Goshawk*, was appointed Sailing Curate to St Andrew's, Gorleston. Phillips also spent some time at sea working with the fishermen. Services were held on board daily when the weather allowed, medical aid was provided, lectures and magic lantern slide shows given, books distributed, free pipes supplied, tobacco sold free of duty, and a scheme of life insurance introduced.[4] These facilities were of course very similar to those provided by the RNMDSF and the SAWCM.

The *Will Morgan* appears to have been highly regarded by the local people who saw it as their own Mission ship. As the ship set off on her second voyage in late August 1895, she was sent on her way amidst great waving and cheering:

---

1. SAWCM Report, 1894, p.84.
2. *Yarmouth Independent*, 15 February 1895, p.3.
3. *Yarmouth Independent*, 25 January 1896.
4. *Norfolk Fair*, June 1969, p.46.

The North Sea Mission vessel, the *Will Morgan*, after having her stores replenished, started on her second eight weeks' voyage on Wednesday morning in connection with her new mission work in the North Sea. There was a large muster on the quay to witness her departure, and still more went out on the tug to see her safely past the sands, on her way to Borkum on the Dutch coast, where the Short Blue fleet are fishing. [. . .] Upon leaving the quay at half past eleven the spectators loudly cheered and wished the vessel and her crew 'Godspeed' on her mission. This was replied by a twenty-gun salute from the tug. Guns were rapidly fired as the vessel left the harbour, which almost drowned the cheers of those gathered on the pier head. [. . .] As the vessel passed the pleasure boats off the beach at Yarmouth, and by the crowded jetty and piers, they attracted the attention of all by the rattling of the miniature cannons from the tug and the repeated cheers of the crews.

A crew member of the North Sea Church Mission wearing the Society's gansey..

Phillips was not slow to take advantage of the opportunity to advertise the Mission's work and, when the ship reached the Cockle lightship, the people in the tug accompanying the vessel were rewarded for their support:

> the 'Cockle' lightship was reached at one o'clock, and here the *Will Morgan* was run almost alongside the tug and then for a few minutes there was a perfect shower of sea biscuits, ginger pop bottles and apples for the smack, which were scrambled for and rapidly devoured by the more hungry members of the party.[1]

This diversion over, the two vessels parted company and the *Will Morgan* set sail for the fishing grounds.

Controversy

During October 1895, Phillips and several of his fishermen friends attended the National Church Congress at St Andrew's Hall, Norwich. He also had the *Will Morgan* towed along the River Yare to Norwich, where it was

---

1. *Yarmouth Independent*, 24 August 1895.

moored by the Foundry Bridge, decorated with bunting and thrown open to the public. The site was about a half mile from the Cathedral, close to the city centre, and directly outside the main railway station – an ideal position to gain public interest – and the public responded with zest. This episode must have irked the other seafarers' organisations represented at the Congress, but Phillips compounded the insult by using the Congress platform to ridicule the work of Nonconformist Missions at sea. He argued that the fishermen:

> must have a Church out there, with a working clergy, and the men must not be left to nothing more than a Salvation Army kind of service. He knew what the unsectarian service was. The seamen were invited to declare at once that they were saved. (Cries of 'No, No!') He was speaking facts, and he would appeal to the seamen at the end of the hall. (Cries of 'No, No!' at the end of the hall) The men were invited to say that they were saved, so that the souls saved might be tabulated together with the fish caught. The Church's work could not be done under dissenting or unsectarian auspices. They must have out there the old Church of the country, with her clergy and her sacraments, and he could assure them such efforts were warmly appreciated.[1]

He went on to tell the audience about a Friendly Society which had been set up to insure the lives of fishermen, of the work of the *Will Morgan*, and of his desire to raise funds to build a Church hospital ship. The comments caused an outcry. The Rev. Charles Hicks, who lived locally and had spent many years working with the RNMDSF and SAWCM vessels, tried to respond at the Congress but was not allowed to do so. He wrote to the local newspapers and gave a full reply to Phillips' claims, and his letter brought others in support from local fishermen. This whole unfortunate episode seems to have done a good deal of harm to Phillips' new venture, because within a year the NSCM was experiencing financial difficulties. Whilst useful for advertising the work of the NSCM, the *Will Morgan* was, nevertheless, an old ship, being 'small, leaky, and unsafe'.[2] Within a few months of her purchase, she was put into dry dock to undergo repairs and it soon became evident that a new vessel was urgently needed.

During the week of the Church Congress, Phillips called a meeting in Gorleston of all those interested in his work. Those present included Admiral Burleigh of the North Sea fleet and representatives from the community, the Church, and the Curates' Aid Society, which was supporting the NSCM

---

1. Church Congress Report (Norwich), 1895, pp.348-51.
2. *Yarmouth Independent*, 5 February 1896.

The Will Morgan *at sea, with the Rev. Forbes Phillips, far right, wearing a trilby.*

financially. Phillips explained that he was enquiring of them whether a new North Sea mission vessel had general support. While they thought it over, a substantial meal was provided along with free coffee, tea, pipes and tobacco – following which the general consensus was in support of the scheme.[1] It was hoped that this vessel would be ready for March 1896. A gift of £2,500 was donated by a lady who wished to remain anonymous to obtain a purpose-built hospital ship, to be called the *Frances*. In the meantime, the *Will Morgan* was condemned as unfit for work at sea and disposed of, and another ship had to be found quickly. The *Elizabeth Phyllis*, a vessel built in 1885, was purchased in January 1896, for £370 and renamed the *St Andrew the Fisherman*,[2] but within a few days it was almost destroyed in a fire. Fortunately, the vessel had been insured two days earlier. The repairs were carried out quickly and the vessel was ready for sea within two weeks, the Bishop of Norwich performing the dedication ceremony on Tuesday, 21 January. Mr Phillips, as usual, made full use of the event to advertise the work:

> The proceedings commenced at 11am, when a large crowd assembled at the Mission Stores. Here, under the superintendence of Dr R.G. Bately, the honorary Secretary, a procession was formed, which marched up to the Church in double file. First came the Volunteer Life-Saving Brigade, under the command of the Chief-boatman Peggs, who were followed by the crew of the Institution and Volunteer lifeboats, headed by their respective coxwains, 'Laddie'

1. *Ibid.*, 12 October 1895.
2. *Norfolk Fair*, June 1969, p.46.

and Joe Woods. A number of smacksmen, fishermen, mechanics, and others brought up the rear. At the Church a large congregation of those interested in the Mission work were awaiting them. The service was an ornate one, and included Holy Communion, and was not concluded before half-past one.[1]

The *St Andrew the Fisherman* performed well and encouraged by this the NSCM Committee set about building the hospital ship.

During the late 1890s there was a great increase in the local fishing population when 89 of Grimsby Ice Company's vessels were added to Hewett's fleet. Phillips said that 'the largest fleets in the North Sea now sail from this parish, making it, I suppose, the largest fishing parish in the world'. The Mission's staff was increased to six, and the Church now officially sanctioned the work: 'Two Bishops are under a promise to go out in our new Mission ship, for the purpose of holding Confirmations, and we have secured the permanent services of a medical man for the Mission work.'[2]

Unfortunately, all does not appear to have gone smoothly with the building of the *Frances*. Originally intended for completion by March 1896, this date was postponed until June. At the Annual General Meeting of the NSCM, in July 1898, the audience was told that the vessel was in course of construction but that many necessary changes had incurred far more expense than had been originally estimated. Fortunately, the original donor had promised a further sum sufficient for the vessel's modifications, fitting out with medical equipment *etc.*, so all looked well. But during 1897 the NSCM appears to have experienced an internal crisis to which reference was made at the 1898 AGM: 'During the past year sufficient funds had been obtained to defray all the working expenses, to pay off some of the liabilities which accrued prior to a change in administration, and to leave a small available balance.' This crisis was more directly referred to at the following year's AGM: '[The Mission's] progress was mainly due to Mr Easterbrook's indefatigable work and untiring energy. He it was who, in the crisis of the Mission, really rescued it from utter collapse.'[3]

All reference to Phillips in connection with the NSCM gradually disappeared from newspaper reports, and it seems likely that he handed over the running of the organisation to others. The crisis may well have come about as the result of the vicar's outspoken views on the Nonconformist

---

1. *Yarmouth Independent*, 25 January 1896,
2. SAWCM Report, 1895, p.82.
3. *The Times*, 12 July 1898; *Yarmouth Independent*, 15 July 1899, p.3.

societies, as all later references by the NSCM Committee to similar work by nonconformist agencies were noticeably complimentary. Local support certainly appears to have abated somewhat, and the Bishop of Ipswich made a particular point of saying at the 1899 AGM that the work was a national undertaking and not merely local. Phillips omitted to send a report to the SAWCM for 1896, presumably because by the spring of 1897 he was no longer directly responsible for the work of the NSCM. The SAWCM Committee, who were no doubt fully aware of the problems facing the NSCM, did not want to have the Mission linked to any bad publicity and included the following comment in its Report for 1896:

> The grant of £40 was continued last year [*i.e.* 1896] to Gorleston, through the new Vicar, but no report of the work for that year having been received, the Committee have not seen their way to a continuance of their support in 1897, especially as the Vicar has started a separate Mission.[1]

By the time of the 1899 NSCM AGM the crisis had subsided and the new Committee hoped to have the new vessel moored beside the *St Andrew the Fisherman* for inspection by those attending the meetings. Unfortunately, further delays had occurred.

The *Frances* had been designed as a sailing ship but, with the rapid growth of steam power, the vessel had to be refitted as a steamer and was eventually launched in July 1899. The modifications had been expensive, costing the NSCM three times the original estimate – a final total of £6,000. The ongoing expenses would therefore be very high.

Decline

By the turn of the century the fishing industry was undergoing a rapid decline and many Gorleston fishermen suddenly found themselves without work when the Short Blue fleet was dispersed c.1901. The NSCM found it more and more difficult to raise funds and after seven years' service the *Frances* was sold.[2]

Following the demise of the NSCM, links were renewed between Phillips and the SAWCM, and a short statement was included in the SAWCM Report for 1908: 'A fairly good result is evident from the renewal of the Society's work in this port. [. . .] The work of the North Sea Church Mission has now been incorporated with the SAWCM, the original parent Society.'[3] The

1. SAWCM Report, 1896, p.11. Reference to the Gorleston work does not thereafter appear in the Reports until 1909 (*i.e.* for 1908).
2. *Yarmouth Independent*, 28 July 1906.
3. SAWCM Report, 1908, p.71.

SAWCM Committee, however, seems to have been wary of the relationship:
literature was supplied by friends rather than directly from the SAWCM,
and there is no record of the earlier annual grant being recommenced.

Although the NSCM appears to have ceased in 1906 with the sale of
the *Frances*, the work of the Institute continued for many years. The great
influx of Scottish fishergirls in the early 1900s, as the herring fishery took
on a new lease of life, gave rise to new needs in the fishing community.
A Deaconess, Miss James, was employed to work with the girls, and a
nurse was in attendance to deal with cuts, sores, and other minor medical
problems, and give advice on health care. Of this changed aspect of the
work, Phillips reported:

> Fishing now – the deep sea part of it – is all done under steam,
> therefore active Mission work on the Dogger Bank and that part
> of the North Sea is no longer possible. In the old days, when Fleets
> were becalmed for sometimes a week, our Mission ship was able
> to hold frequent services. There is no calm under steam, so our
> work now is confined to Mission work ashore and in the river. The
> clergy are welcomed on the ships and smacks; and never do we get
> a surly reception. The work afloat, the memories of Mission work
> under storm and stress on the North Sea, is green in the memories
> of these men, and they are grateful. Literature is welcome, and we
> have to thank many friends for gifts of magazines and books – we
> can dispose of any quantity.
>
> The work of the Scotch fishergirls continues to grow, with the
> result that we have quite another population in the autumn. The
> Club we started for these splendid hard-working women has been a
> favourite rendezvous during the past year. It is open from 9 a.m. to
> 10 p.m. Ladies are always in attendance to give advice and kindly
> counsel to the girls. From time to time concerts are given, and
> the greater part of the programme is always contributed by our
> Scottish visitors.
>
> I am hoping soon to secure the services of a priest who can give
> his whole time to the special work of visiting the ships in harbour. As
> this is a fishing village and port, the work necessarily is of the nature
> which St Andrew's Waterside Mission takes under its special care.[1]

In his report to the SAWCM for the year 1911, Mr Phillips covered
similar ground but concluded in the outspoken manner of his earlier years:
'There is no place for agnosticism in a sailor's life; yet he does not wear
his religion upon his breast. They do appreciate the sober restraint and

1. *Ibid.*, 1909, p.69.

teaching of the Church.' A further comment seems somewhat odd given the amount of work going on in the North Sea by all aspects of the church: 'The supremacy of steam has made Mission work at sea impossible. *There never was much done at any time* [Author's italics]. Ashore one notices an increasing regard for the Church.'[1] With the onset of war in 1914, Phillips worked with the naval personnel, many of whom were fishermen who manned the North Sea minesweepers. But he did not see the end of the war and died at Gorleston on 29 May 1917, aged 51. St Andrew's relationship continued with the SAWCM under the new incumbent, but the links with the NSCM came to an end with the death of Mr Phillips.

---

1. *Ibid.*, 1910, pp.68-9.

Chapter 6
The 'Devil's Mission Ships'

Introduction

Given that the activity of the 'copers' loomed large in the early days of the Mission to Deep Sea Fishermen, the following is an overview of their activity and demise.[1] As with many aspects of the early days of maritime missions, the nature, work and eventual abolition of the copering traffic is fraught with mythological overtones. For example, we are told that the copers (sometimes spelt 'coopers') were mainly Dutch. The facts, however, tell a rather different story. Of the 31 presently known copers, 12 were from Holland, nine from England and ten from other countries. Initially, from c.1820–c.1850, they carried on a respectable trade supplying fish to visiting smacks. The second period, c.1850–c.1878 saw a range of vessels move out beyond the three-mile limit, where they sold and bartered their wares to the North Sea fishermen. A third stage, c.1878–c.1893, was when the full-blown copering trade was active, during which they carried cheap liquor either for sale or barter. It was especially during this period that a good deal of objection to the trade was made by the public, by missions and governments. The Mission to Deep Sea Fishermen played an important role in bringing this trade to the notice of the public and in pressuring the Government to ban the trade – achieved by 1893, although a few copers continued to work their trade for several years.

With a large number of fishermen employed in the North Sea, it became to all intents and purposes a fishing village.[2] But there was little to compare with the comforts of village life ashore. E.J. Mather (the MDSF founder) described the scene by comparing it to a village in the Midlands with the same number of people:

---

1. For a more in-depth study of the copering trade, see Stephen Friend, 'The North Sea Liquor Trade, c.1850–1893', *International Journal of Maritime History*, vol. XV (December 2003), no. 2, pp.43-71.
2. During the 1880s there were between 12,000 and 15,000 men and boys working in the North Sea.

The inland village lay at the foot of a range of hills, with a river flowing placidly by. The North Sea village was constantly tossed to and fro upon 'the grey wilderness of a foaming ocean, swept by winds as pitiless as the hand of death'. The stationary village boasted, for its fifteen hundred inhabitants, two churches, two chapels, four doctors, a new dispensary, a town-hall, a mechanic's institute, and a lending library. The cruising village possessed absolutely none of these various advantages.[1]

Origin and Development of the Copers

The growth of the North Sea fishing industry often brought the fishing smacks of European countries into direct conflict. One writer described the Dogger Bank as having a 'bad name which even that wild waste of waters never deserved. Crews were murdered and smacks sunk, leaving no one to tell the tale of a savage lawlessness which rivalled the winds in dealing death and devastation.'[2] When the sea was calm, the fishermen looked for escape from their mundane existence, the coper, were it around, offered an attractive panacea in the form of distraction, tobacco, liquor and pornographic literature.

During the early nineteenth century (c.1820–c.1854) copers appear to have carried on a respectable trade. The earliest known date at which they bartered tobacco and spirits amongst the North Sea trawling fleets was 1854.[3] Outside the fishing industry, however, no one seems to have taken much interest in their activities. During the next 25 years their numbers increased and they seem to have traded without any significant objection from governments, courts or Christian missions.

The vessels were often known as 'Dutch Copers' (and sometimes as 'Devil's Mission ships', 'floating grog-shops', 'Hells' and 'bumboats'). The term 'Dutch Copers' tended to give the impression that this trading activity was the sole province of men from the Netherlands. But, despite some disagreement among the delegates at The Hague conference in June 1886 (held to discuss ways of getting rid of the copers), it appears that several countries, not least England, were involved in the trade – the Netherlands and Germany openly so because the trade for them was a legal one.[4] Non-Dutch and German copers illegally involved in the trade adopted the simple expedient of flying a Dutch flag.

---

1. Mather, *op. cit.* (1887), p.52.
2. W.M. Colles, 'The Police of the North Sea', *Blackwoods Magazine*, April 1888, p.572.
3. J.A.H. Murray, *A New English Dictionary* (1893), entry on 'Copers', especially the recollection of Mr Wintringham of Grimsby.
4. *British Parliamentary Papers (BPP) vol. XCVIII*, 1888, pp.7, 10; *BPP LXXXII*, 1881, p.19.

Copering activity reached its peak during the late 1870s and early 1880s. Even so, it is unlikely that anyone would have shown much interest were it not for the particular growth and abuse of the trade in liquor. Victorian concern with the abuses of drink, gambling and sex was all associated with the copers, and the wide publicity given to the effects of this trade, not least via the MDSF campaign, caught the public's imagination.

The Nature of the Copers' Trade

While no photographs of copers appear to have survived, there are a few drawings, which were printed in the MDSF's publications. There are also a few good descriptions written during the 1880s that indicate a well-established and sophisticated trading enterprise. Copers were

The coper arriving amongst the fishing fleet.

seldom purpose-built, being more often than not old fishing smacks, which turned to copering as a more lucrative occupation.[1] An account in the Fisheries Exhibition Literature of 1884 described copers as vessels, 'some of [which] are almost as luxuriously fitted up as a gin palace, with mahogany glass-racks, mirrors and couches, almost incredible to those who have not witnessed it'.[2] *The Times* of 17 September 1884 backed up this view: 'A number of finely-built vessels, some of them fitted up in a rather sumptuous manner, have been sailing about the northern coast, all

---

1. J. Dyson, *Business in Great Waters* (Angus & Robertson, 1977), p.21; *BPP LXXXII*, 1881, p.55.
2. *Fisheries Exhibition Literature*, vol. 8 (1884), pp.368-70.

of them well supplied with grog, cigars, and tobacco.' Wilfred Grenfell, in his report of his first trip to sea with the MDSF in 1888, described the coper *Delphin* as

> a small cutter of about twenty tons burden, of double planking vertically placed outside. We must at least credit her skipper with pluck and endurance, as in his tiny vessel he had ridden out all the late bad weather'.[1]

Such descriptions, however, are rare, and most accounts concentrate on the social, economic and moral effects of the trade.

On arrival amongst the fishing fleet the coper would signal its readiness to sell or barter by flying a flag or white rag from her forestay, or by hoisting a basket to the mast-head.[2] This seems to have been an adaption of a method

A fisherman hails the coper, which displays an oilskin frock as a signal that it is open for business.

used before the development of organised fleeting when a skipper would hoist a flag to signal his willingness to load and take fish ashore from other vessels when he was ready to take his own catch to market.[3] The fishing smacks in turn would signal to the coper, and to each other, by hoisting a 'bread-bag or oilskin frock on an oar', – a signal known as a 'creagan' by the fishermen.[4] This term, however, is no longer used or known by fishermen, nor have I been able to trace any older fishermen who remember its use.

---

1. *Toilers of the Deep*, August 1888, vol. 3, p.265.
2. *Good Words*, March 1887.
3. Alward, *op.cit.* (1932), p.30.
4. Mather, *op. cit.* (1887), pp.104, 108.

The word appears to have derived from the Dutch words '*kregen*' and '*krijen*', which mean 'to get', 'receive', 'obtain', 'acquire'.[1] Trade consisted of dice, silk, eau-de-cologne, playing cards, Dutch drops (a popular patent medicine guaranteed to cure all manner of illness), Meerschaum pipes, satins, clogs, concertinas, musical boxes, pornographic books and cards and in some rare instances food.[2] The Government Report of 1881 denied the sale of food although the sale of coffee and tea was not uncommon, and food does appear to have been occasionally sold.[3]

Sails, nets, ropes and knives, which the coper had received in exchange for other items, were also offered for sale at a profit. Lennox Kerr, in his biography of Wilfred Grenfell, suggested that some copers, working off Labrador, also carried prostitutes. Kerr seems to have assumed that, because women were forced into prostitution on the schooners just off the Labrador coast, the North Sea copers must have carried on a similar business. Unfortunately, he does not offer any documentary evidence for this claim, nor have I been able to find any.[4] The kinds and quantities of goods carried by the copers can be seen from inventories drawn up by customs officials when copers were seized. For example, a coper seized off the Kent coast had on board 20,000 cigars, 1,000 pounds of tobacco, 200 gallons of brandy, 100 gallons of gin and 100 gallons of eau-de-cologne.[5] The main business would therefore appear to have been tobacco and liquor.

The initial reason for the fishermen to visit the coper was generally to purchase tobacco.[6] During this period English sailors on long voyages were allowed tobacco out of bond at sea, but fishermen were not (the consequence of an old law dating from the time when fishing was conducted just off the coast). The coper's tobacco was particularly cheap at 1s 6d per pound, compared with 4s 6d on shore.[7] It was sometimes good, sometimes of inferior quality, and the most popular tobacco was known as 'Rising Hope' – a name not without irony given the copers' main business of liquor, aniseed brandy, schnapps, rum, gin and cordials.

1. I am indebted to Charles Lewis, Curator of the Norfolk Museums Service, for this information.
2. Personal letter from Patricia O'Driscoll, 12 January 1988; Chambers' Journal, 4 April 1885, p.233.
3. *BPP LXXXII*, 1881, pp.2, 46 and 54.
4. Kerr, *op. cit.* (1959), pp.41, 54, 104 and 134.
5. *BPP LXXXII*, 1881.
6. *BPP XCVIII*, 1888, p.12 (Report to the Admiralty by Admiral Gordon-Douglas and Mr Malin).
7. Edgar J Marsh, *Sailing Trawlers*, 1953, p.123.

As most fleets had some skippers who had signed the 'temperance pledge' and were a strong influence on their crews, it was not always easy for the captain of the coper to attract custom for his liquor, called 'Chained Lightening' by the fishermen. But most smoked tobacco, and the copers used this as a means of winning trade. The devious captain would offer a free glass of the better quality liquor to those who bought tobacco, only supplying more if payment was forthcoming. Once on the coper few could resist temptation. Barter was an acceptable alternative to cash – knives, blocks, ropes, stores, nets, fish, all found their way onto the coper and into the shops in Dutch and German ports. The hard-bitten fishermen, when they sobered up, were left to return to their own ports minus vital fishing equipment and often blamed their losses on storms or the 'Belgium Devil' (an implement used to cut through fishing nets). Owners could do little but pay out for new equipment.

In 1892 comparative costs of liquor on shore were one bottle of rum (*i.e.* one pint and one quarter) at three shillings, and one quart of gin at four shillings. The copers' liquor, however, was thought to be of an inferior quality. One fisherman said: 'The gin is a vile compound of spirits of wine, vitriol, and sugar. [. . .] I think there is a deal of vitriol in the brandy.'[1] The grog was the vilest possible compound of aniseed and various drugs; its effects were simply maddening, and the loss of life and property directly due to the copers was incalculable. In some cases, fishermen jumped overboard whilst drunk. In one particularly nasty case smacksmen tried to revive their drunken crewmate by pouring turps over him and setting fire to it. Unfortunately, the cure failed and the poor man was burned to death. Other reports talk of the liquor being of good quality. One man, for example, said: 'the gin is very good, but very hot; I got mine out of a long stone bottle, it is quite different to what we get ashore'.[2] The following letter was written to the MDSF on Christmas morning, 1887 by a Hull skipper:

> One case comes fresh to my mind. Five men went to the coper together, three for tobacco and two for a dram, and before they had been long aboard, one of the fishermen was stabbed in three places. In houses ashore where men go for the drink, if they get too much, some policeman will take care of them; but where these horrid copers are trading amongst our fishermen, when a man has tasted their cursed aniseed brandy, he has only to take three strides, and he is in the raging sea, and lost forever.[3]

1. *BPP LXXXII*, 1881, pp.43-4.
2. *Toilers of the Deep*, 1887, p.101; Wood, *op. cit.* (1911), p.206; *BPP LXXXII*, 1881, p.27.
3. *Toilers of the Deep*, vol. 2, 1887, p.68.

Numerous organisations were at work on shore to help people avoid the snare of the gin palace, but little was being done at sea for fishermen who were lured onto the floating grog-shops. The work of the MDSF, however, was gradually making an impact and regular letters and articles by members of this society appeared in national and local newspapers and numerous journals, ensuring that all mention of the copering trade was linked in the same breath to the work of the Mission ships.

Aboard the coper.

Bumboats

Copers were often called 'bumboats', vessels that have a fairly well-documented history as small trading vessels, and that provided supplies for ships in the docks. They were certainly common enough in 1685 for Trinity House to regulate their work on the Thames.[1] They were active at the beginning of the nineteenth century as the following quotation from the Rev. G.C. Smith, c.1817, makes plain: 'I've heard d'ye see, that all the bumboat men and slop sellers [. . .] who come on board at pay-day, are Methodists; because they are such anointed rogues.'[2] Bumboats were such a common sight in ports around the world that by the late nineteenth century W.S. Gilbert was able to create the now well-known figure of 'Little Buttercup', the bumboat woman, in his opera HMS *Pinafore.*

1. P. Kemp, *The Oxford Companion to Ships and the Sea*, 1976.
2. G.C. Smith, *The Boatswain's Mate*, 1817, p.11.

It has naturally been assumed that the more common term 'bumboat' was applied to the less well-known trading vessels, 'copers', simply because bumboats were a well-established phenomenon. Suggestions abound for the derivation of the word – one of the more likely coming from the Fisheries Exhibition Literature of 1884, where A. Beaujon wrote that the word 'bumboat' derived from the Dutch word 'bomschuiten'. These flat-bottomed and square smacks, so designed because they worked from villages with no harbour, thus enabled easy beaching.[1] They were undoubtedly the 'small boats which came off from the shore', referred to by George Alward.[2] Alward also refers to boats 'employed in peddling provisions'. Once the term 'bumboat' was applied to small craft which engaged in trading amongst the fishing smacks just off the Dutch coast during the 1830s to the 1850s, it would be very natural to apply this term also to the later 'copers'.

The Fight against the Copers

The literature of the 1880s gives the impression that large numbers of copers were working amongst the North Sea fleets. This has led some modern writers to assume that a small handful of Mission ships (five in 1885, eight by 1888) could have been of little use in effectively countering the copers' trade. Although the North Sea fishing fleets provided the copers with their most lucrative market, copers also worked in other places, especially around the coasts of England, Ireland, the Scilly Isles and Labrador. In 1886 the delegates at The Hague Conference estimated there to be from 14 to 20 copers carrying on business in the North Sea.[3] It is unlikely, therefore, that there would be more than ten trading at any one time. There were certainly insufficient for each fleet to have its own permanent 'grog-shop'. This figure was suggested by M. Buys, the Netherlands delegate at the earlier International Conference of 14 October 1881, who said in his statement:

> The customs officer cites the names of nine or ten ships making open sale of spirits, of tobacco, *etc.*, in the North Sea. In addition some vessels sailing under the English and Belgium flags and having the same purpose regularly frequent our ports to take on board and renew their cargoes.[4]

1. *Fisheries Exhibition Literature*, 1884, vol. 9, p.441.
2. Alward, *op. cit.* (1932), p.30.
3. *BPP XCVIII*, 1888, pp.7, 12.
4. International Conference Concerning the Policing of the Fishing in the North Sea, held at The Hague, 14 October 1881 (French transcript obtained from the Dutch State Archives at The Hague).

In any case copers seldom remained in one locality for more than a few days, and moved on from fleet to fleet until their stocks were exhausted.[1] There were also numerous fishing smacks which turned to copering for the occasional voyage. It is possible that at least two copers' names are duplicated in the list in Appendix 9, and a number of others were not working at the time of the Conference. Hence, 14 to 20 copers would be a reasonable estimate for that year. Little wonder then that the French delegate, M. Mancel, suggested that the Conference was pointless: 'But taking the higher figure of twenty, in order to avoid any miscalculation, it might be asked if such a number was sufficiently important to warrant measures of repression.'[2] Perhaps not surprisingly, this comment was ignored by his colleagues. With such a relatively small number of copers working in the North Sea, opportunities for trade had to be grasped as and when they could. But this small 'fleet' seems to have had an effect upon the morale of the fishermen out of all proportion to their numbers. Objections to the copers from smack owners and the public authorities which had some association with the fishermen amounted to

- drunkenness at sea – often leading to fights and sometimes death,
- bartering of owners' property (nets, knives, fish) once money had run out,
- smuggling ashore quantities of tobacco, liquor, pornographic literature, eau-de-cologne for sale,
- the immoral nature of the trade – drunkenness, theft, lust, homosexuality *etc.* – and the suffering caused to the fishermen's families on shore.

Responses to the Problem

As owners of a large fleet, the directors of Hewett & Co. were only too aware of the damaging effect of the copering trade, hence Samuel Hewett's request in 1881 that the TCM engage missionaries to visit his Short Blue fleet and the formation of the MDSF. From the public's perspective, the MDSF developed rapidly and by 1884 the Lord Mayor of London, R.N. Fowler, was asking for public support for the TCM's work in the North Sea, arguing that the way to beat the copers was to extend the influence of the Mission ships.[3] This appears to have been one of the earliest mentions, by a member of the TCM/MDSF, of the work of the copers. And perhaps

1. *BPP XCVIII*, 1888, p.12.
2. *Ibid.*, p.7.
3. *Yarmouth Mercury*, 27 September 1884; *The Times*, 28 August 1884.

Mather's first letter on the subject appeared in the *Fish Trades Gazette* on 25 July 1885, although he later claimed to have become aware of the copers' activities during his first visit to the North Sea fleets, and he referred to their work in his short booklet (*Trust Christ More*) in 1884. Despite his assertion that the MDSF was established in part as a direct response to this trade, it is odd that very little is heard in the press or in the TCM's literature about the fight against the copers until 1884. While Mather later claimed to have been made aware of the coopering traffic on his first visit to the North Sea, he does not make any mention of this in his diary notes made on his first visit (Appendix 5).[1]

International attention was drawn to the problem, and the *Yarmouth Mercury* reported, in September 1884, that the Dutch Government had invited European countries with an interest in the North Sea fisheries to attend a Conference at The Hague with the avowed aim of restraining 'the sale of spirituous liquor in the North Sea'. By 11 October the British Foreign Office and the Board of Trade had appointed delegates to attend the International Conference. But the meeting was delayed by Germany which refused to attend until an incident involving one of its copers had been settled – a number of English fishermen were alleged to have boarded the *Diedrich* and stolen tobacco and liquor. Only when these fishermen were taken to court, found guilty of piracy and punished did the Germans agree to attend the Conference. The date of the meeting was set for 8 October 1885 but suffered a series of postponements and did not finally meet until June 1886. The correspondence from this Conference was presented to the British Parliament in March 1888.[2]

During this period the National Sea Fisheries Protection Association also discussed the question of the liquor trade and the forthcoming Conference. The meeting, presided over by Sir Edward Birkbeck MP passed two resolutions: the first urging the British representatives to do all they could to stop the copering trade, and the second:

> That this Association strongly recommends that permission be granted to owners and captains of fishing vessels in the North Sea to have a limited quantity of tobacco out of bond, duty free for the use of their crews while at sea.

Copies of these resolutions were then forwarded to the Foreign Office and the Board of Trade. The latter replied saying: 'the first resolution would be communicated to the British delegates at the Conference, and the second

---

1. TCM Annual Report, 1881.
2. *Yarmouth Gazette*, 15 November 1884.

resolution will be sent to the Commissioners of her Majesty's Customs'.[1] But the Customs office rejected the recommendation on the basis that the law forbade smacks obtaining tobacco out of bond.

On 18 October 1884, an article in the *Yarmouth Mercury* talked of 'floating grog-shops in the North Sea', and asked: 'What is the Remedy?' The writer suggested that a partial remedy would be to raise the duty on German brandy which was intended for consumption in the North Sea.

Tobacco and the MDSF

A newspaper article of Christmas 1884 suggested that Mission ships could supply tobacco to the North Sea fleets. This article appears to have taken up an earlier point made by Mr W. Burdett-Coutts who is reported as saying in November 1884:

> The only effective attempt that has been made to counteract the work of the 'coper' has been carried on through the agency of the mission smacks of the Thames Church Mission. [. . .] Let the mission ship carry tobacco, getting it out of bond if permitted – if not, buying it in a foreign port as the coper does – and sell it at a cost price to the smacksmen. In all probability it would be better in quality and cheaper in price. I should like to go further, and have grog also sold on the mission ship under the careful restrictions as to quantity and frequency of supply.[2]

The latter suggestion is not as strange as it may seem. The Royal Commission on Loss of Life at Sea argued that the provision of a bar at Well Street Sailors' Home in London was a positive help to both the seafarers and the Home, in that it kept the seafarers out of the drinking shops and brought in much needed income to the institution.[3] The dilemma for the TCM/MDSF was whether to provide the very thing they were publicly trying to eradicate. There is, however, a twist to this tale when we later hear that Mather tried to sell ginger beer on board the Mission smacks under the label 'Dogger Ale' – an activity that did not go down well with the Mission Council.

Acting upon Mr Burdett-Coutts' suggestion, Mather appealed to Sir Edward Birkbeck, who in turn agreed to approach the Chancellor of the Exchequer with the request that the Government allow the Mission vessels to carry tobacco out of bond and sell it duty free to the fishermen. By the autumn of 1885 five Mission ships were working in the North Sea, each based with a specific fleet, and such a number could have provided an

---

1. *Chart and Compass*, November 1884, p.329.
2. *Ibid.*, November 1884, p.349.
3. *BPP XLIII*, 1887, questions 15787 & 15788.

effective alternative to the coper's tobacco supply.[1] Sir Edward Birkbeck, acknowledging the potential of Mather's argument, raised the point in Parliament on 30 March 1885, but permission was refused.[2]

By now Mather was convinced that, if his vessels could sell tobacco at a cheaper rate than the copers, many fishermen would be dissuaded from visiting them. The point was constantly made by Mather and also by Admiral Gordon-Douglas and Mr Malin in their reports to the Admiralty and the Board of Trade in November 1884. This report even suggested that 'a great blow could be struck to the trade if fishermen could obtain their tobacco elsewhere at the same price' – a point also raised on behalf of the MDSF in Parliament by Sir Edward Birkbeck. Unfortunately, tobacco was expensive, and the Mission ships could ill afford the outlay, especially as it meant selling it at a loss. There was also some opposition from MDSF Council members, especially Mr Dashwood, to the Mission ships being turned into 'tobacconists' shops'. Some fishermen objected, too, arguing that men boarded the coper for drink and would do so regardless of whether or not tobacco was sold. But Mather disagreed, saying that he was supported by the vast majority of fishermen and smack owners.[3] Admiral Gordon-Douglas and Mr Malin, on behalf of the Admiralty and the Board of Trade, respectively, also implicitly lent credence to Mather's case by stating in their survey of the effects of copering activities that most fishermen boarded these vessels for tobacco.[4] Others also pointed to the value of Mather's scheme:

> We are now convinced that to induce the men to avoid the wretched temptations by which they are now beset will prove a far more effective remedy in the long run that any code of regulations which the International Conference may devise; and in the work they are so manfully undertaking the Mission have our cordial sympathy.[5]

Despite the sympathetic work of Sir Edward Birkbeck MP during 1885, HM Customs, the Board of Trade and the Government, all refused to allow the Mission ships permission to take tobacco to sea out of bond. Mather made a personal approach to the Chairman and Deputy Chairman of the Board of Customs, but achieved little. Determined to overcome the obstacles, he enquired about the condition under which English-manufactured tobacco was exported to the Continent (an idea which he

---

1. Gordon, *op. cit.* (1890), p.75. At least one Mission skipper, Skipper Goodchild, had served on a coper before his conversion (*Toilers of the Deep*, December 1887, p.227).
2. Mather, *op. cit.* (1887), pp.209-10.
3. *Ibid.*, p.208.
4. *Grimsby Times*, 28 June 1884.
5. *The Nautical Magazine*, 1885, vol. 54, p.887.

appears to have taken from Mr W. Burdett-Coutts). Ascertaining that the authorities would not hinder his plans so long as they lay within the law, he was advised to ship a cargo of tobacco to the Continent and arrange for a Mission ship to pick it up in a foreign port.[1]

The German Consul at Ostend agreed to act as Mather's agent by receiving and superintending the consignment of tobacco, and the first three tons were exported on 7 October 1885 on the steamer *Swallow*. Mather travelled to Ostend – only to find that Belgian law prohibited the movement of tobacco onto a fishing smack. Approaching the Consul, Mather informed him that the Mission ships were registered both as fishing vessels and under the Merchant Shipping Act. By agreeing to remove the fishing gear from sight and sail only as a merchant ship, the permit was granted and tobacco stowed on board the *Clulow*. There were no restrictions on trading in the North Sea so long as the vessel was not registered as a fishing vessel.[2]

The *Clulow* set sail for the fishing grounds where she transferred her cargo to the other Mission ships, which then sold tobacco at one shilling and six pence per pound – six pence cheaper than 'Rising Hope'. The tobacco was handed out in half-pound packets, each stating 'For use at sea only' in order not to infringe Custom-house regulations. The fishermen complained, however, that the Mission's 'Cavendish Tobacco' was of an inferior quality to that supplied by the copers, and the supplying company only agreed to provide the MDSF with better quality tobacco at a higher price. This Mather refused.[3]

An encounter with Sir W.H. Wills MP, a partner in the firm W.D. & H.O. Wills, solved the problem. His firm already exported tobacco to the Continent, and he agreed to approach his colleagues on Mather's behalf. Agreement was reached and the company offered to supply tobacco at Ostend, charging only the cost of production. The scheme was a success, the tobacco proved popular with the fishermen – so popular that the suppliers of 'Rising Hope' later approached the MDSF Council offering to supply their tobacco for the Mission ships. The idea was thrown out on the basis that the fishermen preferred that provided by Wills. By January 1888, the MDSF was able to announce that: 'Roughly speaking, we may say that 50,000lbs of tobacco is sold in the year from the Mission smacks.'[4]

We are told that the MDSF's bankers were unhappy with the whole business and insisted that the money obtained from tobacco sales was tainted and should therefore be washed in boiling water before being

1. Mather, *op. cit.* (1887), p.213.
2. *Ibid.*, p.214; BPP XCVIII, 1888, p.12.
3. The coper *Unity* sold 'Cavendish Tobacco' instead of 'Rising Hope', and this may well have added to the vessel's financial problems.
4. *Toilers of the Deep*, January 1888, p.33.

handed over.[1] This tale may seem far-fetched, but an article in *Toilers of the Deep* for 1891(at page 145) offers a likely explanation. It seems that fish was washed before being unloaded to clean off slime. It is only to be expected that money handed over by the fishermen would go through the same process, and bankers might understandably make this request.

On 7 October 1887, Mather received a request from HM Customs that the Mission ships observe the movements of the Dutch coper, *Marie*. He seized the opportunity to raise again the question of tobacco sales, and the Customs official advised him to reapply for permission to take tobacco to sea out of bond. He did so and was granted permission, subject to the consent of the Treasury and the Board of Trade. All these channels were followed up and permission was finally granted in April 1888.[2] With this concession the Mission ship, *Clulow*, was released from its task of ferrying tobacco from Ostend to the other Mission ships, and was fitted out to begin a three-month trial as a 'hospital ship'.

The Demise of the Copers

By the time the International Conference met at The Hague in July 1886, the Mission ships had established their market. Mather, although urging the Conference to abolish the copering trade, claimed that, by the time the delegates met, the Mission had been so successful there remained no traffic to regulate in those fleets that were attended by the Mission vessels.[3] The Conference, nevertheless, felt there was still a problem to be dealt with, and it was agreed that each of the Governments represented should be urged to institute an international law, which banned the coper traffic from the North Sea. The announcement of the Conference's decision was placed in *Toilers of the Deep* for 1886, and pointed out that the delegates had been given a 'detailed statement of the various means adopted by this Mission in fighting the drink traffic; and this was supported by petitions signed by nearly 1,700 representative owners and smacksmen praying for the total abolition of the copers'.[4]

The International Convention was signed at The Hague on 16 November 1887. The Agreement between the six countries represented at the Conference applied to international waters in the North Sea, although each country was expected to apply its own laws to its own territorial waters. The Agreement stated that:

1. Mather, *op. cit.* (1887), p.222.
2. MDSF Council Minutes, 6 April 1888.
3. *Toilers of the Deep*, 1887, p.263; Mather, *op. cit.* (1887), p.224.
4. *Toilers of the Deep*, 1886, p.107.

1. The sale of spirits to fishermen and other persons on board vessels is prohibited;
2. Fishermen are equally forbidden to buy spirits;
3. The exchange or barter for spirits of any article, especially the fish caught, nets, or any part of the gear of 'equipage' of the fishing boat, is also prohibited;
4. Vessels which ply the North Sea for the purposes of selling to fishermen other articles (not spirits) will have to be licensed by the Government of their own country, and to be liable to strict regulations with the object of ensuring their not having spirits on board for sale.[1]

The Governments of the countries represented were asked to bring this arrangement into effect and to punish those who subsequently flouted the law. By 1888 most of the six countries had given parliamentary assent to the recommendations. In Belgium, Brussels followed suit and, on 19 April 1888, *The Times* reported, 'The Chamber of Representatives today agreed to the Convention of 16 November 1887, for preventing the sale of spirituous liquor to fishermen in the North Sea.' France, however, declined to comply and Britain dragged its feet. In the meantime, copers were still to be seen amongst the fleets. One worked amongst the Great Western fleet off Brixham in 1888, although it moved on when the vicar of Brixham arrived in a Church ship, and in the same year a coper was spotted working amongst the herring and mackerel fishermen.[2]

A Bill was eventually brought before the House of Commons in March 1893, by Messrs Mundella and Burt, to put into effect the recommendations of the International Convention of 1886 and the North Sea Act of 1888. This Act had never been brought into force because of the refusal of the French Government to comply with the assent of all the other countries represented at the Convention. The British Bill was an attempt to enforce the Act immediately, leaving France the option of joining later. The Act passed through its third reading in May 1893, and was duly instituted. The terms of the Act referred to non-territorial waters, and set penalties of fines up to £50 or imprisonment for three months for people in British craft selling or bartering liquor to anyone on board a sea-fishing boat. Greater penalties were incumbent upon the person exchanging goods for liquor when such goods were not that person's property. With this Act of Parliament, the final nail was driven into the copers' coffin and, with the

1. *The Nautical Magazine*, 1887, vol. 56, p.1061.
2. 'The North Sea Fishermen', Brussels, *The Times*, 9 April 1888; SAWM Report, 1888, pp.65–6; *Chart and Compass*, vol. X (1888), p.273.

exception of a few pirate floating grog-shops, the trade ceased in the North Sea, although John Dyson says that a coper was seen in the North Sea in 1906.[1] Britain, Germany, Holland, Denmark and Belgium all gave their assent; France abstained.

Retrospect

What exactly were the reasons for the demise of the North Sea copering trade, and what degree of influence did the MDSF have? A number of factors predominate: the decline of the fleeting system after 1880; public outcry during the 1880s; concern by the owners and employees at the worsening situation; national and international legislation; and the work of the MDSF.

Mather suggested that the international cooperation was too late and M. Mancel called it a farce.[2] There would have been no public outcry had the situation not been publicised by the MDSF and local and national newspapers. But, without public and Government support, the MDSF could not have developed its anti-copering work. Certainly, the fishing industry's expansion after 1850, the type of fishing engaged in, the development of the fleeting system and poor working conditions at sea were positive incentives to the copers. But, at the same time, such trade was only really possible because of the poverty of international law relating to the North Sea, and the general lack of concern by owners and Governments for fishermen's welfare.

So, although we may be justified in pointing to a correlation between the rise of the fleeting system and the copers, we cannot draw a similar direct correlation with regard to their *decline*. Other factors played an important role, particularly public demand that something be done to improve conditions at sea, and abolish the trade. Public outcry is always a difficult factor to assess yet, were it not for such interest, there might have been little incentive for Government ministers to take up the case, or for Governments to take action. Nevertheless, given the lack of public awareness before 1884, this fact alone does not account for the enquiries and reports of the early 1880s instituted by the British Government and the report of the Dutch Government presented at the International Conference at The Hague in 1881.[3]

The MDSF, although at the forefront of the battle against the copers, did not come into being as a direct response to the copering trade, but rather as an attempt to improve the spiritual and physical conditions of deep-sea

1. Dyson, *op. cit.* (1977), p.124.
2. *BPP XCVIII*, 1888, p.7.
3. *BPP LXXXII*, 1881, Outrages Committed by Foreign upon English Fishermen in the North Sea; and *XVII*, 1882, Report of a Committee Appointed Under a Minute of the Board of Trade *BPP*.

fishermen. Nor did the initiative for this work come from the TCM, which was by no means eager to get involved in such an undertaking. The response came from Hewett & Co. which, with the support of Mather, encouraged the TCM to respond. Hewett, of course, had good reason to encourage action in that the company was suffering along with other smack owners at the hands of the copers; and religion, if effective, was a cheaper solution to the problem than any radical and expensive change in conditions.

Although the MDSF came into being in 1881, it appears that it was not until 1884 that the society (the TCM) first mentioned copering in the newspapers, via a letter from the Chairman (the Lord Mayor of London) to *The Times*, on 28 August 1884. Mather did mention copering activities in a publication that same year but his first letter on the subject apparently did not appear until a year later.[1] Why, then, was nothing heard of copering activities from the TCM/MDSF until at least three years after the Mission's inception. Such activity was known to the society well before copering activities became its major concern and Mather says in *Nor'ard of the Dogger* that he observed for himself the activities of the coper during his first visit to sea.[2] There was also the very relevant Parliamentary report of 1881, which may well have been on the TCM's bookshelf.

Such a delay may be accounted for without too much difficulty, although it radically changes the commonly perceived history of the (RN)MDSF. The copers presented a specific problem which required dealing with – but it was simply one among many. Judging from later comments by Mather, it would seem that he was astute enough to realise that a fickle public needed a topical cause to support – it was not enough to state that fishermen suffered many hardships.[3] By bringing copering activities to the attention of the public, he could strike the public conscience, gain practical and financial support, and thereby help the Mission ships continue their twofold work of evangelism and physical welfare.

Mather's enthusiasm for innovation was most productive but often brought him into conflict with his Council. This was particularly the case when, following the demise of the copers, he attempted to sell ginger beer under the label 'Dogger Ale'. The MDSF Council put a stop to the practice as soon as they heard of it.[4] In retrospect, the Council's criticism of Mather for this move does seem a little heavy-handed, but the members, no doubt, had an eye to those people who had criticised the Mission in earlier days for

---

1. *Fish Trades Gazette*, 25 July 1885.
2. Mather, *op. cit.* (1887), p.44.
3. MDSF Council Minutes, 8 October 1887.
4. *Ibid.*, 7 June 1887.

'turning the Gospel ships into tobacconists' shops'.[1] Any suspicion that the Mission ships were now retailing liquor would obviously not go down well with either its evangelical supporters or the general public. Nevertheless, it is sobering to remember that Mather appears to have simply adapted this idea from other more radical suggestions and innovations put forward by Mr Burdett-Coutts.[2]

Despite the difficulties Mather faced, the Mission ships provided a viable and publicly acceptable alternative to the copers in meeting the leisure needs of the fishermen, and they appear to have been successful in countering the liquor trade. Even so, international legislation was necessary if a complete abolition of the copers' trade was to be achieved – no one, of course, could have anticipated the very rapidly changing fortunes of the fishing industry. Impetus for the Conference was provided by the MDSF, but the extent of the influence of the latter upon the former is difficult to determine. Although the MDSF only received a brief mention in the Government report of 1888, its publicity campaign no doubt encouraged the British Government earnestly to seek a solution to the copering problem.[3] The Mission ships undoubtedly helped improve conditions at sea for the fishermen; it was not just a case of driving the copers from the fishing grounds but of replacing their negative function with a more positive alternative.

Hewett was aware enough of the problems to attempt to do something about the situation; although it may be argued that the firm's motives were less than altruistic, given that Samuel Hewett merely loaned the funds to Mather (at four per cent interest) to purchase a smack – which his own company then supplied (and this an obsolete vessel).[4] The company, therefore, took no risks, but stood to gain all the benefits from a religious and morally upright workforce. The development of the MDSF was encouraged because this was a good business move – sober men were more hard-working and less likely to sell the firm's equipment to the copers. Nevertheless, Hewett at least recognised the problem and encouraged others to do something about it.

1. *Ibid.*, 2 March 1888.
2. *Chart and Compass*, 1884, p.329.
3. *BPP XCVIII*, 1888, pp.2, 9.
4. Mather, *op. cit.* (1887), p.150.

Chapter 7
Medical Work at Sea

Introduction

Although medical work at sea has a long history, in its early years it was mainly confined to Naval vessels, some of which carried their own doctors. There were also hospital ships which accompanied the fleets, especially in times of war. In October 1821, the *Grampus* was fitted out and opened as a floating hospital at Greenwich, and subsequent vessels (each in turn being named the *Dreadnought*) continued offering medical services to merchant seafarers until 1872. Although some fishermen were given medical aid on board the *Dreadnought*, this service could not possibly meet the medical needs of the vast majority of fishermen on shore, and was largely irrelevant to those at sea.[1]

While little thought appears to have been given to the medical needs of British fishermen, the Dutch had long cared for their fishermen at sea, a hospital ship having worked with the fishing fleet off Shetland as early as the 1830s. The following account of this work was written by Christian Playen in 1839:

> Along with the Dutch Fishing Fleet, fishing off the Shetland Islands, which consisted of heavy round sterned smacks with only one mast, was a vessel called the Hospital Ship, which deserves a more minute description. This ship is appointed to sail about constantly among the Fleet, to render any assistance required. A portion of the hold is fitted up as a hospital, where all the sick from the other vessels are received, and to do the duty of those lying in hospital twelve able seamen are provided. Besides this, this important craft carries

1. *Chart and Compass*, August 1881, pp.229-32; *The Lancet*, 1883; John H. Plumridge: *Hospital Ships and Ambulance Trains* (Seeley, 1975), esp. Ch. 6; A.G. McBride, *The History of the Dreadnought Seamen's Hospital at Greenwich*, 1970; Jane Matthews, *Welcome Aboard*, 1992; Dr J.J. Sutherland, 'The Hospital Ship, 1608–1740', *Mariners' Mirror*, Oct 1936.

also stores of wood, iron, cordage, spars and barrels, and at this last article several coopers work constantly to keep up the stock, lest a sudden great take of fish should occasion embarrassment. There is, moreover, a forge with the necessary workmen on board. I looked with pleasure on this arrangement, and very naturally I am led to draw a comparison between the regulations of other nations for promoting and assisting an important trade and those in force in Faroe.[1]

The British fishermen had no such provision, although the need was great, as Alexander Gordon pointed out in 1890:

Until the humane work now in progress commenced there was nothing beyond the most rudimentary and unskilled treatment for wounds or illnesses to be obtained at sea, which is, it may be added, another way of saying that there was really no suitable treatment whatsoever to be had; and the consequences were simply appalling. For example: a man in cleaning fish sustains a severe gash to his hand from a hidden fish-bone, with the result that poisoning sets in; another slips and falls down the companion, severely bruising his head; a third, in a rough sea, has his leg jammed between the smack's boat and the sides of the steamer; a fourth is suffering from a sharp attack of pleurisy; a fifth is succumbing to acute consumption; but the suffering, the anxiety, and the sorrow must be borne, without comfort and without aid, on the Silver Pits or the dreary Dogger, two hundred miles from England and home.[2]

All the Mission to Deep Sea Fishermen's vessels carried a medicine chest, and the skippers provided some first aid. This work impressed those people who took the trouble to visit the North Sea fleets to witness the Mission's work. One such visitor, the Rev. Dr Stevenson-Moore, commented in 1886:

It could be scarcely affirming too much to say that Christian philanthropy never devised anything more conducive to the relief of human suffering than when it instigated the Mission to furnish their smacks with a medicine-chest, to which fishermen in case of sickness or accident might have recourse free of cost.[3]

---

1. Christian Playen, *Reminiscences of a Voyage to Orkney and Shetland and Scotland in the Summer of 1839*, (translated into English by Catherine Spence, 1896). See *Toilers of the Deep*, Sept 1909.
2. Gordon, *op. cit.* (1890), pp.171-2.
3. *Toilers of the Deep*, Jan 1886, p.9.

In April 1886, Dr A.T. Schofield, of the London Hospital, was appointed Honorary Physician and Surgical Instructor to the Mission, and a regular course of training in first aid and medical care was provided for the skippers and mates of the Mission ships. Following satisfactory completion of the course, they were presented with a certificate of proficiency in the treatment of ordinary surgical and medical cases.[1] The MDSF made full use of the opportunity to publicise its work, and HRH Princess Christian was invited to award the certificates at a special meeting on 6 May, which was attended by several people of note including Frederick Treves, Mrs Oscar Wilde and Edwin Chadwick.[2] The event had its effect and over the next year numerous articles appeared in journals, newspapers and magazines, such as the following in *Good Words* for March 1887:

> Each Mission skipper has received special training, and has at hand a book, issued by the Board of Trade for use of captains at sea, giving clear and explicit directions as to proper remedies and the application of splints, bandages *etc*. Moreover, they hold the certificate of the National Health Society and St John's Ambulance Association.[3]

The training resulted in not only improving conditions for fishermen but gained respect for the Mission's work. Skipper Goodchild of the *Thomas Gray* wrote to the MDSF Council:

> Just a few lines to let you know that the lessons that I had in London at Dr Schofield's have not been in vain, for I had one case come on board with a hand so badly smashed that I could see the patient's bones. I dressed it, not letting him leave without telling him of Jesus Christ, the great physician. The next case happened last Sunday morning: they brought a lad from the smack *Challenger* with his arm broken. By the knowledge derived from Dr Schofield, and by the help of God, I succeeded in putting his arm right, with splints and bandages.[4]

But despite the great benefits, this medical work did not meet the needs of men suffering from more serious illness and injury, and these cases, as Mather pointed out to his Council, had to be sent home to London for hospital treatment, although by the time the patient was in medical hands irreparable damage had often been sustained or the patient had died.[5]

---

1. *Ibid.*, pp.53, 111; 1887, p.134; and 1888, p.96.
2. *Ibid.*, 1886, p.98.
3. Mather, *op. cit.* (1887), p.96.
4. *Toilers of the Deep*, May 1886, p.76..
5. MDSF Council Minutes, 12 November 1886.

The work of the MDSF hospital ships was widely acknowledged as philanthropy at its best. Much of the credit for this innovation belongs with the eminent Victorian surgeon, Frederick Treves, without whom the idea may never have got beyond the drawing board. When Treves joined the MDSF Council, in the autumn of 1886, Mather discussed the idea of a floating hospital with him – and from that point on things moved very quickly. The first doctor began working in the Mission ship *Clulow* in January 1888, and nine months later the first fully equipped hospital ship, *Queen Victoria*, was launched.

Sir Frederick Treves

Frederick Treves (later, Sir Frederick Treves) is perhaps better known today as the doctor who cared for Joseph Merrick ('The Elephant Man') during the 1880s and who, in the twentieth century, performed an operation

on King Edward VII for appendicitis, thereby saving his life and enabling the Coronation to go ahead in June 1902 as planned.[1]

Treves was a surgeon at the London Hospital, where he learned of the MDSF's work from his colleague, Dr A.T. Schofield, who invited him to the meeting in May 1886 at which certificates were presented to the Mission skippers and mates.[2] Treves was already a good sailor and sailed across the Channel to Calais in a small lugger every Boxing Day.[3] He needed little encouragement, therefore, when invited to visit the North Sea fishermen, and responded to the invitation with enthusiasm:

Sir Frederick Treves (1853–1923) at the helm of the Alice Fisher, *January 1892.*

I will take my instrument case, &c., and should like to act as medical officer while I am with the men. I should like also to give some systematic instruction to the men in ambulance work, and in the use of medicines and the treatment of simple diseases. I should be glad, too, if I could add to their amusement in any way.

---

1. For biographical details about Sir Frederick Treves, see Stephen Trombley, *Sir Frederick Treves: the Extra-Ordinary Edwardian* (Routledge, 1989).
2. *Toilers of the Deep*, May 1886, p.98.
3. W. Grenfell, *A Labrador Doctor* (Hodder & Stoughton, 1920), p.61.

I would take out a magic lantern, or apparatus for simple chemical experiments, or give a few short chats about the breeding of fish, &c. I have had a great deal to do with sailors, and should be glad if I could add to the enjoyment of these particular men.[1]

Reflecting upon this visit in November 1886, he said he 'performed one small amputation, and gave letters for the Hospital to three men who were too ill to remain any longer at sea'. He was impressed with the work and expressed great satisfaction with the way the Mission staff at sea carried out their medical duties, and said that: 'At no far distant time I hope that the medical department of the Mission will still be further developed.'[2]

Treves accepted the invitation to join the MDSF Council in September 1886, and subsequently became Chairman of the Hospital Committee.[3] His enthusiasm for sailing eventually led him to seek a qualification in seamanship and in a letter to the Council in February 1892, he said:

In order to put myself in a position to judge the many nautical matters that come before the Hospital Committee, I have passed the Examinations of the Board of Trade in Navigation and Seamanship and have received my certificate of competency as a master mariner.[4]

Hospital Ships

Taking up Treves' suggestion for the further development of the Mission's medical work, Mather, in November 1886, suggested to the MDSF Council that an old hulk owned by the Mission, the *Trusty*, could be anchored off Gravesend and used as a hospital ship for the fishermen – he had already obtained the permission of the Thames Conservators to place a floating hospital for fishermen there. After discussing the project, the Council decided to 'hold it over for fuller discussion at a later meeting'.[5] In the meantime, Mather published an outline of the plan in the December edition of *Toilers of the Deep*:

At present, sorely and even dangerously injured men are continually brought home by these steamers, and not only have to endure the tedious journey up the river to Billingsgate, but the still more painful removal by cab or other conveyance to some London Hospital. Many

1. *Toilers of the Deep*, August 1886.
2. *Ibid.*, November 1886, pp.177-8.
3. *Ibid.*, September 1886, p.142.
4. *Ibid.*, February 1892, p.61.
5. MDSF Council Minutes, 12 November 1886.

hours of acute suffering, and may be, fatal danger, would be saved by their being transferred off Gravesend at once from the steamer to the floating hospital.[1]

The *Fish Trades Gazette* noticed the proposal and carried an article on 5 February 1887, outlining the plan.[2] Given the Council's reticence, members may well have been unsettled at the thought that the plan had perhaps achieved a more fixed prospect in the public's mind than they had intended.

Later, reflecting on events, Mather, in 1888, suggested that the original idea for an extension of the hospital work had been his:

> As long ago as 1881, I formed the opinion, expressed already in print, that a time must eventually come when both the hearts and pockets of Christians ashore would be sufficiently reached to enable the Mission to convert every one of its vessels into a cruising hospital, on board of which a fully qualified medical missionary should receive and succour all who might seek his aid, the patients being retained on board in specially provided cots, where they would receive the full benefit of skilled and tender treatment and careful nursing.[3]

There appear to be no direct references to hospital ships for the MDSF prior to Treves' suggestion in November 1886, although the following statement by Mr Mudd of Grimsby may refer to an incident prior to the above announcement:

> I stood upon Yarmouth sands when I saw Mr Gray going out in one of these vessels. Mr Mather was there at the time, scheming and planning to help on the Mission, and he was then talking about the *Salem* and the *Ensign*, and the others fishing, and how best he would be glad if he could set these vessels apart for merely medical and religious purposes.[4]

The statement in *Toilers of the Deep* for December 1886 may have been the first published suggestion by Mather that the MDSF should branch out in this new direction. Whoever had the original idea for a floating hospital, it was not until Treves joined the Council that the possibility became a real one. Given that Mather made it clear in *Toilers of the Deep* for December 1886 that fuller details of this would be given when the scheme was more matured, it seems appropriate to credit Treves with the innovation. But the idea was not entirely new and it is possible that Mather

1. *Toilers of the Deep*, December 1886, p.192.
2. *Fish Trades Gazette*, 23 October 1886.
3. *Toilers of the Deep*, vol. 3 (April 1888), p.133.
4. *Ibid.*, 1887, p.140.

and Treves had noticed an article in *The Times* in 1883 (and, in Treves' case, also in *The Lancet*), which announced that the Germans were proposing a new experiment in the form of a hospital ship to accompany the Baltic squadron. The vessel was to have 'cots, requisites for the sick and wounded, instruments, and operating tables', and it would be distinguished by being painted white with a red streak.[1]

The MDSF Council suggested caution in this possible new development but, in light of what was published in the December 1886 *Toilers of the Deep*, it would appear that Mather was given permission to explore the idea publicly. The following February a medical sub-committee was established by the Council, consisting of Drs Treves, Schofield, Gilbert-Smith and Mr Mather. The committee was 'appointed to deal with questions relating to the [Mission] work in its medical and surgical aspects.'[2] The Annual General Meeting at Exeter Hall in April 1887 provided an opportunity to advertise the plans via a sympathetic public. Treves informed the audience:

> There is no kind of accommodation even now amongst the fleet for sick men. They have to lie in their own bunks until such a time as they can be carried back by the steam-cutter. If only each Mission smack could provide for North Sea patients, not only would an enormous amount of distress be avoided, but certainly a number of lives would be saved. [. . .] Ladies and gentlemen, this work will never be completed until, as Sir Andrew Clark has said, there is a hospital ship with every fleet.[3]

With such prominent speakers enthusing about the subject, it is not surprising that the hospital scheme achieved wide publicity – even *The Lancet* reported the speech.[4] Mather began to gather support from other influential people and, in *Toilers of the Deep* for 1887, Mr James Runciman, a popular author and journalist, wrote:

> Personally I should like to see a *cruising* hospital ship on the sea before the grip of next winter is on us, for there will assuredly be the usual sad list of accidents. I am aware that the scheme has long been cherished by the Director and the medical members of the Council, but a cruising hospital is but a dream at present, and meanwhile the available mechanism of the Mission can only work according as the public supply fuel.[5]

---

1. *The Lancet*, vol. 2 (21 July 1883), p.118
2. MDSF Council Minutes, 4 February 1887.
3. *Toilers of the Deep*, 1887, p.134.
4. *Ibid.*, 1887, p.156.
5. J. Runciman, *A Dream of the North Sea* (James Nisbet & Co., 1889)(the 'dream'

Having discussed a range of possibilities for the development of the work, the MDSF sub-committee was ready by October 1887 to lay its plans before the Council, and Treves, as Chairman of the Hospital Committee, outlined the recommendations: the Committee envisaged 'a sort of floating Cottage Hospital' in the North Sea,[1] where the men could receive treatment without the need to travel ashore. To develop this work the society's smacks would need to cease trawling, as they did at present, and be adapted for medical work. Treves offered to supply medical officers from the London Hospital each of whom would be at sea for two to three months.[2] This suggestion was later supported by others, including Mr Harrison Mudd, the Hull trawler owner.

Mather followed Treves' statement with the news that HM Customs had given permission (subject to the approval of the Treasury and Board of Trade) for the Mission vessels to take tobacco to sea out of bond. This would free the *Clulow*, which was presently working as a transport ship carrying tobacco from Ostend to the Mission ships among the North Sea fleets, to take on other work – and which could usefully be adapted for this medical work for a trial period of two months. The Council duly gave its support for this trial 'provided it can be done without incurring any further liabilities, or without interfering in any way with the present evangelistic work of the Mission'.[3]

Mather suggested to the Council that it needed a means of going to the public 'with a fresh cry', and events proved the value of this new approach. In the meantime, another Mission ship, the *Sophia Wheatley*, was launched on 12 October 1887. Mather used this opportunity to mention his hope that a Mission ship might be fitted out as a hospital ship. He had already mentioned at the council meeting on 7 October 1887 that he 'had the offer of two months' free service from a surgeon, who would give his skill and services in exchange for board and lodging'.[4]

The public were led to believe that it was only a matter of time before the first hospital ship would be launched, although the MDSF Council had not yet given their formal approval to the plan. Nevertheless, at the meeting of the Council on 16 December, Mather informed members present that the Queen had consented to be Patron of the MDSF was willing to allow her name to be given to the proposed hospital ship, and had donated £50 to the work. This news, coupled with the Agreement of the International

---

being that of a fleet of hospital ships working especially amongst the North Sea fishermen).

1. MDSF Council Minutes, 7 October 1887, p.247.
2. *Toilers of the Deep*, 1886, p.178.
3. MDSF Council Minutes, 7 October 1887, p.48.
4. MDSF Council Meeting, 7 October 1887.

Conference at The Hague, which eventually banned the 'copers' from the high seas, and the publication of Mather's book *Nor'ard of the Dogger*, all gave the MDSF a particularly high status in the public's eyes. But there had been some criticism from the Council: having 'heard it stated that the Mission was engaged in developing the philanthropic at the expense of the spiritual work'. Mather replied that this was a great mistake, but it would have to be made very plain that the proposed hospital scheme would really aid in a material degree, and not hinder the evangelistic work of the Mission. The intention was that it should be virtually a medical Mission.[1]

Mather was treading a very fine line here. On the one hand, he wanted to retain the support of evangelical Christians but, on the other, he wished to gain the support of influential people. In particular, he wished for support from the Royal family – but the Queen was noticeably cool toward extremism. Owen Chadwick stated that:

> She [the Queen] approved neither of evangelicals nor Tractarians. When Davidson became her advisor he was formally instructed that neither of these categories was to be promoted [. . .] the extreme evangelical school do the established church as much harm as the high church.[2]

By building pioneering hospital ships with the direct support of Frederick Treves, and by offering to name one of them the *Albert*, Mather won over the support of Queen Victoria. This statement was a reiteration of the MDSF's standpoint, as an article in *Toilers of the Deep* for February 1886 had stated: 'So the medicine-chest, while ministering relief in pain and suffering, also proves an excellent auxiliary of the direct Mission work.'[3] The Council assented to the proposed scheme, and a Nautical Committee (composed of Messrs Gray, Scott-Moncrieff, Wise and Treves) was established to oversee the construction and the equipping of the Mission's vessels.[4] Treves brought before the Hospital Committee one of his young doctors, Wilfred Grenfell, who was willing to undertake a two months' voyage to the North Sea fleets in January 1888, in order to report on the feasibility of maintaining a hospital ship as distinct from a Mission ship. The Council gave its approval to the scheme and arrangements were made for Grenfell to be accommodated on the *Thomas Gray* (formerly the *Ensign*) with a salary of three guineas per week.[5]

---

1. MDSF Council Minutes, 6 January 1888.
2. O. Chadwick, *The Victorian Church, Vol. II* (A. & C. Black, 1966), p.336.
3. *Toilers of the Deep*, February 1886, p.21.
4. MDSF Council Minutes, 2 February 1888.
5. MDSF Hospital Committee Minutes, 7 January 1888.

In a letter dated 5 March 1888, written from Nice, and published in *Toilers of the Deep* for November 1888, Mather said: 'by the time this letter appears in print a young doctor from the London Hospital will have commenced, on board the *Thomas Gray*, a two months' cruise with the fleets'.[1] In the meantime a letter, signed by Sir Andrew Clark, Thomas B. Miller, Thomas Gray, Frederick Treves and E.J. Mather, was published in many of the London and provincial papers requesting funds for the hospital ships' scheme;[2] and plans were ordered and examined for the proposed vessel, *Queen Victoria*.[3] Public pressure was kept up with details appearing in *Toilers of the Deep* for February 1888 of the numbers of fishermen given treatment at sea: for example, during 1887: '3,902 patients, or more than twenty-five per cent of the total number of North Sea smacksmen'.[4] These figures, however, should be accepted with a good deal of caution. Many patients had treatment more than once and so the actual number of individuals treated probably represented between five and ten per cent of North Sea smacksman – but such figures did not make for good publicity.

Following his return Dr Grenfell gave a detailed report to the Hospital Committee about his experiences and said he was willing to go back to sea for a second voyage on 1 May in the *Clulow*. The Council assented, and encouraged him to write about his experiences for publication in *Toilers of the Deep*. Treves then proceeded to outline his Committee's recommendations as to the future development of the Mission's work, preceding this with support for Mather's earlier comment that the hospital work 'ought to be considered in all points as secondary and subsidiary to the spiritual work of the Mission'.

> For the efficient medical relief of the sick and injured in the North Sea, your Committee is strongly of opinion that each Mission ship should be equipped as a floating Hospital, with not less than *four* beds, and that each should carry a fully qualified Medical Officer. In order to effect this, it is absolutely necessary that trawling by these vessels be abandoned.[5]

Treves also advocated the equipping of a larger ship as a floating hospital to cruise with each of the major fleets – this proposed hospital ship to be called the *Queen Victoria*. He argued that more people could be urged to subscribe to the work – that is, people could be appealed to on philanthropic

---

1. *Toilers of the Deep*, November 1888, pp.92, 253.
2. *Ibid.*, February 1888, p.51.
3. MDSF Hospital Committee Minutes, 29 January 1888, p.5.
4. *Toilers of the Deep*, February 1888, p.51.
5. MDSF Council Minutes, 6 April 1888.

as well as religious grounds.[1] In the meantime, the *Clulow* could be used as a temporary hospital ship. Mather wrote a well-illustrated pamphlet about the envisaged work and distributed this widely in order to raise funds for the scheme.[2] The Hospital Committee also advocated the presence of a doctor at sea during the winter months and, referring to Dr Grenfell's work on board the *Thomas Gray*, Treves said that the Medical Committee undertook to draw up rules clearly defining the role and responsibilities of the medical officer. He urged the immediate modification of all Mission vessels,[3] and the appointment of medical officers to work with each fleet, directly under the control of the Mission skippers. Enthused by Treves' words, the Council agreed that following the successful completion of the experiment on the *Thomas Gray*, a further two-month trial should be undertaken on the *Clulow*. The experiment was successful and two purpose-built hospital ships soon followed: the *Queen Victoria* and the *Albert*.

The Queen Victoria *(1888)*

Dr Grenfell wrote a full report of his experiences at sea and this appeared as a *Toilers of the Deep* article for July 1888.[4] This publicity proved very successful, and other doctors working on the Mission ships were encouraged to follow Grenfell's example. With 18,000 readers in November 1888 (rising to 20,000 by January 1891), there was a good ground-swell of support for the scheme, and a desire to read more about this work. Readers were especially encouraged by a donation of £3,500 given in August 1888, for the construction of a second hospital ship to be called the *Albert*.[5]

The *Queen Victoria* was launched at Great Yarmouth on 29 September 1888,[6] with all due pomp and ceremony. The Queen later visited the ship – although the visit was marked by a certain amount of chaos. Dr Schofield recorded the details in his book, *Behind the Brass Plate*:

Being one of the six founders of the Mission to Deep Sea Fishermen, I took an active part in its proceedings. At that time we had just launched our Hospital Ship for the North Sea, completely fitted out to perform most operations on the deep without bringing the patients back to land. We were very proud of her and the Queen expressed a wish, equivalent to a command, to see her before she was used, and that the vessel should be brought to Cowes for her

---

1. *Ibid.*, 6 January 1888.
2. First published in *Toilers of the Deep*, April 1888, pp.133-46.
3. MDSF Council Minutes, April 1888.
4. *Toilers of the Deep*, 1888, pp.238-43.
5. *Ibid.*, pp.307, 348-51.
6. *Ibid.*, pp.353-7.

inspection. The Secretary gave orders for the boat to be sent from Yarmouth, and asked me to show it to the Queen. I accordingly left Waterloo at five o'clock in the morning, and walked round the shore from Southampton West to the steamer. Just then a cab drove up, with a gentleman on the box in a cap, muffler, frock coat, and slippers, who was said to represent the London Press. From the inside, besides the secretary – an exceedingly dapper young man emerged – the artist of *The Graphic* and *Illustrated London News*.

We all embarked, and drawing near to Cowes saw with our glasses Captain Goldsmid, of the *Alberta*, with a Royal launch awaiting our arrival. My first painful duty was to place our Press representative in the care of Captain Goldsmid, as he was, even at that early hour, somewhat exhilarated. So the captain put him in a boat with orders that he was to be rowed about and not allowed to land until the inspection was over. The three of us were taken over to the Queen's yard at East Cowes, and Captain Goldsmid very naturally asked the secretary whereabouts the Hospital Ship was lying. The secretary, however, did not know. The boat had been ordered to Cowes, and he presumed she was there.

The hospital ship was eventually found but further mishaps followed and then a message came from the Palace that the Queen had postponed her visit until the next day. Unfortunately, even with another day to consolidate arrangements, events remained chaotic:

> To attend my practice perforce I returned to town, and in my place Sir Frederick Treves went down the next day to Portsmouth. Being told there by wire that he must cross by an Admiralty tug to Osborne, he got over to Gosport with some difficulty, and eventually arrived at the Admiralty Yard.
>
> 'What name?' said the Orderly-in-waiting, and his card was sent in to Sir Edmund Commerell, and he was told to enter. With some difficulty Sir Frederick explained he wanted an Admiralty tug to take him to Osborne Bay (where the Hospital Ship now lay). Sir Edmund, much irritated by the events of the day before, became very indignant.
>
> 'We have no tugs for private gentlemen,' he said, 'you should have crossed by the Ryde steamer.'
>
> 'But it's just gone,' said Treves meekly.
>
> 'Well, you've a chance still,' said Sir Edmund. 'The Queen's yacht *Elfin* is at the Victualling Yard, and, will take you straight across if you hurry up.' So Sir Frederick dashed off into the rain and

arrived in a state of exhaustion only to see the *Elfin* just leaving her berth. There being no hope in this quarter, he in despair returned to the Admiralty Yard, and, undeterred by some uncomplimentary remarks from Sir Edmund which he overheard when his name was sent in, once more declared 'he must be transported to Osborne Bay by the Queen's orders'. Unable to swim or fly, he 'looked to Sir Edmund to transport him'. This gentleman at last, though himself transported with rage, telephoned up and down for a torpedo boat. But alas! none had steam up, and his final advice to Sir Frederick was to go to the George Hotel, and get the best breakfast he could, and take the first train back to London; which he did; and no one but the secretary showed the Queen and the Prince of Wales over the Hospital Ship.[1]

Apart from day-to-day medical care of non-serious cases, the *Queen Victoria* provided accommodation for ten patients. The dispensary carried a wide variety of drugs, surgical appliances, an instrument chest and linen.[2] The ship carried a skipper, seven or eight crew members and a doctor, plus visiting missionaries and a regular contingent of reporters and guests.

The Question of Trawling

In November 1888, a Resolution was passed by the Council to the effect that all the Mission vessels would permanently discontinue trawling. The trawling gear was removed and the MDSF fleet became a Medical Mission to the North Sea fishermen.

Opposition to these changes was again voiced in the Council meetings, and Alexander Gordon recorded that there was a general feeling there had been 'an error of judgement' in stopping the Mission ships trawling.[3] There were two important factors here: first, by ceasing to trawl alongside the other smacks, the Mission's vessels and staff lost some of the intimate contact which they had formerly had with the fishermen; and second, the extra income accruing from fishing was lost. This point gained force when the *Cholmondeley* was refitted with trawling gear for a period in January 1890 and after two months brought in a profit of £50 to the Mission's funds. The fishing did not interfere with the medical work carried out on board and the critics felt amply justified in their views.

---

1. Schofield, *op. cit.* (c.1915), pp.146-8.
2. Gordon, *op. cit.* (1890), pp.176-9. The development of the hospital ships inspired one member of the office staff, Mr J. Darke, to design a hospital ambulance for use on the Mission vessels. The Council bought the rights for this from Mr Darke and paid him the sum of £25. MDSF Council Minutes, 7 December 1888.
3. Gordon, *op. cit.* (1890), pp.98-9.

Nevertheless, the change in status to that of a Medical Mission had its compensations. The mortgages on the older vessels had been paid off by early 1888 and the new hospital ships' scheme inspired the public to support the work. By the spring of 1889 the Mission could record that it was completely free of debt.[1] The figures for this period are impressive: nearly £600 spent in medical officers' salaries and purchases of medicine; and 112 fishermen treated as in-patients and 8,145 as out-patients.[2]

Trawling was resumed on all the vessels other than those fitted as hospital ships.[3] And later further problems ensued: some skippers became unhappy because, when they did not fish, crews lost income. Mr Miller, the Chairman, visited Yarmouth to discuss the issue, and wrote a letter to Dr Grenfell, the Superintendent and all Mission skippers, again reinforcing the Mission's raison d'être:

> But the Gospel work must stand first, and wherever trawling interferes with this the gear must remain on board, and a corresponding entry should be made in the log, which will be submitted to you when the vessel returns to port, and payment made for the time lost according to the average voyage.[4]

The issue, however, became ever wider in that, whilst some Mission vessels fished, the hospital ships did not. The question of fairness was raised and Miller suggested that skippers could change vessels each year, thereby giving all a chance to experience the different aspects of the work.[5] Other discussions followed, and the Council took up the suggestion of a previous meeting held at Yarmouth with the skippers that Miller's recommendation be squashed.[6]

Throughout 1889 there is little mention of the hospital ships in the MDSF Minutes, for the Council spent many months tackling the question of Mr Mather's relationship with the Mission, which culminated in his resignation in July 1889. Although the MDSF Council was deeply disturbed over this period, it was fortunate in having several people able to perform Mather's functions in the short term.

The success of the first two hospital ships led to increased support for the MDSF's scheme, and an appeal was launched in 1890 for a new hospital ship, to be called the *Alice Fisher* (launched in 1891) in memory

---

1. *Ibid.*, p.101.
2. MDSF Council Minutes, 17 January 1890.
3. *Ibid.*
4. *Ibid.*, 10 June 1891.
5. Letter in MDSF Council Minutes, 10 June 1891.
6. MDSF Council Minutes, 5 February 1891.

of a lady who had donated one third of the cost of the vessel. Inevitably further debts were incurred but by February 1892 the MDSF Council was again able to say it was free of debt.[1] Other hospital ships followed: the *Alpha* in 1899, the *Queen Alexandra* in 1901, and the *Joseph and Sarah Miles* in 1902.

Wilfred Grenfell

Having performed his duties to the satisfaction of all, Wilfred Grenfell was appointed doctor to the MDSF in 1888 at a salary of £300 per year and in December 1889 he was appointed Superintendent of the Mission with responsibility for much of the deputation work which had previously been done by Mather:

> Dr Grenfell entered the service of the Mission at a very opportune period. Mr Mather having been lost to the work it was necessary that some temporary appointment should be made to bridge over the interim pending the engagement of some permanent officer. This Dr Grenfell had very efficiently done in the matter of addressing Drawing Room and Public Meetings.[2]

On his appointment as Superintendent, Grenfell was based at Great Yarmouth, and along with responsibility for administering the Mission's field-work he had oversight of the work of the 'Ships' Husband', responsibility for the vessels and their equipment, appointment of crews and oversight of the medical work and missionaries. As Superintendent he would be equal in status to the Secretary, each being responsible for their own spheres of work and each answerable to the Council. With so many responsibilities away from Great Yarmouth, it was perhaps inevitable that problems would occur with personnel. Dr Grenfell appears to have been a very able member of staff, if somewhat difficult to control. There were numerous clashes between Grenfell and the Council although these appear to have emanated more from his enthusiasm for the work than from any mischievous intent.[3]

During 1890 the MDSF sent Wilfred Grenfell to visit the Irish fishermen and to establish the Mission in Ireland. This successful work was followed up by several more visits in 1891.[4] There had, however, been some earlier

---

1. *Toilers of the Deep*, January and March 1891; and 1892, p.60.
2. Statement by F. Treves, MDSF Minutes, 6 December 1889.
3. For example, MDSF Council Minutes, 4 July 1890: problems with public speeches about the funding of the new Gorleston Institute; 5 February 1891, and conflict between Grenfell and a local medical practitioner.
4. *Toilers of the Deep*, 1891, pp.86-93, 141-5 *etc.*

mission work in Ireland. The Irish had for many years watched French, Manx and Cornish fishermen benefit from the wealth of fish in the Irish seas. Then about 1880, an Irish priest, Father Davis, intervened:

> Boats had first to be secured, and this meant money. Ireland might be poor, but Father Davis knew that England was rich – he knew she gave with a free hand. [. . .] Baroness Burdett-Coutts came to the rescue, and Baltimore has gone forward with leaps and bounds ever since.[1]

Following the Baroness's intervention, others offered their help to Father Davis and among his ventures a school was established for 120 fisherlads. By the 1890s the West Coast fisheries were thriving – but success brought less welcome guests, for example, the coper which could no longer work the North Sea fishing grounds. Grenfell, nevertheless, found he was made welcome and throughout 1890–91 regularly visited the Irish fishermen in the *Euston* and provided medical aid.

While developments with the hospital ships were going smoothly the MDSF Council once again entered a period of crisis. The Secretary, Alexander Gordon, who had been with the work since its inception, wrote to the Council on 1 March 1892 to admit to embezzling £426 over the years to satisfy his 'taste for fine wines' and offering his resignation.[2] The Council accepted it put the matter in the hands of the Mission's Solicitor. Mr Francis Wood was appointed to the post of Secretary, and it was largely due to him that the Society's personnel problems were quickly overcome. Meanwhile, with Dr Grenfell's many commitments, the MDSF Council thought it wise to appoint a Deputation Secretary to ease the burden and Colonel Wroughton was appointed to the post in May 1891.[3]

During 1891 Francis Hopwood (later, Lord Southborough) visited Canada on behalf of the Board of Trade. He was also a member of the MDSF Council. While visiting Newfoundland and Labrador, Hopwood made extensive notes and later submitted a report to the Council in which he described the condition of the local fisherfolk. The report was timely because a severe gale in 1892 resulted in a large number of Newfoundland cod fishers losing their lives. The Lord Mayor of London launched an appeal and the poor conditions of the Newfoundland and Labrador fisherolk quickly came to the notice of the public.[4] A local clergyman had asked the MDSF to extend its work to the Newfoundland and Labrador coasts as

1. *Ibid.*, pp.88-9.
2. MDSF Council Minutes, 4 March 1892.
3. *Toilers of the Deep*, 1891, p.131.
4. *Ibid.*, 1891, p.233.

Sir Wilfred Grenfell (1865–1940).
The picture was taken in the North Sea
on board the Alice Fisher, *January 1892.*
The setting appears to be the same as that
for Dr Frederick Treves, on page 162.

early as 1886[1] and this link, Francis Hopwood's report and the recent tragedy, all encouraged the MDSF Council to send one of its hospital ships for an exploratory visit. Dr Grenfell volunteered to go and the *Albert* departed on 12 June 1892.[2] On arrival at St John's on 22 July, Grenfell was confronted with a disaster of mammoth proportions: 2,000 of the 11,000 houses had been destroyed by a fire, and numerous people were in urgent need of medical care. It was five weeks before the *Albert* left to visit the Labrador coast.

Grenfell met large numbers of immigrants from Devon and Cornwall who called themselves 'Liveyeres' – because, they said, 'We all live here!'[3] The work, however, proved expensive, and Grenfell argued that a smaller vessel was required. The *Princess May*, a steam launch of 45 feet, was provided and served well, although in due course Grenfell acknowledged the need for a fully equipped, and purpose-built hospital ship.[4] Following a brief period in England, he returned to Labrador where he became so absorbed in the work that the Mission Council had to write in January 1896, requesting his immediate return home.[5] Grenfell launched a fund, and by 1898 the *Strathcona* was built. The steel hull was reinforced for protection against ice and the vessel was fitted out with a hospital ward in a similar manner to the *Queen Victoria*. X-ray equipment, electric lights and all the latest in medical equipment was fitted, and Marconi presented a wireless set.[6] The vessel served well

1. MDSF Minutes, 3 December 1886: The Rev. Henry How of Newfoundland suggested, 'that an arrangement might be made by which his communicants might be registered as Honorary Agents of the Mission'.
2. Log Book of the *Albert* (Norwich County Archives).
3. Kerr, *op. cit.* (1959), p.61.
4. Grenfell, *op. cit.* (1920), Chs 6 and 8.
5. MDSF Council Minutes, 24 January 1896.
6. Plumridge, *op. cit.* (1975), p.77.

until 1924 when it was replaced by the *Strathcona II*. In 1925 Grenfell formed the International Grenfell Association (IGA) under the aegis of the RNMDSF and the IGA became an independent association in 1934.[1]

The period leading up to the separation of the two societies was fraught with difficulties, not least because of Grenfell's growing sympathy with liberal theology and away from the Mission to Deep Sea Fishermen's emphasis on conservative evangelicalism. But, despite occasional problems with Grenfell and other members of staff, the society gave the public the impression of being a well-organised and efficiently run organisation. As a result, the great value of the work was acknowledged by Queen Victoria in 1897 when she bestowed the title Royal on the society.

---

1. Rompkey, *op. cit.* (1991), p.233

Chapter 8
Ebenezer Joseph Mather: Resignation

Introduction
The following statement appeared in *Toilers of the Deep*, October 1889:

The Severance of Mr Mather's Connection
with the
Mission to Deep Sea Fishermen

Statement of the Council

Having regard to the large number of enquiries which have been made as to the reason of the severance of Mr Mather's connection with the 'Mission to Deep Sea Fishermen', the Council think it right to inform the subscribers and friends of what has occurred.

Complaints of a serious nature having been made with regard to Mr Mather's conduct in certain matters connected with the Mission, the Council felt bound to call upon him, as a paid officer of the Society, for explanations.

These explanations being unsatisfactory, the complaints were considered by a Sub-Committee of the Council, and were reduced into certain specific charges, which were forwarded to Mr Mather, with the suggestion that they should be referred to the investigation of an independent Arbitrator. This Mr Mather refused. The Council, therefore instructed the Sub-Committee to investigate and report on the charges.

The Sub-Committee reported that a *prima facia* case was made out on each of the charges.

No satisfactory answer being forthcoming, and the proposal for investigation by an arbitrator having been refused by Mr Mather, the Council, having lost confidence in him, unanimously decided that they had no alternative but to permit him to resign.

The Council cannot forget Mr Mather's past services to the
Mission; but whilst regretting the painful necessity which has led
to his severance from the Society, they confidently assure its many
well-wishers that the work will, under the blessing of God, be
prosecuted with undiminished energy and vigour.

Signed by order of the Council
Alexander Gordon
Secretary
October 15, 1889.

Although there had been rumours, this was the first the public officially
knew of Mather's severance from the MDSF. Further details about the
circumstances of his misdemeanours were made available on request
(Appendix 11). The charges suggest gross abuse of his position and
raise many questions, but the problems did not begin in 1889. Mather's
forced resignation was largely of his own making, although the enemies
he made during his rise to fame contributed to his downfall. One person
in particular, George Lionel Dashwood, played an important role in the
development of events.

George Lionel Dashwood

Dashwood was one of the first businessmen after Hewett to finance the
purchase of the TCM's Mission ships. But in October 1884, following a
disastrous trading year, Mather repaid the various partners their investment
and became the sole managing owner of the four vessels. When the MDSF
later began to prosper, Dashwood's hostility took on a sinister aspect:

> Mr George Lionel Dashwood (now a Junior Partner at Child's
> Bank) was originally a warm supporter of the Mission. Eventually,
> however, he became bitterly hostile to Mr Mather. Nevertheless,
> he was, in February 1887, elected a member of the General
> and Finance Committees of the Mission; but he was soon so
> unanimously regarded by the other members of the Committee
> (which numbered 13) with such disapproval that he was obliged
> to retire from it on 1st April, 1887. His hostility was thenceforth
> directed against the Council of the Mission as well as against Mr
> Mather, and he has in many ways made insinuations and created
> suspicions far and wide greatly to the discredit and detriment of
> the Mission.[1]

---

1. Document in the RNMDSF Archives. The first mention of Dashwood appears in
    the TCM Minutes for Wednesday, 21 February 1883. In *Nor'ard of the Dogger* (1887),
    Mather does not explicitly mention either Dashwood's financial support nor the

On 6 January 1888, a letter from Dashwood appeared in *The Record* complaining about misrepresentation concerning his relationship with the MDSF. His main bone of contention centred on his sponsorship of the Mission ship, *Edward Auriel*, which had originally been purchased by Dashwood but was sold to Mather on 30 December 1884. Although happy to sell the *Salem* and the *Cholmondeley*, Dashwood was not at first very keen to part with the *Edward Auriel*, but Mather insisted: 'My conditions are, first, that the three vessels be sold – I repeat I am fully prepared to buy the three ships, not two, but the contract must be signed today.'[1] Dashwood was adamant that he wished to retain the *Edward Auriel* as it had been named after his cousin and had other sentimental associations:

> My relations gave the harmonium, medicine chest, and other little things to furnish the '*Edward Auriel*' memorial vessel, which, by the way, was christened at Bideford by my eldest daughter, and afterwards was dedicated at a religious service in London by Bishop Tozer on behalf of the Bishop of London, and to make all complete, as I thought, Mr Weston, of Sandgate, gave an enlarged photograph of this aged servant of God (the late Revd Edward Auriel, of St Dunstan's, Fleet-street), which was placed in the cabin.[2]

Mather seems initially to have acknowledged Dashwood's claim upon the vessel, and, on 24 October 1884, replied:

> Since you are anxious to retain the *Edward Auriel*, I will agree to purchase the other two. If you will send me a line saying the price you are prepared to accept for the two vessels, my solicitor shall prepare a form of contract for signature.[3]

But he later changed his mind, saying that the MDSF could not be instituted as an independent society if Dashwood retained the smack, it being necessary that all the vessels be owned by the society, although they would be registered in Mather's name as managing owner. Dashwood eventually acceded to Mather's wish but, on conclusion of the sale, he had misgivings and later said that he and the other former owners had been 'somewhat misled' and had '[given] up a very considerable sum'.[4] The vessel was later renamed the *Clulow* (ostensibly to comply with the condition of a donation of £1,000 from a Mrs Howard of Blackpool)[5] which also irked Dashwood:

Thames Church Mission.
1. Supplement to *The Record*, Friday, 6 January 1888, p.27.
2. *Ibid.*
3. MDSF Council Minutes, 2 March 1888.
4. *The Record*, 6 January 1888.
5. MDSF Council Minutes, 12 November 1888.

I am not surprised at the clergy feeling hurt at a religious Society sweeping away the honoured name of one of their body without the Council having even the common courtesy of writing to one of those who gave liberally towards it, or to me, who was formerly one of their Committee, and who worked for the Society before any member of the Council except Mr Mather himself.[1]

It should also be noted that the changing of the name of a fishing vessel, like sailing on a Friday, was regarded as bad luck by fishermen. The MDSF, however, appeared to enjoy tempting fate; it broke many of the fisherfolk's long-held superstitious beliefs – the *Ensign* had its maiden voyage on a Friday, women were invited to sail on the Mission ships, clergymen were employed on the vessels and so on.

As if to add insult to injury, the *Clulow* was also the first vessel to transport tobacco from Ostend to the fishing fleet – another source of Dashwood's antipathy, he had at one point accused the MDSF of being 'little more than a tobacconist's business'. The Rev. C. Bevan supported Dashwood and in 1887 wrote to the Mission Council arguing that although it had done nothing illegal in giving the *Edward Auriel* a new name, there was, nevertheless, a moral obligation. Dashwood suggested the compromise of renaming the *Salem* the *Edward Auriel*, but the essence of this claim seems to have been lost in the ensuing debate about financial irregularities.[2]

Dashwood's letter to *The Record* received a reply from Thomas Gray the following week, 13 January 1888, commenting merely on the financial issue raised by Dashwood. It seems the vessel cost £2,000, and Dashwood was reimbursed £1,900 – it being purchased 'with her liabilities', which amounted to £685. There was further public correspondence on this matter in which Dashwood argued that the Mission had bought her from Mather with this debt:

> In May, 1884, she went to sea for the first time costing £2,000. In December 1884, I sold her for £1,900, thus leaving £100 in my memorial ship. How could, in seven months, her debts be £685? Mr Mather sailed her 2¼ years before 'we paid' this sum – *i.e.* the Council has not been yet one year in existence.[3]

A letter from the council to Dr Gilbert-Smith on 7 April took up this point, arguing that:

---

1. *The Record*, 6 January 1888.
2. MDSF Council Minutes, 3 February 1888.
3. Letter to Sir Andrew Clark, 29 February 1888 (RNMDSF Archives).

as the first meeting of the Committee of the *MDSF* was held on 24th November, 1884, and that from that date until the Society was licensed by the Board of Trade, the Committee continued to meet from time to time as was deemed to be necessary. The members formerly met as Members of the Committee, but since the Society has been licensed by the Board of Trade, they now meet as Members of Council. There has been no break in the continuity and no change in the name of the Society, and, therefore, no new Society has been formed.[1]

Dashwood received the money from the sale of the *Edward Auriel* in December 1884, the MDSF Council stating in a letter to Dr Gilbert-Smith: 'that is the £1,900 agreed upon was paid on the 31st December (and 5th and 8th January), or six weeks after the first Committee meeting'. Hence, it was argued, Dashwood sold the vessels to Mather not as an individual but as the Agent acting for the Mission – because 'a Society cannot be registered at the Custom House as owners of vessels'. As to Dashwood's claim that he knew nothing of the liabilities until they were mentioned by Mr Gray in his letter to *The Record*, it was pointed out that he signed a 'Contract for Sale' of the *Edward Auriel*, in which there is a provision to the effect that 'the purchaser should take over the liabilities'. As Dashwood was elected a member of the General and Finance Committees on 4 February 1887, this gave him the opportunity of ascertaining all the facts relating to the transaction of the *Edward Auriel* and, after a thorough and searching enquiry 'conducted with the assistance of a firm of Chartered Accountants', he 'signed, with other gentlemen', a report which completely exonerated the management.[2]

With regard to the £685 liabilities of which Dashwood claimed ignorance until 11 January 1888, it appears that the details were discussed at the Finance Committee meeting of 15 February 1887, and the Minutes for that meeting 'contain a distinct remark by Mr Dashwood on this very item'. The MDSF Council also maintained that, when Dashwood sold the vessel in December 1884, he signed a contract with 'the express provision that the purchaser should take over all the liabilities'.[3] As a member of the Finance Committee Dashwood had every opportunity to check this but omitted to do so. He attended six Council meetings, but was eventually asked by the Council members to resign on Friday, 1 April 1887.

---

1. Copy of letter in RNMDSF Archives dated 7 April 1888.
2. Copy of letter to Dr Gilbert Smith, dated 7 April 1888 (RNMDSF Archives).
3. *Ibid.*.

Receiving no satisfaction from his public and private correspondence, Dashwood began spreading malicious rumours about the Mission's finances. Frustrated with their ineffectiveness he wrote, in December 1888, an anonymous letter to Sir Henry Ponsonby, equerry to the Queen, suggesting that the MDSF was misleading the public.

On 22 December 1888, Sir Henry Ponsonby wrote to Mather, saying that he had received an anonymous letter suggesting that the MDSF was a Joint Stock Company in which the members themselves received profits. This was a misunderstanding of the nature of the Memorandum and Articles of Association, of 1886, which allowed the MDSF to be a 'Company Limited by Guarantee'.[1] The Memorandum and Articles of Association limits the liability of the Trustees, and does not allow them to receive profits; nor does it permit the society to use the words 'Limited Company' after its name. The anonymous writer implied that the MDSF was trying to mislead the public. Mather replied to Sir Henry Ponsonby:

> I cannot do better than enclose for your perusal, a copy of the Memorandum and Articles of Association under which this Society received the incorporating license of the Board of Trade. You will notice how exceedingly stringent are the terms by which every member is bound, and you will at once recognise the legal impossibility of our doing what your anonymous informant alleges.[2]

Mather pointed out that the MDSF had for some time been annoyed by malicious rumours but had failed to identify the source. He asked to be allowed an inspection of the anonymous letters as he felt this 'might be the means of bringing the offenders to justice'. Sir Henry forwarded the anonymous letter to Mather and gave permission for the MDSF to take whatever action was necessary. It took Mather very little time to identify Dashwood's handwriting, 'in disguised form'. However, when we compare the anonymous letter with the one in Dashwood's handwriting, there would appear to have been a good deal of bluff on Mather's part. Nevertheless, convinced that Dashwood had written the letter, Mather and the MDSF Council took legal advice. In presenting their 'Case for Counsel's Opinion', they argued that, assuming proof of handwriting, the MDSF should press for libel against Mr Dashwood. Counsel replied:

> I should deem it improbable that Mr Dashwood did write such an anonymous letter to Sir Henry Ponsonby. Surely a partner in Child's Bank would know the difference between a company licensed under Section 23, and an ordinary trading Company Ltd.[3]

1. Copy of letter in RNMDSF Archives.
2. *Ibid.* It appears that this was one of a series of such letters.
3. Copy of letter in RNMDSF Archives.

Nevertheless, he admitted that, if the case could be proven, such an action was indeed libellous, although Dashwood could justifiably claim ignorance of the Companies Act. But, as the partner in a bank, such a claim would obviously have caused him great personal embarrassment. It was recommended that the MDSF obtain a written admission from Dashwood and that 'Criminal proceedings must certainly *not* be taken' – *i.e.* until and unless the evidence was watertight.[1] The MDSF called Dashwood's bluff and, when confronted with the facts and the threat of court proceedings, he signed a statement admitting his wrongdoing. He was now left entirely at the mercy of the MDSF Council, which had no real desire to bring the case before the public. The correspondence regarding the matter ended with one final letter from Dashwood's solicitor requesting that the MDSF should not publish, circulate, or make generally known the details of Dashwood's misdemeanours. In return, Dashwood promised to 'promote actively the interests of the Society and to undo the harm he [had] done'.[2]

Although greatly pained by his experience, Dashwood no doubt felt some satisfaction in hearing of Mather's forced resignation from the MDSF only a few months later. Ironically, Dashwood remained involved in charitable work with seafarers, continuing his membership of the TCM and later with the Missions to Seamen when the two societies amalgamated in 1904.

Mr Mather's Resignation

On 4 January 1889, the MDSF Council concluded its meeting by recording its 'sense of gratitude for the wonderful blessing which had been vouchsafed to the Mission during the past twelve months'.[3] Alexander Gordon said that all the mortgages on the older vessels had been paid off in early 1888, and that the society would be completely free of debt by the spring of 1889.[4] The Council had good cause to rejoice but just when the future looked promising the Mission's Founder and Director was forced to resign.

The events surrounding Mather's resignation are confusing. He appears to have been somewhat 'economical with the truth', and rather careless in his attitude to finance. He was certainly in need of censure, and the charges were perceived to be sufficient justification for his separation from the MDSF, but there remain several unanswered questions and, during the eight months of discussions prior to his resignation, events would take a

1. 'Case for Counsel's Opinion' written by Dr W. Blake Odgers, dated 1 January 1889 (manuscript in the RNMDSF Archives).
2. Letter from Mr Hewlett, Dashwood's solicitor, dated 21 January 1889 (copy in RNMDSF Archives).
3. MDSF Council Minutes, 4 January 1889.
4. Gordon, *op. cit.* (1890), p.101.

number of complex twists and turns. At the Council meeting on 30 January
1889, just prior to the reading of Dashwood's apology, Mather made a
surprise announcement:

> The Director, having made a brief statement as to the general
> Mission work during the previous month, then mentioned that
> in future he proposed to do all he had previously done for the
> Mission, without remuneration. This was no new idea, but had
> been constantly before his mind. Indeed he had never signed
> a receipt for any payment to himself from the Society's funds
> without the feeling of strong dissatisfaction. Hitherto, however,
> he had not been in a position to devote his time to the cause of
> the smacksmen without receiving remuneration from the Mission
> funds. But circumstances had arisen which would enable him to
> do so. He wished the arrangement to take effect from January
> of this year, since which date he had been acting as Honorary
> Director.
>
> On the basis of the amount received in 1889, the saving to
> the funds of the institution would be £1,000 per annum, and
> he would ask the Council to be good enough to pass that yearly
> amount in monthly portions to the 'In Memorium Endowment
> Reserve Fund', which he had inaugurated at the last Annual
> General Meeting, and as to the increase of which he was most
> anxious.[1]

The Council members were stunned. At the following meeting, on
1 March, Mr Gray proposed that legal advice be sought regarding the
Constitution of the Mission before proceeding further.[2] The Secretary was
instructed to forward a copy of the resolution to Mather who was at that
time in France. The news was not well received. The Council replied saying
that members had: 'received his telegram with much regret, and postponed
its consideration until his return with a view to friendly conversation on
the whole subject in order that if possible any difficulty which now exists
might be cleared away'.[3]

On 15 March Mather attended a special meeting of the Council,
which had been called by Gray and Campbell, and he: 'voluntarily and
spontaneously offered to give up his direction of the Mission and confine
his efforts to advocating the claims of the Institution before the public'.
This offer was rejected in a rather hastily drawn up resolution:

---

1. MDSF Council Minutes, 30 January 1889.
2. *Ibid.*, 30 March 1889.
3. *Ibid.*, 1 March 1889.

That this Council having considered Mr Mather's generous offer to give his services gratuitously to the Mission begs to offer him its best thanks, but regret that it is unable to accept it as it is strongly of opinion that the best interests of the Mission require that he should give defined and exclusive service as advocate of its claims and continue to receive his present salary.[1]

Following the meeting, Treves, Wise and Schofield felt that the resolution had been put before the Council without due notice, and wrote to the Secretary calling another special meeting for 22 March. After discussion, a sub-committee was appointed to consider, in consultation with Mather, the administrative and other duties which he would in future perform on behalf of the MDSF. Prolonged discussions ensued over the next three months, but each meeting finished inconclusively. Mr Hopwood appears to have talked the situation over with Mather in an attempt to resolve the difficulties and, on 7 June, a memorandum was put before the Council in which Mather said he was willing 'to defer to the manifest wish of his friends on the Council that he should receive remuneration for his services to the institution'. But he qualified this with a number of requests, notably:

1. That a Resolution be passed by the Council clearly expressing their conviction that the remuneration is justified in consideration of the nature and extent of the services rendered and that he be furnished with a signed copy of such Resolution;
2. That the words 'exclusive service' contained in the Resolution of March 15th do not appear in the Resolution proposed in Section 1 of this memorandum.[2]

Messrs Gilbert-Smith, Robertson, Treves and Schofield proposed that this memorandum act as the basis for discussion and consideration at the next Council meeting. But this was countered by Campbell who said that he intended to move a personal resolution at the next Council meeting. At this point it becomes clear that the discussions of the previous three months had involved a number of factors not so far mentioned in the Council Minutes and which include charges mainly brought before the Council by Campbell:

That this Council having heard with surprise and regret the charges of irregularity and untruthfulness brought against Mr Mather by members of the Council and having investigated the various matters are of opinion that Mr Mather has been guilty of serious irregularity in: (summary of the charges)

---

1. *Ibid.*, 15 March 1889.
2. *Ibid.*, 7 June 1889.

1. Travelling 3rd class whilst claiming 1st class fare in his account to the Mission.
2. Taking £200 from the cash in hand of the secretary in anticipation of a cheque which he expected to receive from the Finance Committee.
3. Untruthfulness in denying to the Council on March 15th that he had any connection with the Pure Water Company, and denied any knowledge of this Company's manufacturing a drink known as 'Dogger Ale' [a ginger beer manufactured by the Pure Water Co.] for sale among the fishermen.
4. Denied any knowledge of 'Dogger Ale' having been ordered to be sold on board the Mission smacks.
5. Making a false statement to Drs Schofield and Gilbert-Smith re. the £200 cheque mentioned above.[1]

These charges had already been put to Mather, and he had replied in a lengthy letter explaining his actions. His letter reveals a poor relationship with Campbell, the origin of which may well have dated from the foundation of the new Council in July 1886. At this time, Campbell, who was then Chairman of the Finance Committee, had donated £2,300 towards the purchase of a new vessel but added the request that the MDSF become known as 'non-sectarian' and avoid proselytising. This marked an important change in the nature of the MDSF, although Campbell emphasised that the main object of the Mission was 'to save souls for Christ'.[2] Whatever the origin of the poor relationship between Mather and Campbell, it had reached a climax by May 1888, when Campbell made charge one against the Founder and Director. Mather says that the issue had been discussed at that time and the situation resolved without recourse to the Council and he was therefore indignant that Campbell should persist with this charge:

> It is painful to me that this matter should, again after the lapse of 13 months, be dragged up, after an assumed burying of the hatchet. It was fully discussed at the time and I naturally said, without an instant's hesitation, that I would of course not again travel in any class but that for which expenses were allowed. At the time I felt very indignant indeed with Mr Campbell for imputing dishonourable motives to me and but for being dissuaded by Messrs Gray and Miller I should have brought the matter up at the next Council meeting.[3]

1. MDSF Council Minutes, 7 June 1889.
2. Gordon, *op. cit.* (1890), p.80.
3. MDSF Council Minutes, 7 June 1889.

Campbell presumably felt that he had no choice but to raise these charges in the light of later irregularities. In response to Mather's letter, the Council requested that he be present at their next meeting – but Mather failed to appear. His letter of 7 June, however, referred to some misunderstandings which had arisen as a consequence of statements being mistranslated from the Secretary's shorthand notes, and the Council responded by calling in an independent shorthand writer to keep a full report of future meetings. By 8 July, Campbell had refined his resolution and suggested an amended version. Following some discussion, and an aborted amendment put by Robertson which said there were insufficient grounds for censure,[1] a vote was taken on Campbell's motion with eight in favour and four against. The Council members, however, were unhappy with the situation, and at the next meeting, on 12 July, Mr Archibald suggested:

> That the charges against Mr Mather, to be defined by a sub-committee of the Council, be referred to an arbitrator, or two arbitrators, and an umpire in the usual way under the Common Law Procedure Act as between the Council and Mr Mather.[2]

The sub-committee consisted of the Chairman of Council (T.B. Miller), the Chairman of the Finance Committee (Thomas Gray) and Mr Archibald. The operation of the resolution of 15 March (regarding Mather's position in the Mission) was duly suspended pending the sub-committee's report.

The Council met again, on 2 August, when the sub-committee presented its report. A letter had been received (dated 11 July – the day before the previous Council meeting) in which Mather offered his resignation for the second time, although he appears to have had no real desire to leave. His letter, however, was superseded by the decisions made at the 12 July Council meeting. On 15 July Gordon replied to Mather's letter by simply forwarding copies of the two resolutions which referred to the setting up of a sub-committee and named the people elected to serve on it. Mather was not impressed with the idea of arbitration:

> Under God I was permitted to initiate a work which has still a great future before it. Shall I now risk the shattering of that whole edifice by consenting to an arrangement which must inevitably drag 'domestic difficulty' before the public, and whatever the result cause infinite damage to the work.[3]

---

1. *Ibid.*, 8 July 1889.
2. *Ibid.*, 12 July 1889.
3. *Ibid.*, 2 August 1889 (letter dated 16 July 1889).

He again pointed to his willingness to resign and pleaded with the
Council to adjourn the whole matter until the autumn when he hoped to
be sufficiently recovered to attend meetings and to discuss all the points
raised. His offer was rejected. On 20 July a further letter to Mather from
Gordon enclosed a copy of the charges which were to be submitted to
arbitration, and Mather was requested to accept this procedure. By the 29
July no sufficient reply had been received and Gordon wrote urging a reply
by the following Friday (2 August), saying that 'the matter is one which the
Council cannot allow to stand over'.[1] On 1 August Mather replied, once
again rejecting arbitration and accepting his defeat:

> I wish it to be clearly understood that my proposal of 13th January
> still remains, and will ever remain open to the acceptance of the
> Mission. In the meantime, I hold myself officially disconnected
> from it, and never one whit the less on that account, or any other
> account, bound heart and soul in earnest prayerful sympathy with
> its work, and long desire to further its cause.[2]

Gordon replied saying that Mather's answers to the charges were
unsatisfactory, and pointed out that the Council members: 'are unable to see
how the proposed arbitration which would have been of a private character
could have become, as you suggest, detrimental to the work of the Mission'.[3]
Mather was taken aback: 'neither of your two former communications gave
the most distinct hint that the suggested arbitration was intended to be of a
private character. It was merely described as being under the Common Law
Procedure'. The sub-committee reported to the 9 August Council meeting
that a *prima facie* case had been made out on each of the charges, and Mather
acknowledged that his link with the Mission was severed:

> For my own part, I hope, if it please God to restore my health, to
> take up other labour for the benefit of fisherfolk, and that will be
> the reason I shall always furnish those who ask an explanation of
> my being no longer actively engaged in the work with which my
> name has hitherto been associated.[4]

Mather's resignation was accepted. Gordon informed him of the
Council's decision and pointed out that there were several sums of money
charged in his expense book, which, in spite of several requests, had not
been properly accounted for. There also appeared to be some excessive

---

1. *Ibid.* (letter dated 29 July 1889).
2. *Ibid.* (letter dated 1 August 1889).
3. *Ibid.* (letter dated 3 August 1889).
4. *Ibid.*, 9 August 1889.

expenditure in charges for advertisements. Details of a cheque to Nisbet & Co., but forged and banked by Mather, also came to light in November. By October supporters of the Mission were enquiring as to Mather's position and a sub-committee was appointed to draft, with advice from the society's solicitors, a statement suitable for publication; this was ready by 15 October and published in the November issue of *Toilers of the Deep*. This must have been a stunning blow to Mather who apparently never expected a public proclamation of his faults – his own wish to have people think he had retired because of ill-health was rejected. Not surprisingly, perhaps, he left England for a trip to Australia two months later.

Financial Irregularities

The charges in the statement issued by the Mission's solicitors appear quite damning, and they were unlikely to have been questioned too closely by those members of the public who received a copy (Appendix 11). The charges baldly stated are misleading: charge six (four above), for example, gives the impression that Mather was selling strong liquor rather than ginger beer; and charge five (two above) suggests that he stole £200 from the Mission's funds. He was undoubtedly guilty of evasion and untruthfulness, but the impression given in the charges is much more serious. Indeed, Mather's solicitors (Lawrence, Walden and Webster) wrote to the MDSF Council protesting against this impression:

> Mr Wood had hoped for and would still suggest, the possibility of the Council refraining from objection to some short published statement by Mr Mather to negative the impression (widely derived from what has already been published) that Mr Mather's errors (of which we would be the last to speak lightly) are of a more serious nature than they really are.[1]

Was Mather guilty of fraud or theft? The charge of fraud was certainly true, as the case of Nisbet's cheque shows (see below – although this came to light after the formal charges had been written out), but the charge of theft is disputable.[2] There is also the further question as to whether Mather did wrong intentionally? With responsibility for developing a complex and expensive organisation such as the MDSF, with a large number of employees, he must have been under considerable pressure, a situation not helped by the ongoing troubles of the MDSF throughout the 1880s. The stress resulted in ill-kept personal expense accounts, oversights, recklessness and occasional outbursts of anger.

---

1. MDSF Council Minutes, 6 December 1889.
2. *Ibid.*, 8 November 1889.

The forgery of Nisbet's cheque is significant in that it throws some light on the other charges. The details of this incident are outlined by the author ('Sleuth') of a series of articles in the monthly journal *Truth*, relating to Mather's separation from the Mission. It seems Mather was experiencing some financial difficulty in October 1888. He consulted Nisbet & Co about his account, but found there was nothing outstanding (*i.e.* royalties on book sales). A few days later, on 27 October, he countersigned a cheque made out in Nisbet's name for the amount of £418 and paid it into his own account. When the Mission Secretary pointed out the impropriety of this transaction, Mather wrote another cheque to Nisbet on 31 October – but asked his bank to hold it over for several days before payment. The cheque did not clear his bank until 7 November. Why did he perform this action when, as 'Sleuth' pointed out, 'Mather knew that what he had done must come to light sooner or later.'[1] 'Sleuth' argued that Mather's object was to obtain one week's credit for this amount, that he was 'in desperate straits'[2] and needed to raise money quickly. When Nisbet's cheque passed through his hands in late October, he saw a means of obtaining the necessary funds. This event is linked directly to the charge in the MDSF statement of: 'Taking £200 from cash in the hands of the Secretary in November 1888, irregularly and without authority.'

At the Council meeting on 2 November 1888, Mather asked Treves to propose a resolution requesting payment of £200 for business unconnected with the Mission, which he had had to give up. Following the meeting Mather requested that the Secretary let him see the resolution in the Minutes and said that the record was incorrect – the Council having granted him the money. Mather suggested referring the matter to the proposer of the motion (Frederick Treves) and subsequently produced a note from Treves purporting to sustain his view.[3] The Secretary duly amended the Minutes and paid Mather the cheque – which was then used to repay the amount 'borrowed' from Nisbet & Co.

At the next Council meeting, on 7 December, the Minutes were read and confirmed without any change to the resolution which Mather is purported to have altered. This raises the question as to why, if the recorded Minute was incorrect, it was not challenged? Yet the Council later accused Mather of 'taking £200 from cash in the hands of the Secretary, in November 1888, irregularly and without authority'. The question of what Mather wanted

---

1. *Truth*, 23 January 1890, p.160. Articles appeared in *Truth* on the following dates: 14, 21 and 28 November 1889; 9, 23 and 30 January 1890; and 13, 20 and 27 February 1890. A letter also appeared in *Vanity Fair* on 15 February 1890.
2. *Truth*, 23 January 1890.
3. *Ibid.*

the money for may well be important – although this is never stated. It is quite astonishing that, whilst in November 1888, he was in financial difficulty, yet in January 1889, he was offering his services to the Mission free. There appear to be two possibilities. He may have required the money to purchase the consignment of 'Dogger Ale' from the Pure Water Co. – which also ensured the company's offer to him of a directorship. Given that he later claimed it was never his intention to take any profits from the sale of 'Dogger Ale', he may have expected to receive sufficient return on his shares in the company, plus a director's salary, to compensate for his salary with the MDSF. The other possibility is some financial commitment to the building of a 'Fishermen's Institute' at Great Yarmouth with which he was involved.

The Council's request that Mather give 'exclusive service' to the Mission indicates a concern that his loyalties could well have been divided should he be involved in a variety of enterprises. There was no doubt also the worry that, should he attain the position of a Council member on a par with the other members, he would have too much control over the direction and development of the MDSF – a point which had concerned Council members at an earlier date.[1]

The sale of 'Dogger Ale' appears to have been a determining factor in that Mather did not tell the Council of his request that the Mission skippers 'push the sale of this article'.[2] Without these sales, Mather had no directorship with the Pure Water Co. and presumably no other immediate source of income. Why, then, did he not resist resigning his post with the Mission? It appears he had begun developing a 'Fishermen's Institute' in Great Yarmouth and he sailed to Australia in January 1890, initially with the aim of collecting funds for his Institute.[3] So in the autumn of 1890 there still appeared to be some options open to him. Unfortunately, two factors militated against him: first, the MDSF had published details about his separation from the Mission; and second, 'Sleuth' published several articles in *Truth* during early 1890 warning the British and Australian public against Mather's schemes and this effectively put an end to his charitable endeavours.

Mather's Critics and Friends

When the MDSF Council called Mather to account because of financial irregularities, these did not initially include the forged Nisbet's cheque (which came to light only after he had resigned); but the Council's action explained several of the charges. This sequence of events is important

---

1. MDSF Council Minutes, 15 March 1889.
2. *Ibid.*, 7 June 1889.
3. *Truth*, 23 January 1890; and 27 February 1890.

because, although each charge initially made against Mather can be reasoned away as of little importance, with the benefit of hindsight we can see that his actions taken altogether had worried Council members for some time. Dashwood had obviously been right in his criticism of Mather, although he spoilt his chances of success by being unscrupulous. Had Mather not resigned, it is quite likely that the Council would have insisted on his resignation as more details of his activities came to light. And Mather had made far too many enemies by this time for him to have much chance of being let off lightly. Indeed, Mr Miller, the MDSF Council Chairman in 1886, had referred to Mather as a 'one-man band': 'if Mather were to dispense with the committee tomorrow it is not clear what redress could be obtained except perhaps to apply to the High Court of Justice. [. . .] The Society is at present Mr Mather and no one else.'[1]

Among the major critics of Mather were the Thames Church Mission Committee, Sir Edward Birkbeck, the British and Foreign Sailor's Society and the Family Welfare Association. The Minutes of the TCM Committee meetings have occasional references to animosity against Mather by other members of staff. The Rev. J.F. Guthrie, for example, 'made several shameful charges against him'.[2] There were also numerous problems that came to light following Mather's separation from the TCM when the MDSF became autonomous. Some of the people who moved from the TCM to the MDSF with Mather, such as Alexander Gordon, also found him difficult and autocratic, and the MDSF Council Minutes record there being some difficulty between the two. The details regarding Sir Edward Birkbeck's concerns were never fully spelled out, though they appear to centre around the MDSF's finances. The MDSF Council had numerous meetings with Mather and appear to have placated him to some extent.[3]

In the BFSS magazine *Chart and Compass* for 1884, there is an article entitled the 'Bethel Flag'. In this article the author comments:

> We rejoice in any work done by kindred societies, and observe with pleasure that one is said to have three smacks fishing six days a week, and on board of which services are held on Sunday. [. . .] It is perhaps untrue to say that they have three vessels, because they are owned by gentlemen who make as much money out of them as other smack owners.[4]

---

1. MDSF Minutes, 1886.
2. TCM Minutes, 20 April 1883.
3. MDSF Council Minutes, 7 January 1887.
4. *Chart and Compass*, 1884, p.104.

Alexander Gordon also suggests, in his book *What Cheer, O?*, that Mather was profiting from the Mission ships. This is borne out by a letter from Dashwood to Mather in 1882 suggesting that each of the financial backers plus Mather should receive one fifth of the profits from fishing. If, therefore, Mather was guilty of profiting from this enterprise, so also were other members of the MDSF Council – although, following the incorporation of the MDSF as a 'Company Limited by Guarantee', all future profits from the vessels were expected to be put into the Mission's work.

In December 1889 *Chart and Compass* reviewed Mather's book *Nor'ard of the Dogger*. The BFSS critic remarked on the oddness of Mather's sudden departure, and criticised the Mission for spending over £12,000 on advertising and administration – compared with £6,698.0s.2d on maintenance of nine Mission vessels.[1] This question of finance was taken up by the investigator for the Family Welfare Association, which compiled several reports on the MDSF during the late 1880s. The reports for 1889 indicate great dissatisfaction with the state of the accounts for the two years April 1887 to April 1889. There was particular concern that the 'Summary of Receipts and Expenditure' showed a difference of nearly £9,000. This deficit was made up of a range of omissions and inaccuracies. There were also other worrying omissions, for example, no published account of receipts for the annual Public Meetings – yet it was to be expected that gate money would have brought in a considerable sum (in 1887 tickets were issued at 10s 6d each). In an FWA letter dated 18 July 1898, and signed 'E.C.', there is again criticism of Mather:

> He [Mather] stole and forged and played all kinds of hanky panky with the Mission vessels, and other property. One or two of his successors failed in honesty. The present Secretary (Mr Wood) has made a distinctly favourable impression upon me. [. . .]
>
> There is no doubt that the vessels are now properly registered, and I notice a very large decrease in expenditure on advertising, apart from TOD.[2]

Another FWA letter, dated 4 July 1898 (unsigned), states that: 'Mr Wood mentioned another example of Mather's sharp practice in selling the same picture blocks twice over.' Other charges remain vague, such as charge number nine on the statement of charges by the MDSF (Appendix 11), in which Mather is accused of 'untruthfulness in his statements to Mr

---

1. *Ibid.*, December 1889, pp.368-71.
2. Letter in the Family Welfare Association Archive file: MDSF, dated 18 July 1898 (now in the GLC Archives).

Scott-Moncrief relative to the British and Foreign Bible Society'. No other reference is made to this item, and the Minutes and other correspondence of the BFBS do not throw any light on the charge.

Despite his numerous enemies, Mather did retain the respect of a number of close friends, not least R.M. Ballantyne, Alfred Schofield and James Runciman – although Runciman eventually saw Mather as a rogue. R.M. Ballantyne's correspondence for 1889–90 reveals some interesting details.[1] In November 1889, Ballantyne received a letter from Mr Frank Wilson, who appears to have been a close friend of Mather (and was also married to a daughter of the explorer and missionary Dr David Livingstone). Wilson was concerned to engage the support of other friends in order to publish a statement urging leniency by the MDSF Council. Ballantyne replied saying he was not willing to put his signature to any such letter as was being proposed, and he continued: 'In a conversation with Mr Mather – when I was in partial ignorance of his private means – I advised him to go to the colonies, but there is no absolute necessity for his taking this course.'[2] Ballantyne displayed a good deal more rationality than James Runciman – but this, no doubt, was due to his unwillingness to allow himself to become so emotionally involved in the affair (or perhaps because he was unwilling to put himself in direct opposition to other members of the MDSF Council). Ballantyne seemed to retain some respect for Mather, as he called him, 'Our friend', and said, 'work should not be too difficult to find for a man of his talents'. This implicit support is made explicit by Ballantyne's wife, who wrote a comment on the back of his personal copy of the Council's Statement of Charges against Mather: 'RMB always defended him [Mather] from intention to do wrong.' In a letter to his wife, dated 20 September 1889, Ballantyne said:

> The letter in *The Christian* from Mather is amazing to me. How can he go on in the circumstances is past my comprehension. It seems to me incompatible with guilt! If he succeeds he will be more the fishermen's friend than ever and may sail in their smacks as such – yet, dismissed from the Mission as a liar!!! The position is outrageously absurd.[3]

The letter in *The Christian* (6 September 1889) was entitled 'Deep Sea Fishermen Mather Fund'. This fund, originally the Royal Fund for the Relief of Orphans of Sea Fishermen, had been established at the suggestion

---

1. The Ballantyne correspondence is in the possession of his grand-daughter, Mrs Karasek.
2. Letter from R.M. Ballantyne to Mr Frank Wilson, dated 9 November 1889 (in possession of Mrs Karasek).
3. Ballantyne correspondence.

of the Prince of Wales by investing the £18,000 surplus of the International Fisheries Exhibition of 1883. Mather had offered to raise £50,000 of behalf of the fund and this effort was called the Mather Fund.[1] When the details of Mather's dismissal were published in *Toilers of the Deep* in November 1889, he wrote to the Fund asking that his name be withdrawn.

Dr Alfred Schofield had been at school in Wales with Mather[2] and knew him better than other Council members. He accepted Mather's guilt – and indeed voted to censure him – yet he remained on friendly terms, and Mather spoke of him with respect in his later biography, *Memories of Christian Service*.[3] Sadly, there appear to be no other extant personal documents by Schofield which might have given us some insight into his personal feelings about Mather.

A third friend, Mr James Runciman, provides us with a great deal more insight. He was a popular author and journalist during the 1880s and, although not a Christian, admired the work of the MDSF in general, and Mather in particular. Following a visit to the North Sea fleets he wrote several articles on the work and a book entitled *A Dream of the North Sea* – in which the 'Dream' was of a fleet of hospital ships. During 1889 he contracted tuberculosis and gradually deteriorated. Mather's resignation came as a blow to him and this exacerbated his already poor health. As a result of this condition, Runciman did not always act rationally and he wrote letters to the MDSF Council and various journals and newspapers defending Mather to the hilt. He seemed unwilling to acknowledge Mather's guilt, other than as a minor aberration, and protested in a letter to *Vanity Fair* at the injustice of the treatment Mather was receiving:

If TRUTH would be content with attacking me, all right, I am a trained slogger, and I am quite ready to counter pretty hard when my chance comes. I should not care if TRUTH came out with an acre of abuse – or even truth, if that were possible – regarding me, for I should only grin; but, in the name of manhood, let them leave a broken, helpless wretch like Mather alone. A fighter would be hissed if he went on punishing his man after he got him beaten; but TRUTH keeps on at an unhappy fellow who cannot reply; a poor woman and a batch of harmless girls suffer worse than death.

Mather committed a forgery, and repaid the money in a week. There is the plain fact, and when you have stated that and driven your man out of life, why go on girding at him? I never thought

---

1. *The Christian*, 6 October 1889.
2. Schofield, *op. cit.* (c.1915), pp.39ff.
3. Mather, *op. cit.* (c.1922).

that Mather would be fool enough to commit himself, for he was
a hero of mine, and I suffered hard as any man could when I knew
of his folly. But ruin is ruin, is it not? Can a man drink deeper
of bitterness than that? Let the poor soul go, and, in Heaven's
name, give us some sort of manliness. When I have shown all his
old friends that he was not a rogue; when I have proved that his
fault was a solitary fault, then he drops out of life for me, and I
shall think of him as a noble man, who broke his life, and sent his
children to the workhouse by playing the fool.[1]

Runciman knew that other charges had been levelled at Mather, although
he does not at this point appear to have seen them, and wrote to *Truth*
saying that: 'Charges have been hinted at, and these *charges* are not worth
considering.' 'Sleuth' disagreed:

There are other charges. They *have been* specified, and, in spite of
Mr Runciman's opinion to the contrary, I *do* think them 'worth
considering'. They are charges which impeach the bona fides of Mr
Mather's philanthropy, and suggest a strong suspicion that his zeal
was not unmixed with a practical solicitude for Mather.[2]

Despite Runciman's protests, by late February he was beginning to have
doubts – not least because by that time Mather had sailed for Australia.[3] In
a letter published in *Truth* on 27 February 1890, he asked for evidence of
Mather's having begun work on an Institute at Great Yarmouth. 'Sleuth' refused
to divulge details given to him in confidence but suggested Runciman contact
Yarmouth solicitors and architects. Runciman wrote to Alexander Gordon,
the MDSF Secretary, in March 1890, asking for evidence and Gordon replied
saying that, when Runciman saw the documents in the solicitor's hands
relating to Mather, he would no longer respect him.[4] Little more is heard from
Runciman until August when he wrote to Gordon saying that he was now
in possession of all the facts: 'Mr Frank Wilson was unable to give me any
information regarding Mr Mather, but I have now learned everything. I only
learned all the sordid and hideous truth today, and it has all but killed me.'[5]

Exactly what Runciman learned is never divulged. The phrase 'sordid
and hideous' implies something more damning than has so far been
discussed – but none of the extant documents add anything to what is

1. *Vanity Fair*, 15 February 1890, p.142.
2. *Truth*, 20 February 1890, p.370.
3. Mather sailed on the *Port Denison* for Sydney, then on to Adelaide where he spent a
   few months before returning home to England.
4. Letter in RNMDSF Archives.
5. *Ibid.*

already known. Nevertheless, given Runciman's poor state of health, and his over-reactions in his letters, it is possible that his use of language here is simply a reaction to confirmation that he had been duped by Mather. His letter to Gordon supports this view. If this is the case, Runciman had simply learned that Mather was in fact planning an Institute for fishermen at Yarmouth and had sailed to Australia to collect funds for the project. Mather had led Runciman to believe that he was incapable of any such work. On seeing the full list of charges against Mather he presumably drew the conclusion that 'Dogger Ale' was liquor – hence the strong language in his letter to Gordon. Nevertheless, this still leaves the question open as to why it took Runciman so long to obtain all the evidence – and a nagging doubt remains that all has not been revealed. Sadly, Runciman's ominous note, that the truth had all but killed him, was followed by his death from tuberculosis a few months later.[1]

Assessment

What can we make of this saga? 'Sleuth's' point, that the charges against Mather impeach his *bona fides* and suggest a suspicion of selfishness and greed, has a ring of truth about it: many pioneers are egocentric and extremely difficult to work with. When responsible for such a large organisation as the MDSF, with all the attendant difficulties, it was too easy to be careless about day-to-day items such as keeping personal accounts and recording events. Add to this the enormous stress that Mather suffered, and some of his omissions and activities become understandable. That stress did take its toll is evidenced in his constant attacks of illness – mainly rheumatism – suffered during the months of investigation by the MDSF Council, as well as the failure of his marriage. But, as 'Sleuth' indicates, the recorded evidence was surely only the tip of the iceberg. That the details regarding Nisbet's cheque only came to light after Mather's resignation, strongly supports this suspicion. The Council members were therefore vindicated in their concern to reach the truth – although some members, such as Campbell, were pleased to be rid of a man they had ceased to respect and whom they now saw as a hindrance to the work. In light of the evidence, the Council's position is understandable but it is impossible not to feel some sympathy for Mather. He had borne the brunt of the difficulties and had established a magnificent work against incredible odds. Yet, just when the many difficulties had been overcome, and the work of the Mission looked set to make great leaps forward, he was forced to resign and was subsequently prevented from engaging in any other charitable work.

---

1. Obituaries in *The Illustrated London News*, 18 July 1891, p.71; *The Schoolmaster*, 11 January 1891, pp.44-5.

It is difficult, nevertheless, to avoid the conclusion that in the end he was the victim of his own insatiable scheming and that the complex financial web, which he created, eventually snared him. Whether he should be judged guilty of deceit and dishonesty depends very much on one's perspective. Other members of the TCM and MDSF Committees saw nothing wrong in benefiting financially from profits made by the Mission smacks; and many supporters of the Mission lent money on the basis of repayment with a profit. Mather's fault, therefore, may lie in his vulnerability as a figurehead. This, of course, is not an unusual situation – most prominent public figures are expected to be morally superior to other people, and the rise or fall of any one depends upon the effectiveness of his publicity machine and the support of colleagues. When either of these factors deteriorates, the fall from grace is often only a matter of time.

Ironically, Mather outlived most of his contemporaries, dying on Canvey Island, Essex, almost fifty years after his separation from the MDSF. Like the Rev. George Charles Smith before him, he died in poverty, having received little personal benefit from the long years of struggle – although a Civil List pension of £50 a year was awarded to him in 1918.[1] In 1924 following his wife's death, he married his nurse (thirty years his junior), with whom he spent a few happy years before his death in 1927. Following his death, a room was named after him at the RNMDSF headquarters and a photograph of Mather in old age, donated by his relatives, hangs there. This photograph has been endlessly copied for the society's publicity – which is strange, given that a picture of Mather at the time he established the MDSF was published in *The Christian* and *Toilers of the Deep*.

There are, perhaps, other ironies. If Mather had succeeded in his schemes, many of which appear to have depended upon his being given a directorship and holding shares in the Pure Water Co., he may in due course have faced great financial difficulty because the company went into liquidation in the early 1890s.[2]

---

1. *Fish Trades Gazette*, 6 July 1918.
2. 'The Pure Water Co', The National Archives, Kew, DCs Ref. no. BT31, 4220/27314.

Chapter 9
The Roman Catholic Concern
for Seafarers and Fishermen

General Overview

Peter Anson has noted that: 'When the non-sectarian Port of London Society for Promoting Religion among British and Foreign Seamen was founded at London in 1818, it had no competitors anywhere in the worldwide Roman Catholic Church.' There were nevertheless a number of small initiatives taken by individual Roman Catholic clergy:

> In 1759 a little chapel was opened at Gosport on the west side of Portsmouth harbour, replaced by a larger building in 1781. Dr Talbot, Vicar Apostolic of the London District, wrote in 1790 that it had been most useful to sailors, especially during the war. In 1793 the Abbé de la Rue, an émigré French priest, built a very humble chapel at Portsmouth, which he served until his death in 1827. At Chatham the Abbé Salmon opened a chapel in 1793, and the Abbé Guibert acted as unofficial chaplain to sailors at Plymouth after 1806. From 1795 to 1822 French seamen in particular were cared for by the Abbé Duboisson at Weymouth. Another French priest – the Abbé Bellisant – ministered to mariners at Margate from 1804 to 1808.[1]

These chapels presumably attracted fishermen, especially in ports such as Plymouth and Margate, although Anson says little about this.

When the 81-year-old Ultramontane Cardinal Manning acted as peacemaker during the London Dock Strike in August 1889, his action had far-reaching consequences.[2] *Punch* depicted the Cardinal standing over two bowed dock employees and, although many Protestants felt antagonistic towards the Catholic presence in England, the cartoon symbolised a growing

---

1. Anson, 'Final Manuscript of *The Church Maritime*', Apostleship of the Sea Archives, Hull History Centre, HIST/7, 195.
2. T. McCarthy, *The Great Dock Strike, 1889* (1988).

tolerance.[1] Manning's views, however, were not shared by the majority of the Roman Catholic hierarchy, who feared anything that had overtones of state socialism. Nevertheless, Edward Bagshaw, Bishop of Nottingham, allied himself with Manning's views and had earlier (in 1885) published a pamphlet entitled *Mary and Justice for the Poor*.

Roman Catholic concern for fishermen in Britain was, like the Nonconformists' work in the early 1800s, awoken by the more general call for a mission to seafarers – and the call came from a seaman rather than a priest. In 1889 a sailor called on the Rev. Lord Archibald Douglas at South Queensferry, Scotland, and urged him to do something for Catholic bluejackets. Lord Archibald followed this up in January 1890 with an article in *The Messenger of the Sacred Heart* (the official organ of the Apostleship of Prayer) entitled 'Jack Wrecked at Sea', in which he appealed for help in responding to the needs of Catholic seafarers.[2] Lord Archibald's letter has been seen as the start of the Catholic Sea Apostolate in Britain, although he said the real founder was the anonymous sailor who had visited him. Unknown to Lord Archibald, Pope Leo XIII had selected 'Men of the Sea' as his Special Intention for members of the worldwide Apostleship of Prayer for May 1890 and, with this action, Catholic concern for seafarers began to gather momentum.[3]

Father Goldie SJ, editor of *The Messenger of the Sacred Heart*, published an article during the same month also making a plea for Catholic action on behalf of seafarers, referring to the zeal of the Protestant missions to seafarers and pointing to the apparently complete apathy of Roman Catholics:

> No one class of our people is perhaps as destitute of spiritual aid, nor more in need of it. Sailors are difficult to get at; even to estimate the number of Catholics among them is almost impossible, since it is part of their condition that they are dispersed beyond all hope of being gathered into congregations. [. . .] Our Catholic soldiers are now supplied with chaplains; the claims of the pauper and even of the convict are recognised; but the soul of the sailor is unattended still. The difficulty is great, no doubt, even to devise a means, still more to provide one. But prayer and charity can accomplish all things; and it is still no small sign of the Divine Mercy that our prayers are directed by the Holy Father to this intention; the prayers of our associates will draw grace into zealous and charitable hearts, whose efforts will do the rest

---

1. *Punch* Magazine, 1889.
2. Anson, *The Church Maritime*, p.200.
3. Anson, *The Sea Apostolate of the Port of London* (published posthumously by the Apostleship of the Sea, 1991), p.47

For several months there seemed to be little effect, although letters about concern for seamen continued to appear in *The Messenger*. Then in early 1891 a Catholic blue-jacket wrote a forceful letter:

> I have a suggestion to make. If all the Catholic communities were to distribute all their out-of-date religious papers to ships on foreign stations, I think that it would do some good, as we hardly ever get anything of the kind, unless our relations send them to us, and, as a rule, most likely they do not trouble about us in that way.
>
> Now the Church of England Missions sends to every man once a month, a large parcel of books and papers; and it is natural that Catholics, not having anything of the kind of their own should read them. Then some of them through doing this, I am sorry to say, often fall away altogether. I think it is a standing disgrace to the Catholics of England that they can't do something for us in the way of good, sound, moral literature. Perhaps you will think I am rather impertinent, but I have just recovered from a sickness, and the doctors had given me up. I was down with typhoid fever; the only religious book I had to read was *The Messenger*, and it did me some good to see that a blue-jacket is not always forgotten.[1]

Father Dignam SJ, the National Director of the Apostleship of Prayer, took up the suggestion and began appealing for suitable literature. In June the Catholic Truth Society (CTS) formed a committee that took responsibility for providing literature for Catholic seamen. Mgr John Virtue, Bishop of Portsmouth, was elected Chairman, and the Hon. Mrs Georgina Fraser was appointed Secretary.[2] Some members of the *Apostleship of Prayer*, led by Miss Mary Scott-Murray and Miss Margaret Stewart responded to the call, established the 'work for Catholic blue-jackets', and sent out the first batch of literature on 31 July 1901.[3]

Father Goldie agreed to compile a prayer book, which he called 'A Guide to Heaven for Use of those at Sea', and this was accepted as the official Roman Catholic prayer book in the Royal Navy. The initiative by the Catholic Truth Society and the Apostleship of Prayer was followed up on 3 June 1892 with a meeting of the CTS Congress at Liverpool, where the topic for discussion was 'How can we help our seamen?' – and this included the fishermen, as reference was made to the work of local

---

1. Reprinted in Anson, *op. cit.* (1948), p.49.
2. William Redford and Michael J. Knight, *Jacob's Ladder: The Rise of a Catholic Community, 1848–1913* (St Mary on the Sea, Grimsby, 1996), pp.82, 91-2, 115, 119 and 122.
3. *Ibid.*, pp.50-1.

committees in several ports such as that of Canon Hawkins at Grimsby. Nevertheless, the main comments appear to have centred upon the needs of the Royal and Merchant Navies. In his speech, Fr Goldie argued that the work should be organised under local confraternities rather than being left to the often overworked parish priest; and he argued for the establishment of homes similar to those run by Miss Agnes Weston at Portsmouth and Devonport.[1] It was also proposed that reading matter be supplied to men of the Mercantile Marine in all parts of the world.[2] In April 1894 Fr Goldie published an article in *The Month* arguing the case for a trained Catholic Sea Apostolate, similar to the *Société des Oeuvres de Mer* in France.

During the early 1890s other initiatives occurred: the Society of St Vincent de Paul began work amongst seafarers in Bristol, Sunderland and Tyneside during 1893; the first Roman Catholic Club for Seamen was opened at Montreal in May 1893; and the first club in Britain opened at Wellclose Square during July 1893.[3]

A seamen's branch of the Apostleship of Prayer was established in 1895 by Fr Gretton SJ (the recently installed National Director of the Apostleship of Prayer – following Fr Dignam's death) and this continued for several years but had lost much of its impetus by the dawn of the twentieth century.[4] At the CTS Annual Conference in September 1895, the Hon. Mrs Fraser presented a paper entitled 'General Aspects of Work for Catholic Seamen', in which she outlined the growing number of initiatives at home and abroad and gave an overview of the current state of the work.

By the end of the century Roman Catholic seamen's clubs and homes had been established in Glasgow, Sydney, New York, Genoa, Naples, Port Said *etc.*; and the Society of St Vincent de Paul established work among seafarers in Cardiff, Hull, London and in the United States. Then in 1901 a special magazine for seafarers, the *Stella Maris*, was published and copies distributed free to all vessels of the Royal and Merchant Navies.

All these developments continued with an ever-expanding range of groups and organisations. On 31 July 1917 Brother Richard (Peter Anson), an oblate with the Caldey Benedictines, attended lunch with Miss Scott-Murray. She invited him to take over the directorship of the Apostleship of Prayer and he agreed. After several years of running this organisation, and research investigating the history of Catholic work amongst seafarers, he published an article in *The Universe* of 30 April 1920 entitled 'A Plea

---

1. *Ibid.*, p.60.
2. P. Anson, *The Sea Apostolate in Ireland* (Office of the Irish Messenger, 1946), pp.9-10.
3. *Ibid.*, p.10.
4. Anson, *op. cit.* (1948), pp.46-76.

for Catholic Seamen: Catholic and Protestant Activities – a Contrast'. The response was overwhelming and, with the help and support of Fr Goldie SJ and others, Anson established the Apostleship of the Sea (more properly known as Apostolatus Maris) as a worldwide society for seamen. It took over the work of the now defunct seamen's branch of the Apostleship of Prayer and was given the authority of Pope Pius XI on 17 April 1922.[1]

Canon Hawkins of Grimsby

While the Roman Catholic concern for fishermen (like the early Protestant work) was subsumed under a general concern for seafarers, work was going on quietly in the fishing ports around Britain. One important example, was the work of Canon Hawkins with fishing apprentices at Grimsby. By an Act of 1862 children could be removed from workhouses and placed in Catholic institutions at the expense of the local poor rate. Yet this requirement was clearly ignored by the local councils and Catholic clergy were left to follow up the contacts as best they could. One such response was the Confraternity established by Canon Hawkins.

At the CTS Conference in 1891, in the midst of concern for Catholic seamen, Canon Hawkins (who was in the USA) charged a colleague to speak on his behalf about the young fishing apprentices in Grimsby who were largely ignored by the Catholic Church. There was no national response, however. Canon Hawkins appears to have been left to his own devices, although supported by the Hon. Mrs Georgina Fraser, and was responsible for the establishment of St Joseph's Confraternity in 1891, with the aim, among others, of caring for the Catholic apprentices. The Confraternity appears to have relied largely upon the goodwill of several young men who begged reading material and passed this on to the fisherlads before they left for the fishing grounds. A Club Room was also opened and the fisherlads were made welcome to use its facilities. Of this work Canon Hawkins wrote in *The Tablet* in 1893:

> To be chained for long years in apprenticeship to the hard calling of deep-sea fishers [. . .] penned for ten, twelve or fourteen weeks at a time within the narrow compass of the trawler, the Catholic fisherlad stands unsupported often among a coarse and ignorant crew – the mark of ribald jeers, his religion the target for every species of contumely. And joined to this is the insidious whispering of would-be proselytisers – the Protestant Chaplain or the self-elected 'Evangelist' of the mission ship.[2]

---

1. *Ibid.*, Ch. VII.
2. *The Tablet*, 20 October 1893.

The first *Report of the Confraternity*, published in 1893, gives a number of reasons for the lapsed faith of many young Catholic fisherlads:

1. There was an almost total failure to notify the removal of boys from schools, union, reformatories *etc.* to the parish priest or other Catholic authority in the fishing ports. Out of 100 lads on the register of St Joseph's Confraternity, only 26 had been notified as coming to Grimsby.

2. Although the usual age was thirteen to fifteen, only the smallest percentage of these boys had any definite knowledge of the Catholic faith. This want of instruction was the most important factor working for their spiritual death. It was rare to find one who had been confirmed, rarer still to meet one who had received the Sacraments of Penance and the Holy Eucharist. Only fifteen lads were entered as confirmed.[1]

By the mid-1890s the number of fisherlads under the care of the Confraternity was reduced, mainly because of the failure of a large Grimsby fishing company during 1895–6, which resulted in the sale of a hundred fishing smacks. The Annual Report of the Seamen's Branch of the CTS in 1895–6 stated that, as a result of the sale, 100 fisherlads lost their employment – 40 of whom were said to be Catholics.[2] The last entries in the register of the Confraternity appear in 1897, following which the organisation appears to have ceased and the Club Room closed. Of the 100 lads on the register it seems that almost all were subsequently lost to the Catholic Church.

Although other priests followed Canon Hawkins' example, there was no coordinated Roman Catholic approach to caring for fishermen and in this the British Roman Catholic work was left far behind that of other European countries. It was not until well into the twentieth century, and the advent of the Apostleship of the Sea, that Catholic fishermen found themselves cared for by a national Roman Catholic organisation.

---

1. Anson, *op. cit.* (1948), pp.55-6.
2. Quoted in *ibid.*, p.58.

Chapter 10
Missions Influenced by the RNMDSF

Introduction

The work of the Royal National Mission to Deep Sea Fishermen's hospital ships was so successful that other nations followed its example, France, Scandinavia (Denmark, Norway and Sweden), the Netherlands and the United States. *The Société des Oeuvres de Mer* in France fitted several hospital ships for work around Newfoundland, Iceland and the Faroes, including the *Saint-Pierre*, launched in 1897, although this vessel was sunk by an iceberg, and the *Saint-Paul* suffered a similar fate in 1899. The *Saint-Francis d'Assise* fared much better and served until 1913, when it was replaced by the more modern vessel, *Saint-Jehanne*, and this was joined by the *Notre-Dame de la Mer*.[1] The Dutch launched the *De Hoop* in 1898; and a number of mission vessels were established in the US. Various mission vessels were also established by Scandinavian countries.

France

The RNMDSF tended to concentrate on British fishermen, with only occasional medical help given to fishermen of other nationalities. The development of the society's work, however, was watched with particular interest by the French and the Dutch, although there was clearly some influence from other earlier mission work among fishermen. In 1859 two French priests, Abbé Bernard and Abbé Beaudouin, were given permission to work among the Icelandic fishermen and were subsequently committed to caring for the Icelandic fishing community, many of whom spent the season working away from their homes in Brittany and Normandy. Of these fishermen Anson says:

> For many years fifty to sxty *goëlettes* (schooners) and *dundees* (ketches) had been setting forth from Paimpol on the north coast of Brittany, each with a crew of eight or nine men and boys. They

---

1. Anson, *op. cit.* (1948), pp.80-1.

were away from home for the whole of the summer. Conditions on these small craft were squalid. No lifeboats were carried. The crews were in constant dangers from sudden changes of weather. Here was a hitherto neglected maritime mission-field, where four to five hundred seamen were left without the sacraments for at least six months on end. No Catholic priest had been allowed to set foot in Iceland since the sixteenth century.[1]

Following the return home to France of Abbé Bernard, Abbé Beaudouin, leading the life of a hermit, continued serving the fishermen until his death in 1876.

Between the years 1859 and 1878 some French and Dutch priests worked among fishermen on the Orkney and Shetland Islands and formed what became known as the Apostolic Prefecture of the Arctic Missions (embracing Orkney, Shetland, the Faroes, Iceland, Lapland, Greenland and Caithness on the mainland of Scotland). The Prefect of this work, a Polish priest, Dr Stephen de Djunkowski, known more widely as Monsignor Etienne, recognised the need for a vessel to visit his widely-spaced parish, and set about raising support for this initiative, but a pamphlet published in 1865 failed to gain the relevant support.[2]

There was also some important earlier work by the French. The Confrérie du Saint-Sacrement was established in 1662, with its base at l'église Notre Dame in Le Havre, and worked solely with the captains, mates and pilots of fishing vessels especially those engaged in the Newfoundland cod fishery.[3] This work came to an end in 1727 when the list of administrators stopped. Alain Cabantous says that the demise of the Confrérie was partly the result of declining numbers of Newfoundland cod fishermen. With the resurgence of this fishery in the late eighteenth century, it would appear that no significant religious provision was being made by any country for fishermen around Newfoundland at that time.

The anonymous English author of *The Early History of a Sailor*, 1819, worked as a fisherman in Newfoundland during the years 1796–1798 and drew attention to the poor religious situation there, although he noted the work of the Methodists and Moravians and he encouraged the establishment of marine Bible associations.[4] It is possible that the memory of Catholic involvement with fishing vessels in Newfoundland during the earlier part

---

1. Anson, *op. cit.* (1974), p.199; also: Anson, *Mariners of Britany*, J. M. Dent and Sons Ltd., London, 1974, p. 99.
2. *Ibid.*, p.200.
3. Cabantous, *op. cit.* (1983).
4. Anon., *The Early History of a Sailor*, published by the author, 1819 (copy in the possession of Stephen Friend).

of the eighteenth century was passed down as oral history and influenced Protestant development of organised seafarers' missions in the early nineteenth century. The author of *The Early History of a Sailor* says nothing about such a link although his very presence in Newfoundland as a cod-fisher suggests the possibility of an awareness of oral history of the earlier Christian concern for fishermen. However, Miller has pointed out that in 1893 Abbé Theodore Garnier and his Confraternity of Notre Dame de la Mer was influenced by the work of the Confrérie du Saint-Sacrement and 'opened *foyers* (clubs) at various points along the French coast'.[1] Further influence came from Fr Goldie, the Anglican Fr Charles Hopkins, the work of the Order of St Paul and the work of Wilfred Grenfell in Labrador. Hence, in 1894 the Augustinians of the Assumption began a similar work to that of the Confrérie du Saint-Sacrement, working especially with the Newfoundland fishermen.

Miller has referred to the relationship between the *Société des Oeuvres de Mer* and the Augustinians of the Assumption as working side by side, with the latter providing the chaplaincy and the former being more of a secular organisation. This relationship proved to be important for the *Société* in that, while the French Third Republic (1870–1940) generally viewed the Church with suspicion, it supported its social and medical work[2] and in due course the *Société* was awarded the *Frère Eugène*.[3]

The *Société des Oeuvres de Mer* was formed after one of its founders, Bernard Bailly, had observed the work, during the 1890s, of the Royal National Mission to Deep Sea Fishermen (the prefix 'Royal National' having been added in 1897). However, prior to the advent of the *Société*, Henry Cook had worked along the French canals in his sailing church during the 1870s, and this may well have been another factor in influencing the development of the French maritime mission. There were also even earlier examples of maritime missions along the French canals with the establishment of various auxiliaries to the Bethel Unions set up by the Rev. G.C. Smith. While the French *Société* was influenced by the work of the RNMDSF, it does not appear to have worked in British ports – focusing much more, like its predecessors, on the coasts of Newfoundland and Iceland. Launched in December 1894, the *Société* defined its object as: 'to bring medical, social, moral and religious assistance to French seamen and those of other nations, especially men engaged in deep-sea fisheries'.[4]

These various initiatives demonstrate that the Roman Catholic Church was not entirely lacking in concern for the welfare of seafarers, especially fishing,

---

1. Miller, *op. cit.* (2005), p.268.
2. Miller, *op. cit.* (1995), p.89.
3. Miller, *op. cit.* (2005), p.272.
4. Anson, *op. cit.* (1974), p.203.

communities, although it was not until well into the nineteenth century that events began to move towards the development of an international Roman Catholic movement for seafarers. Subsequently, in 1930, the *Société des Oeuvres de Mer* became a constituent member of the Apostleship of the Sea.

The Netherlands

The Dutch established medical work at sea using hospital ships for their fishing fleet during the 1830s, thus anticipating the work of the RNMDSF by half a century. During the late 1890s the master of the Dutch vessel, *Dolfyn*, observed the work of the RNMDSF's hospital ships in the North Sea and was so impressed that he spoke with a clergyman friend, Domine Van der Valk, of the Dutch Reformed Church. He in turn invited those clergymen of his church who worked in fishing ports to a meeting to discuss the possibility of setting up a society to care for Dutch fishermen. The response was positive and a committee was formed with Domine Van der Valk elected as Chairman. The new society began researching the needs of the country's fishermen and collecting funds for the purchase of a suitable vessel to act as a hospital ship. Despite some initial criticism, the new society persevered and established a fundraising committee under the control of two ladies in Amsterdam and The Hague. The joint ladies' committee issued a statement to the effect that the 'medical mission was not a pretext for spiritual work, but was itself a distinct object', whilst the spiritual work was not ignored.[1] The Dutch work was in marked contrast to the work of the RNMDSF, which consistently repeated its prime motive as being 'evangelistic', although the words 'Preach the Word' and 'Heal the Sick' on the bows of the British vessels pointed to a growing national concern with practical aid.

The Dutch fundraising initiative was effective and a vessel was obtained and launched for work on 17 June 1898, when the *De Hoop* set off on her maiden voyage to the Shetland Islands where she began work amongst the 600 Dutch fishing smacks.

Scandinavia

The Scandinavian countries had some early experience of maritime missions. A Danish Church was established in Wellclose Square, London, in 1696 and was followed by a Swedish Church in 1728. During the early nineteenth century an important pioneer in modern Scandinavian work among seafarers was the Rev. Carl von Bülow.[2] Following service as an army

---

1. *Toilers of the Deep*, vol. 15 (1900), p.140.
2. Kverndal has provided a helpful biography of von Bülow's life and work in his *Seamen's Missions* (1986), pp.260-3. See also Kverndal, pp.591-610 on the

officer in the Napoleonic Wars, von Bülow left Denmark for Edinburgh to undertake study and training as an evangelist and in 1819 returned to Scandinavia where he visited fishermen and other seafarers along the coast. Returning to London in 1824, he received sponsorship from the British and Foreign Seamen's Friend Society and Bethel Union, and subsequently worked as a missionary to foreign seamen in the London Docks. In 1826 he returned to Scandinavia, bought a small sailing vessel, fitted it out for mission work and set off along the coast where he ministered to seafarers. Kverndal says that von Bülow's mission activity was 'destined to become the forerunner of the Norwegian Missionary Society'.

In Norway a fishermen's mission was established in 1880 in Bergen (one year ahead of the advent of the Mission to Deep Sea Fishermen) and this Norwegian Home-Port Seamen's Mission was the initiative of the fishermen. Later the Mission established a series of Bethel Ships based on the model of the MDSF.

Denmark had preceded the Norwegian work with the establishment of the Danish Seamen's Church in Hull in 1871 (many Danes had previously joined the German Church in Hull). Later the Danes followed the example of the Norwegians and established a Bethel ship ministry in 1881. The Danish Home-Port Seamen's Mission was subsequently established in 1905.

Other Scandinavian missions, and also missions for fishermen from Finland and Iceland, were established in a number of British fishing ports especially where Scandinavian fishermen and their families had relocated. The Danish mission in Grimsby, for example, opened in May 1927 (opened by the Danish pastor from Hull) during the postwar heyday of the Grimsby fishing industry when many Danish fishermen visited the town;[1] and the Finnish mission in Hull, established in 1883, worked with each society's own countrymen, a number of whom had established small communities in the British ports.

The United States of America

Numerous American societies were also influenced by the RNMDSF, including the American Seamen's Friend Society and the Gloucester Fishermen's Institute. This latter society published a monthly journal, *The Fishermen*, and made regular references to the work of the RNMDSF, in particular following the RNMDSF's lead locally in pressing for the purchase and fitting out of a Bethel ship, which appears to have been obtained in 1898 and named the *Pastime*.[2]

---

development of Nordic maritime missions.
1. *Grimsby Evening Telegraph*, 19 May 1967.
2. 'The Fisherman', *Gloucester Fishermen's Institute*, October 1897, pp.150-1; and 1901, p.117.

Chapter 11
Conclusion

In this conclusion a number of threads from the foregoing material will be drawn together, looking particularly at the reasons for the rise of missions to fishermen during the later years of the nineteenth century, the factors that led to the monopoly of the Royal National Mission to Deep Sea Fishermen in its social and spiritual concern for fisherfolk, and the relationship between the various maritime mission societies as their work developed during the 1890s.

The reasons for the rapid expansion of the fishing industry during the nineteenth century were complex: the development of an appropriate infrastructure, technological innovations, a comprehensive support network and the discovery of new and lucrative fishing grounds, were all important. But these changes also led to a number of social developments such as the rapid expansion of fishing communities and the influx and employment of people, such as apprentices, who had no previous experience of involvement with the fishing industry. Inevitably this led to social and economic problems, especially when economic depression began to set in during the late 1870s.

The initial response of seafarers' missions, however, was aimed at winning converts, it being assumed by many middle-class Victorian Christians that poverty was the consequence of sin and that social, economic and political changes would follow on from spiritual change – despite the fact that many studies had drawn very different conclusions. There was also the problem of finance as few seafarers' missions had sufficient funds to spare on social work after the needs of evangelisation had been met.[1] Views, however, were changing. The Government reports on the social conditions in fishing ports and at sea set the scene for later similar reports by individuals and groups. With the growing number of missions in fishing ports, many of them supported by the Missions to Seamen and the British and Foreign Sailors' Society, one would have expected to see them reaching out to the

---

1. Kennerley, *op. cit.* (1989), p.254.

expanding floating population but, prior to 1881, only individual chaplains and lay-workers visited fishermen at sea, there being no serious attempts to ensure a sustained presence among the fishing fleets. The Thames Church Mission did not begin such work until 1881, when the Mission to Deep Sea Fishermen was founded, and at a time when the fleeting system had reached its peak. The initiative also followed the Government's introduction of legislation intended to improve conditions at sea. The Payment of Wages Act of 1880 allowed apprentices to give two days' notice in the event of their refusal to sail and abolished criminal proceedings against apprentices. While this solved some of the apprentices' problems, it caused others for employers when apprentices deserted and left the industry with a labour problem. The resulting outcry from fishing vessel owners and employers led to the Board of Trade Enquiry of 1882.[1]

Two factors are important here: not everyone was convinced of the necessity for developing such work; and the cost of obtaining, fitting out and running a vessel for work amongst the fishing fleets seemed to be prohibitive. Despite the concerns expressed in local and national newspapers, and by fishing companies and the Government, the TCM Committee was not convinced that such a new development as a sustained presence at sea was necessary, and Committee members were understandably reticent to branch out into new spheres of work. The Thames Church Mission was after all a small society when compared with the Missions to Seamen and the British and Foreign Sailors' Society. Even so, with the increasing number of official reports about abuses at sea, the situation clearly required some sort of response, if the costs could be met – but there was concern that the necessary funds would not be found on the basis of evangelical claims alone. Thus, it is especially curious that no direct response from the seafarers' missions occurred during the 1870s, although these organisations did by this time have a presence in most of the country's fishing ports.

Lord Cholmondeley, the TCM's Chairman, had direct links with the work of a number of pioneer maritime missionaries who had obtained their own vessels for work at sea, including Carl von Bülow, Thomas Rosie and Henry Cook. This was no doubt an important factor in eventually convincing the TCM Committee of the viability of the scheme to establish a North Sea Mission. The TCM Secretary, Ebenezer Joseph Mather, was already aware of the work of these pioneers, and the methods currently in use on the floating churches and chapels in the country's seafaring ports were easily adapted for use on the Mission ships at sea. Nevertheless, when the TCM Committee was eventually convinced of the viability of the scheme, it was based on a number of factors: funding from a fishing

1. *BPP XVII*, 1882.

fleet owner, Mr Samuel Hewett; Mather's willingness to accept personal responsibility for the vessels; and the use of the envisaged 'Bethel ships' as fishing smacks and later as hospital ships. These Bethel ships were vessels adapted to act as sailing chapels that were crewed by seafarers who worked as evangelists when their day's fishing was done. In this way costs were kept to a minimum and the TCM was absolved of ultimate responsibility. Extra income was then generated by appealing to the moral conscience of evangelicals and the public. The impression was given that the MDSF was a truly innovative mission, the work being necessary if abuses were to be curtailed.

While it may seem strange that a dedicated mission to fishermen did not come into being until the early 1880s, the evidence so far discussed suggests that this view is an oversimplification. Clearly, the maritime mission societies had been active since the 1860s in providing and encouraging staff to visit the fishing fleets and to minister to the needs of the fishermen. Indeed, missionary W. Jary of the British and Foreign Sailors' Society visited the Short Blue fleet at sea and hoisted his Bethel flag there for meetings.[1] The Missions to Seamen also occasionally sent a chaplain to visit the fleets. A desire for a full-time Church ship working among the fishing fleets was mooted at the Church Congresses for 1874 and 1879, with Canon Scarth of the SAWM arguing on several occasions for a chaplain to work with fishermen at sea. The genius of the founder of the Mission to Deep Sea Fishermen lay in his ability to bring together several disparate factors, to engage a number of influential and important Victorian figures with the work and to 'sell' his vision to the TCM/MDSF committee. He was also perhaps fortunate in that a number of relevant factors aided his task. The changing theological emphasis, from the Atonement to the Incarnation, encouraged many Christians to acknowledge their social responsibilities. The publication of several newspaper articles, books, official documents and Government reports outlining the poor conditions of fishermen and their apprentices was effective in generating sympathy for the maritime missions. Two of the main drives of the Mission to Deep Sea Fishermen, after its primary aim of evangelisation, were its fight against the copers and the development of its medical work at sea. Practical concerns also struck a moral chord with the public. Mr Mather's charismatic personality and his use of publicity had the effect of drawing funds from a wide section of the public.

It has been shown that the emergence and development of the MDSF during the 1880s was directly related to the social, economic and technological changes that occurred during the period of the British fishing

1. Pike, *op. cit.* (1897), p.238.

industry's expansion. But the development was also influenced by changing attitudes within Victorian religion – something that was especially noticeable in the later years of the nineteenth century, when radical changes were necessary if the MDSF was to survive. During the 1890s representatives of the Victorian High Church (notably the SAWCM and the NSCM), but also the evangelical Salvation Navy, developed their own fleets of Mission ships for work amongst the fishermen, and a period of competition ensued between the various missions. This situation resolved itself to some extent towards the end of the nineteenth century when these organisations found that financial constraints made it increasingly difficult to sustain their work at sea – although later developments, such as W.F. *Stewart's Albatross* Mission remained active until well into the twentieth century.

By the beginning of the twentieth century the MDSF, which had over ten years' start on the other Christian missions' work at sea (and now the RNMDSF), found itself with a monopoly of work among fishermen at sea – although other small organisations and individuals did from time to time send out Mission ships to the fishing grounds. As technological, social and economic changes continued to affect the British fishing industry, and the fleeting system came to an end, the RNMDSF expanded its shore-based work, such as its development of accommodation for fishermen visiting and working from ports other than their own.

Inevitably the social and economic problems remained acute, and the various seafarers' missions responded in a variety of ways. These developments continued well into the twentieth century, with the Scottish Episcopal Church developing a Mission to work specifically with the Scottish fishergirls. Others worked with apprentices, navvies and dock labourers, and there were numerous local initiatives such as the work of clergy at Grimsby, Brixham and Hastings.

While the MDSF had quickly developed a fleet of Bethel ships, this appears to have been the result of an economic opportunity that presented itself to several businessmen rather than Mather's own idea. And later, when he eventually found himself solely responsible for the growing fleet of vessels, this was the direct result of economic difficulties faced by the businessmen. Nevertheless, as has been shown, mission work with fisherfolk had been going on quietly in the fishing communities from the early years of the nineteenth century, although changing attitudes, especially theological views, to Christian social action provided a motive for extending more intensive work among the North Sea fishermen. With the MDSF released from its dependence on the TCM in 1886, the society, under Mather's leadership, was able to make a number of innovative changes – not least restructuring the Committee to include influential writers, doctors and fishing fleet owners. The publication of a popular monthly journal, *Toilers of the Deep*, and later the employment of a charismatic doctor, Wilfred Grenfell, whose work among the North Sea fishing fleets, and fisherfolk in Ireland and Labrador, kept the public interested in the work, despite Mather's fall from grace and his resignation in 1889.

The rising militancy of fishermen also began to worry the fishing companies. Such militancy became of national importance in the early part of the twentieth century when whole communities, such as those at Grimsby and Fleetwood, saw the fishing fleets being laid up for a considerable time. The very nature of their occupation, however, with long periods at sea, generally prevented them from engaging in radical actions such as strikes. Theoretically, therefore, fishermen were of necessity generally conservative and as members of a stable social group within the working class they ought to be thought of as inherently religious. However, in 1851 they did not meet the requirements of Horace Mann who considered church attendance as the major criterion of religious commitment – and working-class people were not generally supportive of regular church attendance.

Religious commitment is difficult to assess. Nevertheless, sustained conversions were present in fishing communities, such as at Filey in 1823, when local support for new converts was readily available. But even here there was a significant falling away from newfound faith. More research, therefore, needs to be undertaken before any comprehensive explanation can be offered as to the nature of religious commitment among fisherfolk, and the degree and type of success achieved by the maritime missions. Given that the data compiled by the various maritime mission agencies was, and is, naturally intended to publicise their missionary work and to encourage financial support, it would appear that further in-depth studies of particular fishing communities will provide an appropriate focus for future research.

Appendix 1a

The Development of British Seafarers' Missions during the Nineteenth Century

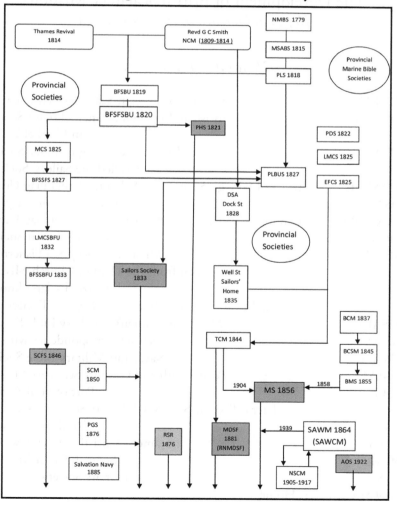

Appendix 1b

The Development of British Seafarers' Missions
Key to abbreviations in Appendix 1a

Nonconformist Missions

BFSBU	British and Foreign Seamen's Bethel Union
BFSFSBU	British and Foreign Seamen's Friend Society and Bethel Union
BFSS	British and Foreign Sailors' Society (now called the Sailors' Society)
BFSSBFU	British and Foreign Sailors' and Soldiers' Bethel Flag Union
DSA	Destitute Sailors' Asylum
LMCSBFU	London Mariners' Church Society, or Bethel Flag Union
MCS	Mariners' Church Society
MDSF	Mission to Deep Sea Fishermen (separated from the Thames Church Mission in 1886 – later known as the Royal National Mission to Deep Sea Fishermen)
MSABS	Merchant Seamen's Auxiliary Bible Society
NCM	Naval Correspondence Mission
NMBS	Naval and Military Bible Society
PGSM	Portsmouth and Gosport Seamen's Mission
PHS	Port of Hull Society (later called the Sailors' Children's Society – see SCS)
RSR	Royal Sailors' Rests
SCFS	Seamen's Christian Friend Society
SCM	Scottish Coast Missions
SCS	Sailors' Children's Society (see PHS)
Well Street Sailors' Home	

Church of England Missions

BCM   Bristol Channel Missions
                    (later known as the Bristol Channel Seamen's Mission – BCSM;
                                         and the Bristol Mission to Seamen)
ECFS   Episcopal Floating Church Society
LMCS   Liverpool Mariners' Church Society
MS   Missions to Seamen
NSCM   North Sea Church Mission
PDS   Port of Dublin Society
PLBUS   Port of London and Bethel Union Society
PLS   Port of London Society
SAWM   St Andrew's Waterside Mission
            (later known as the St Andrew's Waterside Church Mission – SAWCM)
TCM   Thames Church Mission

Roman Catholic Missions

St Joseph's Confraternity   (a confraternity founded in Grimsby
                                                     for Roman Catholic fisherlads)
AOS   Apostleship of the Sea (founded in 1922)

Appendix 2

The Port of Hull Society:
Average Sunday Attendance on the *Valiant*

Date	Morning	Afternoon	Evening (Summer)*

1821: The *Valiant* was berthed in Queen's Dock and the first service held on board was on 3 October 1822.

Date	Morning	Afternoon	Evening (Summer)*
1822	250		
1823–7	-	-	-
1828	247	357	
1829	247	385	136

1829: Prince's Dock was opened and the Valiant transferred here, where she spent the rest of her life

Date	Morning	Afternoon	Evening (Summer)*
1830	251	437	
1831	267	472	209
1832	292	523	245
1833–6	-	-	-
1837	242	251	383
1838	250	521	
1839	306	546	
1840	312	541	220
1841–50	-	-	-

1851: The *Valiant* was taken out of service and broken up, the vessel being 'thoroughly worn out'. The services were thereafter held in the Institute, which had been recently erected for the Port of Hull Society (PHS Report, 1851, p.7).

*Services were not held on the *Valiant* on Sunday evenings during the winter because no lights were allowed on the Dock (PHS Report, 1822, p.16).

The statistics here are drawn from the PHS Annual Reports – the Minute books for the early years could not be found when I visited the Sailors' Children's Society in September 1990. Unfortunately, attendance statistics were not recorded every year in the Reports, hence the gaps. The figures given are all exclusive of children.

(Source: PHS Annual Reports)

Appendix 3

Rules and Regulations
of the Thames Church Mission Society

1. That this Society shall be designated *The Thames Church Mission*
2. That the object of the Society shall be to promote the spiritual welfare of seamen remaining on board the vessels which lie at the different sections in the River Thames, between the Pool in London and the Anchorage at Gravesend, awaiting their turn to go up and deliver their cargoes in the metropolis.
3. That a vessel shall be provided, and so fitted, that Divine Service, at the usual times, may be performed on board on the Sabbath-day; and that a Chaplain shall be appointed to conduct the public worship of 'God' at such services, whose duty it shall likewise be, to visit from section to section on the weekdays and impart religious instruction to the sailors, by all means that circumstances may place at his disposal.
4. That this Society shall be arranged by a Committee, a Treasurer and Secretaries. The Committee consisting of twenty-four members, four of whom shall go out by rotation at the first meeting of the Committee in the year, the outgoing members to be eligible to re-election.
5. That the Committee shall meet once a month, for the general business of the Society, or more frequently, if requisite, and that the presence of 'three members' shall form a quorum.
6. That all meetings held by this Society shall be commenced by prayer.
7. That the Chaplain appointed to conduct the Mission, shall be a clergyman of the Established Church, to be nominated by the Committee, subject to the approval of the Bishop of London.
8. That a donation of two pounds; or an annual subscription of one pound, shall constitute Membership. A clergyman contributing half the above sums, shall be entitled to the same privilege.

9. That an Annual Report of the proceedings of the Society, shall be printed under the sanction of the Committee, together with a balance sheet of the receipts and expenditure duly audited, also a list of contributors to the Society.

10. That a General Meeting of the Members of the Society, at which not less than eleven shall constitute a quorum, may be called at the requisition of the Committee; or by any thirteen members, on addressing a letter to the Secretary, specifying the purpose of the meeting.

Ten days' notice of any such meeting, and the design, in three public newspapers, and this shall be considered affording sufficient publicity to the intended meeting and the object for which it is called.

May 10th, 1844

Read and Confirmed,   William Waldegrave, Chairman

(Source: Thames Church Mission Minutes — Mission to Seamen Archives, Hull History Centre, 10 May 1884)

Appendix 4

E.J. Mather's Address
to the Newcastle Church Congress, October 1881

E.J. Mather (Secretary of Thames Church Mission, London)

My lord, – All here who have ever had the pleasure of listening to Miss Weston's interesting narration of work among the blue-jackets in the Royal Navy, must heartily regret her inability to be present; but I for one am thankful that her absence has enabled Commander Dawson to read his very able paper upon 'Church Work amongst Seamen in the Diocese of Durham', for no one is better qualified than he to deal with the question according to the terms of the programme, his society having for many years occupied stations in these great northern ports.

The Committee's invitation to me allows great latitude, and your lordship will perhaps permit me to confine my observation entirely to Church-work in the Diocese of London, which has been for many years carried on by the oldest Church society for the benefit of seamen – the Thames Church Mission.

From the year 1829 to 1847, the *Brazen*, an old sloop-of-war, fitted out as a church, was moored off the Tower of London, in the hope that seamen in large numbers would attend the spiritual provision made for their benefit. It was found, however, that sailors who had returned from long voyages preferred remaining on shore; and so in this respect the *Brazen* proved a failure. In a higher sense, however, she was successful, as this anecdote will prove: After the last annual meeting of the Thames Church Mission, an aged sea-captain introduced himself to me, stating that forty-one years ago he attended the *Brazen* service one Sunday night on his return from the West Indies. God met with him there: the Gospel preached by the officiating clergyman reached his conscience and heart, and he left England again a changed man, 'to live no longer to himself, but to Him who died for him and rose again'. Here is a practical commentary on the text, which has been the Society's motto: 'Cast thy bread upon the waters, for thou shalt find it after many days.'

In 1844, several members of the *Brazen* Committee met for prayer, and to consider what further steps could be taken to meet the desperate need of sailors entering the Port of London, and the outcome of that prayer-meeting was a second application to the Admiralty, who kindly granted the *Swan*, a cutter which had seen service in the Baltic. She was forthwith fitted as a cruising church, and with a resident chaplain, licensed by the Bishop of London, and a crew of five pious men, she sailed forth – as the old report expresses it – 'to do battle for the Lord of Hosts against the powers of darkness for the soul of the sailor'.

The conditions of the river-traffic differed entirely from those of to-day. Instead of vast docks extending for many miles below London Bridge, the shipping (and especially the colliers) lay in seven sections between London and Gravesend, awaiting their turn to go up and discharge in the Pools.

Here were met the north-country sailors, hailing from the Diocese of Durham. We Londoners depend largely on the northern coal-fields – 5,225 cargoes of coal have entered the Thames during the present year, chiefly in steamers; but in the early days of the Thames Church Mission, the coal was conveyed in a fleet of brigs of from 100 to 500 tons burthen, manned by some 3,500 sailors. Many of these poor fellows were not merely ignorant, but terribly ungodly and profane, with hearts as black as the coal in which they traded. At first they met the chaplains and his band of lay-helpers with insult and abuse, for a notion was prevalent that the Government were attempting to force religion down the sailors' throats, and that the next step would be the imposition of a tax to cover the cost of maintaining the *Swan*.

However, through God's great goodness, this opposition ceased, in a great measure owning to the conversion of a captain who had been the bitterest opponent, but afterwards became one of the most ardent supporters of the Mission Church, never failing to attend the services himself and using every effort to take others with him, beyond doubt, we shall meet many – very many – of them in that day when 'the Lord shall make up His jewels'.

Now, the *Swan* no longer cruises, but a mission-room with library *etc.*, assistant-chaplain, five lay missionaries, and four colporteurs (all except the clergy themselves being seamen). With this staff the daily visitation of shipping of all nationalities is carried on, both on the river and in the docks. No fewer than 27,281 visits were paid last year, while 3,226 services were held, at which there were 94,624 attendants. The same spirit of devotedness is maintained as in earlier years; the same earnest desire to win souls for Christ – and, thank God, the same blessed results.

The senior chaplain resides at Gravesend, and you would be greatly interested in details of his services with seamen and emigrants, were there time to relate them. Those held with the latter class are often deeply affecting. 22,559 English and foreign emigrants have left the great Port of London during the present year; and it is no small satisfaction that as far as can be ascertained (and the leading shipowners give every facility to the mission-staff) every emigrant has been presented with a copy of the New Testament. Gospels, or Psalms, together with suitable tracts, in his own language. Similar gratuitous distribution was, by the courtesy of the Admiralty, effected on board the transports which conveyed reinforcements to the Cape at the beginning of the year; so that each soldier took a New Testament and tracts as part of his kit; and no fewer than 4,524 copies of the Word of God and 800 Prayer-books were purchased by the seamen during the past year.

Services are also held on the Lord's-day, and Bible and Confirmation classes during the week on board the cadet-ship *Worcester*, and the training frigates *Arethusa*, *Chichester*, and *Cornwall*, whose captains speak in the highest terms of the spiritual results upon their youthful crews. And let us hope the eighty *Worcester* cadets, and one hundred and seventy boys from the other ships who annually enter the merchant-service, carry away in their hearts the precious seed which has been sown, to bring forth fruit for God in their after lives.

But there is one point to which I must refer in the few moments which remain, the fact – and it is undeniable – that so large a proportion of those sailors who have been converted during the past thirty-seven years have lapsed into Dissent. A sailor recently remarked to me, 'When I go to church I never feel comfortable; no one notices me, or if they do it is to find fault with my clothes; but if I enter a chapel, some one comes forward to grasp my hand and show me to a seat. I am made welcome; and if unable to find the hymns, the person next to me will do so for me. I feel at home, sir, and my heart is warmed up.'

My lord, very much could be said as to the causes and remedies of this secession; but nothing more to the purpose than those words in your lordship's opening address, referring to the earnest Christian men who seceded from the Established Church one hundred and fifty years ago: 'What regrets for the past and what warnings for the future does it not suggest to us! What lessons of *organisation*, of *sympathy*, of *adaption* does it not read to us! Why should not this great spiritual mechanism have been retained within the Church to which it owed its being?' Let me earnestly appeal to the sympathies of the members of this Congress on behalf of the sailor. Oh, carry back with you to your several spheres a truer sense of your responsibilities towards those brave seamen to whom we owe so much, and who merit our thoughts and our care in spiritual things.

When the day arrives that 'Mariners' Churches' shall have been erected wherever there are sailors to attend them; when larger numbers of clergy, unhampered by the care of a parish, shall devote themselves exclusively to the sailors; when to quote the Archbishop of Canterbury, 'the recommendations of Convocation shall have been vigorously acted upon', and an army of lay readers have been appointed from the ranks of spiritual-minded officers on the mercantile marine, to conduct the services of the Church on board ships when away at sea, thus connecting our brethren afloat by closest ties with those who worship ashore – then, and not till then, will the Church win back and retain within her borders the hundreds of godly seamen who ought never to have been permitted to leave her communion.

(Source: Church Congress Report, 1881)

Appendix 5

E.J. Mather's Diary Notes,
TCM Annual Report for 1881

Tuesday[1]

Left London in the fishing smack steamer *Supply*, to visit the fishermen on board of the smacks at the Dogger Bank. I had a very nice time for conversation with the men on the passage down to Rainham, where she took in ice and coal; left at 7pm for the North Sea.

Wednesday

At night, when the men had done for a time, I went down the forecastle, when, an opportunity presenting itself, I held a meeting, which was of an interesting character. At the close three of the men offered up prayer that God's blessing would rest on my labours among their brother fishermen, and that the Lord would bless the Mission with which I am connected.

Thursday

Morning being fine we joined the fleet of smacks, and about eight boats came alongside, having three or four men in a boat. I then showed the men and lads what a deep interest the Thames Church Mission Society felt in them. I gave to them four hundred Gospels and five hundred tracts. Speaking to the men and lads about their souls, I sold three Bibles, two Testaments, and twenty 'Gospel Compass' cards. I then boarded the smack [. . .] and had a very interesting meeting; fourteen fishermen were present. A nice prayer meeting followed. I felt my own soul blessed. The men thanked me, and spoke with gratitude of the Society for taking such a work up. I then waited to see where next, when up came the master of the [. . .] saying, 'You must come with me, for the blessed Lord has answered my

---

1. The dates here are puzzling as Mather gives Saturday 27 August for his departure. However, see Chapter 5.1 'Nonconformist Missions', footnote 22.

prayer by sending you out to us. I have prayed for this three days, that the Lord would send someone to me that they may speak to my son, and now I thank God for sending you.' I then wished all a good-night, and went on board the smack [. . .] to stay a short time. I was received very kindly by all on board, where I gave my address, and we had a good time in prayer.

Friday

Westerly wind; very fine indeed. At 10am hoisted the Bethel flag for a meeting, and twenty-three met with us to hear the truth as it is in Jesus. We spent a happy day; sold two Bibles and a number of 'Gospel Compass' cards.

Saturday

Went on board of the smack. [. . .] Mr [. . .] held a meeting with fourteen men, and after the address I held a long prayer meeting, and it was good to be there. I gave a good number of portions of Scripture and tracts and returned to the [. . .]

Sunday

Morning boarded the smack. [. . .] Mr [. . .] hoisted the flag; a strong wind; a very great interest taken by the Christian masters to get a good number to meet with us in the morning; twenty-two came; a warm address and prayer meeting that God's good blessing might rest on all present. Boarded the [. . .] to get my dinner, and then returned to the Bethel Ship; forty met with us – a very good meeting; after the address a long prayer meeting that the Lord would bless us, and we felt it good to be there. Returned to the [. . .] gave address and prayers, then speaking of the love of Jesus, and urging them to seek the Lord.

Monday

Returned to the *Supply* to go home: wind and sea strong SE wind; 11.45am left here for London; arrived at East Greenwich at 7pm next day, feeling sure that our gracious Lord has blessed the means used out on the Dogger Bank to the souls of not a few of the poor fishermen, who appeared to be truly grateful that the Thames Church Mission had sent and are going to send out suitable men to preach the Gospel to them.

(Source: Thames Church Mission Annual Report for 1881, British Museum Library)

Appendix 6

Letter to the Archbishop of Canterbury
from the Rev. A.R.C. Smith

The Rectory
Chadwell St Mary
Grays

March 30th, 1883

My Lord Archbishop,

Under a supreme sense of duty I venture to bring to your Grace's notice, as briefly as possible, a few publications of the Thames Church Mission Society which, having hitherto enjoyed the Patronage of the late Archbishop of Canterbury, will no doubt make application to your Grace for a continuation of that valued favour.

I do not presume to express any opinion by an earnest hope that, before committing yourself to this Society, your Grace may find it possible to examine directly for yourself the statements contained in the accompanying prints.

The matter was brought under my own notice a few months ago when the new deep water docks at Tilbury (in this parish) were commenced. Then the Secretary, Mr Mather, wrote to me asking my co-operation in a mission amongst the navvies on the works. As we already had our own Mission I was somewhat surprised at the request and on making particular enquiry I found that Mr Mather is an avowed Plymouth Brother and that their tenets largely if not exclusively prevail in the Thames Church Mission Society. Consequently I declined to co-operate and gave information to the Archdeacon and the Bishop (St Albans) both of whom when appealed to by the secretary in company with Admiral Fishbourne, directly and unhesitatingly upheld the view which I had taken not to sanction the operations of the TCM on this side of the water. I should add that the TCM is not to be confused with the Saint Andrew's Waterside Mission from which most valuable Society our work amongst the navvies has from the first received substantial encouragement and support.

I have the honour to be
My Lord Archbishop
Your Grace's humble Servant

A.R.C. Smith
Rector of Chadwell St Mary

(Source: Lambeth Palace Archives)

Appendix 7a

Visits to the St Andrew's Mission Rooms, Grimsby, by Fishermen and Fisherlads

Year	Month	Visits to the Mission Rooms
1883		
1884	February	131
	March	297
	April	16
	May	61
	June	147
	July	188
	August	184
	September	260
	October	390
	November	489
	December	429
1885	January	501
	February	486
	March	477
	April	257
	May	340
	June	300
	July	254
	August	261
	September	346
	October	599
	November	480
	December	395

1886	January	733
	February	498
	March	510
	April	566
	May	514
	June	591
	July	550
	August	841
	September	866
	October	1158
	November	899
	December	929
1887	January	976
	February	998
	March	947
	April	1121
	May	820
	June	645
	July	918
	August	635
	September	940
	October	1010
	November	897
	December	1229
1888	January	901
	February	956
	March	703

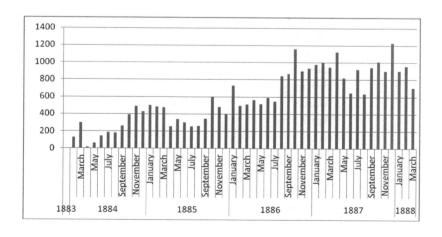

Appendix 7b

Visits to the *Water Kelpie* by Fishermen and Fisherlads
(The vessel was opened for use by the fishermen
in October 1891)

Year	Month	Visits to the Mission Rooms
1891	November	430
	December	405
1892	January	708
	February	750
	March	400
	April	548
	May	512
	June	258
	July	
	August	
	September	
	October	
	November	
	December	
1893	January	
	February	
	March	500
	April	
	May	
	June	
	July	
	August	
	September	
	October	

	November	
	December	385
1894	January	350
	February	400
	March	756
	April	389
	May	408
	June	384
	July	314
	August	257
	September	145
	October	
	November	480
	December	228
1895	January	
	February	300
	March	500
	April	940
	May	732
	June	811
	July	246
	August	
	September	
	October	291
	November	267
	December	569
1896	January	
	February	497
	March	456
	April	262
	May	171
	June	96
	July	116
	August	77
	September	73
	October	70
	November	48
	December	226
1897	January	154
	February	92

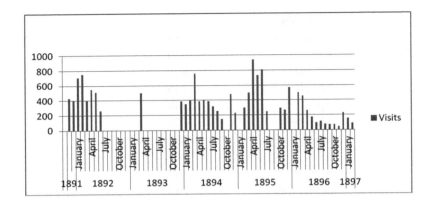

Appendix 8

Appointment of Mr E.J. Mather as Secretary to the TCM
(Thames Church Mission Minute Book, 9 February 1880)

Appendix 9

List of all known Copers

Name of coper	Port	Known date of activity	Notes
The Netherlands			
Nettle	The Texel	c.1881	
	Nieuwediep	c.1881	
Greensider	Schiedam	c.1884–5	
	Ditto	Ditto	
Noordstar	Ditto	Ditto	
	Dordrecht	Ditto	
Cosmopoliet	Ditto	c.1884–6	
De Kenau	Schiedam & Nieuwediep	Ditto	Formerly the *Merchant* of Grimsby
Eva	Helder &	Ditto	
Mary	Nieuwediep	c.1884–7	
	Schiedam		
Merchant	?	April 1888	
	Rotterdam	July 1900	
Zwaluw (Swallow)			
De Maria			
Delphin			
Regina			
Germany			
Diedrich	Geestenmunde	c.1880–5	Formerly *Billow of Grimsby*
	Ditto	c.1884	Formerly *Christobel* of Colchester

Caroline	Ditto	Ditto	Formerly *Majestic* of Hull
	Ditto	c.1884–5	Formerly of Hull; Skipper Brocklesby
Delphine	Ditto	c.1884	Formerly *Earl of Yarborough* of Grimsby Formerly *Two Sisters* of Grimsby
Christina (Martha)	Ems	Ditto	
Anna Helene			
?			

England

?	Dartmouth	c.1878	Described as a 'Dartmouth Dandy'. Skipper Bennington
	?	c.1878	
Josephine	?	c.1881	Just one trip as a 'coper'
Margretta	Gt Yarmouth	c.1881	
*Warrior	Ditto	c.1881–8	Lost 21 May 1888
Annie	Humber	c.1881	
	Grimsby	May–Sep 1882	
Angelina	Colchester	1885–8	Formerly of Ymuiden
	Ditto	c.1887	English for three months
Dora			
Unity			
*Thorn			
Perseverance			

Belgium

Telegram	Antwerp	c.1878	Formerly of Hull
	Ostend	c.1882–1906	
Kenan	?	c.1888	This reference may be to the Kenan
	Ostend	c.1890	
?			
Marie Louise			

Denmark

Long Betsy	Copenhagen	c.1881–3	

Sources:

E.J. Mather, Nor'ard of the Dogger

Walter Wood,North Sea Fishers and Fighters

J. Dyson, Business in Great Waters

A. Gordon, Helping the Trawlers

A. Gordon, What Cheer O?

Edgar J. March, Sailing Trawlers

Fisheries Exhibition Literature

Toilers of the Deep

Chart and Compass

Newspapers, e.g., Yarmouth Gazette, Yarmouth Mercury and the Grimsby News

British Parliamentary Papers, especially BPP Vol. XCVIII, 1888, p17, and LXXXII, 1881, p19

(See Chapter 6 for further details.)

*The HM Customs account of the seizure of the Warrior on 13 July 1881 is to be found at the National Archives, Kew, under the reference CUST 97, Yarmouth, p.87.

*The Thorn generally traded under a foreign flag and sold wares in foreign ports. It was formerly of Ymuiden, but was registered in 1884 at Colchester, 'so that according to circumstances this vessel could represent herself as a fishing-boat or as a trading vessel. She took in her supply of spirits at Amsterdam.' (HMSO, 1888, pp. 7, 12)

Appendix 10

Official letter in reply to enquiries regarding Mr Mather's separation from the MDSF
(Sent out with the list of charges in Appendix 11)

> Mission to Deep Sea Fishermen.
> 181, Queen Victoria Street,
> London, E.C.
>
> Dear
>
> In reply to your enquiry for further information as to the reason of the retirement of Mr Mather from the Mission to Deep Sea Fishermen I am instructed to send you herewith copy of the original charges formulated against him, and which, as you are aware he refused to submit to the investigation of an impartial person. I would further wish to bring to your attention the matter which is referred to in the two accompanying letters, which, although it was not discovered until after the severance of Mr Mather's connection with the Society, further shews the extremely improper nature, not to use a stronger term, of some of Mr Mather's proceedings.
>
> I am, Dear Sir,
> Yours faithfully,

(Source: RNMDSF Archives)

Appendix 11

Copy of the charges against Mr Mather
(Sent out with the covering letter in Appendix 10)

Statement of Charges

1. Excessive and unwarrantable expenditure in connection with travelling, subsistence, and other items.
2. Absence of vouchers for expenditure.
3. Inaccurate, evasive, and misleading explanations in regard thereto.
4. Travelling third class and charging first-class fare, contrary to the terms of his employment and the arrangement of the 26th August 1887 that only the expenses actually incurred by him whilst on the service of the Mission should be charged.
5. Taking £200 from cash in the hands of the Secretary, in November 1888 irregularly and without authority.
5* Untruthfulness, want of accuracy, or evasiveness in statements to Dr Gilbart Smith and Schofield with reference to the matter of the preceding charge.
6. Making arrangements for trading in and giving orders for the sale of Dogger Ale by the Mission Smacks on the North Sea, contrary to the Resolution of the Council with regard to trading.
7. Untruthfulness, want of accuracy, or evasiveness in connection with the matter of the preceding charge.
8. Untruthfulness, want of accuracy, or evasiveness in connection with his proposal to establish a store at Yarmouth.
9. Untruthfulness in his statements to Mr Scott Moncrieff relative to the British and Foreign Bible Society.

(Source: RNMDSF Archives)

Appendix 12

Letter to Alexander Gordon of the RNMDSF
from James Runciman

A. Gordon Esq.

Kingston on Thames
13 August 1890

Dear Sir,

Mr Frank Wilson was unable to give me any information regarding Mr Mather, but I have now learned everything. It appears that I have done you and Mr Miller much wrong in my heart. My only motive was to defend a man whom I regarded as honest and weak. A long statement framed with all the bitterness of my mind and soul is now in type, and I fear that I cannot stop it from appearing. All I can do is state as publicly as possible that my article, should it appear, was written when I was being deceived by a man in whom I wholly trusted. I only learned all the sordid and hideous truth today, and it has all but killed me:– certainly I am very nearly mad today, when I think of the affair. For a man of the world like me to be taken in like a mere firkin is humiliating: while Mr Mather's folly and deceit are heart-breaking. If I could make you any reparation I should be only too glad; but I can do nothing except repent in rage and bitterness during the brief remnant of my life.

With sincere apologies to you for my savage accusations made against you.

I am,

Yours Truly,

James Runciman

(Source: RNMDSF Archives)

Bibliography

Primary Sources

Anon, *Church Work Amongst Sailors in 64 Home Ports*, Convocation of the Lower House of Canterbury, February 1878.

Anon, *The Early History of a Sailor,* published by the author (Copy in the possession of Stephen Friend).

Anon, *The Fisherman's Refuge for the Whole of the Yorkshire Coast from Redcar to* Bridlington, published privately, 1836 (Copy in Leeds City Reference Library Ref.: 361 F53Y).

Anson, Peter F., *Life on Low Shore: Memories of Twenty Years Among Fisherfolk at MacDuff, Banffshire, 1938–1958* (Banff: The Banffshire Journal Ltd, 1969).

Anson, Peter F., *The Church Maritime*, unpublished manuscript, 1974, in the Apostleship of the Sea Archives, held at Hull History Centre.

Fleming, Baldwin, 'The Treatment of Pauper Apprentices to the Grimsby Fishing Trade', 19 June 1873 (Report drawn up for the Government and submitted to the Rt Hon. James Stansfeld MP, President of the Local Government Board), copy held in the Local History section of Grimsby Public Library, PRO MH/32/99.

Fleming, Baldwin, 'International Conference Concerning the Policing of the Fishing in the North Sea', French transcript held at The Hague, 14 October 1881.

Fleming, Baldwin, Logbook of the *Albert*, held in Norwich County Archives.

Mather, E.J., Trust Christ More, *The Sunday at Home*, c.1882 diary notes, TCM Annual Report, 1881, held in the British Library.

Mission to Seamen Archives, Letters signed by 'G.F.T.', held at Hull History Centre. Typed history of the Thames Church Mission (unsigned), held at Hull History Centre.

Royal National Mission to Deep Sea Fishermen Archives, 'Deed of Covenant', 1886, held at Hull History Centre.

'Partnership of Agreement', copy held at Hull History Centre.

Setterfield, H.G., *The Conversion of a North Sea Fisherman*, published privately, c.1914.

Stewart, A. (ed.), *The Albatross Yacht Mission*, published privately, (No Date). (Copy held by Stephen Friend).

Taplow, W. P., in Maclaren, Hamish (ed.), *The Private Opinions of a British Bluejacket* (London: Peter Davies, 1929).

Archives

The Anson Library, Buckie
Apostleship of the Sea, Hull History Centre
The Bristol Channel Mission Reports, Hull History Centre, under Mission to
    Seafarers
The British and Foreign Bible Society, Home Correspondence
The British and Foreign Sailors' Society, Minutes, Reports *etc.*
The British Museum Library
County Records Office, Newport, Isle of Wight
Essex Records Office
The Family Welfare Association, GLC Archives, London
GLC Record Office and History Library, London
Hereford and Worcester County Records Office
The Howley Papers, Lambeth Palace Library
Hull History Centre, University of Hull
Lambeth Palace Library, especially the Fulham Papers: Howley Collection, vol. 14
Lincolnshire County Archives, Lincoln
The Maritime Museum of East Anglia
The Mission to Deep Sea Fishermen, Hospital Committee Minutes, RNMDSF
    Archives
The Missions to Seamen, Annual Reports, Minutes *etc.*, Hull History Centre
The National Archives, Kew
The National Library of Scotland, Edinburgh
The Norfolk Records Office, Norwich (SO4/5 and SO4/6)
North Shields Archives
Norwich Records Office
The Port of Hull Society, Annual Reports, Hull History Centre
The Pure Water Company, Documents, the National Archives, BT 31, 4220/27314
Royal Commission Archives, Quality House, Chancery Lane, London
Royal Library, Windsor Castle
The RNMDSF Archives, London
The Sailors' Children's Society, Port of Hull Society, Minutes, Reports *etc.*, Hull
    History Centre
The Sailors' Orphan Society of Scotland, Centre for Business History in Scotland,
    University of Glasgow, GUAS Ref. UGD 187
St Andrew's Waterside Church Mission Archives - SAWCM Minutes, Reports, etc.
    (Missions to Seamen, London)
The Seamen's Mission Archives, Minutes, Reports *etc.*, London
South Humberside Area Record Office, Grimsby
Strathclyde Regional Council Archives, Glasgow
Thames Church Mission Archives, Minutes *etc.*, in the Mission to Seafarers Archives,
    Hull History Centre; some of the TCM Annual Reports are also kept in the
    British Museum Library
Time and Tide Museum, Great Yarmouth

Journals, Magazines and Society Annual Reports

British and Foreign Bible Society, Home Correspondence
British and Foreign Sailors' Society Reports
The Catholic Federalist
Chambers Journal, 1885
Chart and Compass, published by the British and Foreign Sailors' Society from 1879
    (a continuation of *The Sailors' Magazine*)
The Christian
The Church Congress Reports, 1869–95
The Church of England Temperance Chronical, 1887
The Church Times
Church Work Among Sailors in 64 Home Ports, held at the Lower House of
    Canterbury, February 1878.
Convocation of the Church of England Reports
Crockford's Clerical Directory
The Evangelical Magazine, especially 1818
Fish Trades Gazette, especially 1885, 1888, 1889 and 19 March 1921
The Fishermen, Gloucester Fishermen's Institute, October 1897
The Fisheries Exhibition Literature, 1883–4
Good Words, 1887
History today, December 1983
The Illustrated London News
International Labour Review, September 1944
The International Journal of Maritime History, vol. XV, no. 2
Labrador Studies
The Lancet, 1883
The Mariners' Mirror
The Messenger of the Sacred Heart
The Mission to Seafarers, Annual Reports
The Missionary Register, 1827, copy kept in the British Museum Library
The Month
The Monthly Packet
The Nautical Magazine
The Naval and Military Bible Society, 1826
The New Sailors' Magazine, 1827–63 (titles vary)
Northern History
Our Own Magazine, the Children's Special Mission, London, vol. VI, 1885
Norfolk Fair
Notes and Queries, Seventh Series, vol. XII, July–December 1891, pp.45, 387, 435,
    451-452, 496, Eighth Series, vol. I, January–June 1892, pp.32, 217, 342
The Penny Post
Punch Magazine
Report of the Proceedings of the Port of Dublin Society, 1837–42, Dublin
St Andrew's Parish Magazine, 1890s, St Andrew's Church, Grimsby
St Andrew's Waterside Church Mission Reports, Hull History Centre
The Record

The Sailors' Magazine, London, January 1820–7 (continued under various names)
The Schoolmaster
The Seamen's Family Society (began as the Port of Hull Society)
The Tablet
Toilers of the Deep, first published by the MDSF in 1886
Truth, 1889–1890
Vanity Fair
The Word on the Waters, published by the Missions to Seamen
The War Cry, Supplement II, 18 March 1978
Wesleyan Seamen's Mission Quarterly Papers
Word and Work

Government Papers and Reports

Archival material held at Algemeen Rijksarchief, Tweed Afdeling [State Archives,
    Second Division], The Hague, Holland.
Conference International Concernant la *Police de la Peche dans la Mer du Nord*, held
    at the Hague, October 1881.
BPP LXXXII, 1881, c.2878: Higgins, W.H., 'Outrages Committed by Foreign upon
    English Fishermen in the North Sea', (Hansard 23 May 1881).
BPP XVII, 1882, c.3432: Report of a Committee Appointed by the Board of Trade
    to Inquire Into and Report: Whether Any and What Legislation Is Desirable
    With a View to Placing the Relationships between Owners, Masters and Crews
    of Fishing Vessels on a More Satisfactory Basis.
BPP XLIII, 1887 North Sea Fisheries Convention, 1883 (Questions 157 & 15788
    (Hansard 2 August 1887, Vol. 318, cc933-5).
BPP XXVIII, 1888, c.5412: Second Annual Report [. . .] for 1887, Sea Fisheries
    (England and Wales).
BPP XCVIII, 1888, c.5263: Correspondence: report to the Admiralty by Admiral
    Gordon-Douglas and Mr Malin. Respecting Liquor Traffic in the North Sea,
    (Hansard, 24 April 1888, Vol. 325, cc391-413).
Hansard, 1800-1890.
Merchant Seamen's (Payment of Wages, &c.) Act 1880, 43 & 44 Vict. c16. BPP
    LXXXII, 1881. BPP, XVII, 1882.
The Proceedings of the International Conference held at the Hague in October 1881,

Acts of Parliament

Merchant Seamen's (the Payment of Wages, &c.) Act 1880, 43 & 44 Vict.c.16.

Newspapers

The Aberdeen Newspaper Weekly Journal
Gosport Evening News
Grimsby Evening Telegraph

Grimsby News
Grimsby Times
The Hampshire Telegraph
Portsmouth Evening News
The Times
Yarmouth Gazette and *North Norfolk Constitutionalist*
Yarmouth Independent
Yarmouth Mercury
The Yorkshire Gazette
Weekly Scotsman

Reference Works

Boase, George Clement, and Courtney, William Prideaux, *Bibliotheca cornubiensis: A catalogue of the writings, both manuscript and printed, of Cornishmen, and of works relating to Cornwall*, Vol. 2 P-Z, Vol. 3 Supplement (1882)(London: Longmans, 1878, 1882).
The Fisheries Exhibition Literature, International Fisheries Exhibition, 1883, 14 volumes (London: William Clowes & Sons Ltd, 1884)
Funk I. K., *et al.*, *Standard Dictionary of the English Language* (New York: Funk & Wagnalls, 1946).
Matthew, H.C.G, and Harrison, Brian (eds), *The New Dictionary of National Biography* (Oxford: Oxford University Press, 2004).
Murray, J.A.H., *A New English Dictionary* (1893).

Books

Abrams, L., *Myth and Materiality in a Woman's World: Shetland 1800–2000* (Manchester: Manchester University Press, 2005).
Aflalo, F.G., *The Sea Fishing Industry of England and Wales* (London: Edward Stanford, 1904).
Alward, G.L., *The Development of the British Fisheries During the 19th Century, with Special Reference to the North Sea* (Grimsby: a lecture published by Grimsby News Co. Ltd, February 1911),
Alward, G.L., *The Sea Fisheries of Great Britain and Ireland* (Grimsby: Albert Gait, 1932).
Anson, Peter, *Fishing Boats and Fisher Folk on the East Coast of Scotland* (London: J.M. Dent, 1930), *Fishermen and Fishing Ways* (London: G.G. Harrap, 1932).
Anson, Peter, *The Sea Apostolate in Ireland* (Office of the Irish Messenger, 1946).
Anson, Peter, *The Church and the Sailor* (London: John Gifford, 1948).
Anson, Peter, *Scots Fisherfolk* (Banff: The Saltire Society, Banffshire, 1950).
Anson, Peter, *The Sea Apostolate in the Port of London* (published posthumously by the Apostolate of the Sea, 1991).
Atholz, J.L., *The Mind and Art of Victorian England* (Minneapolis: University of Minnesota Press, 1976).
Ballantyne, R.M., *The Young Trawler* (London: James Nisbet & Co, 1886), *The Lively Poll* (London: James Nisbet & Co, 1886).

Boggis, R.J.E., *History of St John's, Torquay* (Devonshire Press, 1930).

Booth, Charles, *Life and Labour of the People in London* (London, 1889).

Booth, William, *In Darkest England and the Way Out* (London, 1890).

Boswell, D., *Sea Fishing Apprentices at Grimsby* (Grimsby Public Libraries, 1974).

Bruce, Stanley, and Harris, Tina, *Back to the Sea* (Bard Books, 2009).

Bullen, F.T., *The Palace of Poor Jack* (London: James Nisbet & Co., 1900).

Chadwick, O., *The Victorian Church, Vols II & III* (A. and C. Black, 1966).

Clark, Alexander, *A Short History of the Shipmaster's Society* (Aberdeen: Wm Smith & Sons, 1911).

Clark, D, *Between Pulpit and Pew* (Cambridge, 1982).

Cocceiana, Cassii Dionis, *Historiarum Romanarum Quae Supersunt,* edited by U.P. Boissevain (Berlin, 1901).

Danielou, J., *Primitive Christian Symbols* (Compass Books, 1961).

Davies, P., *The Beach and Harbour Mission – The Beachman's Church and St John's Church, Great Yarmouth* (published by P. Davies, 2011).

Defoe, D., *A Tour Through the Whole Island of Great Britain*, first published in 1724 (Harmondsworth: Penguin, 1971).

Dodds, J., *Coast Missions: A Memoir of the Rev. Thomas Rosie* (James Nisbet & Co., 1862).

Down, W., *On Course Together: the Churches' Ministry in the Maritime World Today* (Norwich: The Canterbury Press, 1989).

Durrans, M., *The Life and Times of Miss Dora Walker, FRSA, 1890–1980* (Whitby Literary and Philosophical Society, 1998).

Dyson, J., *Business in Great Waters* (Angus and Robertson, 1977).

Forbes, Athol, *Cassock and Comedy* (C. Arthur Pearson, 1898).

Forby, R., *The Vocabulary of East Anglia* (1830).

Gilbert, A.D., *Religion and Society in Industrial England: Church, Chapel and Social Change, 1740–1914* (Longman, 1976).

Gillet, E., *A History of Grimsby* (Hull: University of Hull Press, 1969).

Gollock, G.A., *At the Sign of the Flying Angel* (Longmans, Green & Co., 1930)

Gordon, A., *What Cheer, O?* (James Nisbet & Co., 1890).

Grenfell, Wilfred, *A Labrador Doctor* (Hodder & Stoughton, 1920).

Hadley, Michael L., *God's Little Ships: a History of the Columbia Coast Mission* (Madeira Park, BC, Canada: Harbour Publishing, 1995).

Heasman, K., *Evangelicals in Action* (London: Geoffrey Bles, 1962).

Hicks, G.F., *The Bishop of the North Sea*, published privately, c.1930 (copy in Great Yarmouth Reference Library).

Hope, Ronald, *A New History of British Shipping* (London: John Murray, 1990).

Kemp, P., *The Oxford Companion to Ships and the Sea* (Oxford, 1976).

Kent, John, *Holding the Fort: Studies in Revivalism* (London: Epworth Press, 1978).

Kerr, J. Lennox, *Wilfred Grenfell: His Life and Work* (G.G. Harrap & Co. Ltd, 1959).

Kingsford, M.R., *The Mersey Mission to Seafarers, 1852–1956* (Abingdon: 1957).

Kverndal, R., *Seamen's Missions: Their Origin and Early Growth* (Pasadena, CA: William Carey Library, 1986).

Kverndal, R., *The Way of the Sea: the Changing Shape of Mission in the Seafaring World,* (Pasadena, CA: William Carey Library, 2008).

Kverndal, R., *George Charles Smith of Penzance* (Pasadena, CA: William Carey Library, 2012).

Latourette, Kenneth Scott, *A History of the Expansion of Christianity, Vol. 4* (London: Harper & Row, 1970).

Lewis, C., *Great Yarmouth: History, Herrings and Holidays* (Poppyland Publishing, 1981).

Lewis, Donald M., *Lighten Their Darkness: the Evangelical Mission to the Working Class of London, 1828–1860* (Greenwood Press, 1986).

Lummis, Trevor, *Occupation and Society: the East Anglian Fishermen 1880–1914* (Cambridge: Cambridge University Press, 1985).

March, Edgar J., *Sailing Trawlers* (Percival Marshall, 1953).

Mather, E.J., *Nor'ard of the Dogger* (James Nisbet & Co., 1887),

Memories of Christian Service (Marshall Brothers, c.1922).

Matthews, Jane, *Welcome Aboard: the Story of the Seamen's Hospital Society and the Dreadnought* (Buckingham: Quotes/Baron Birch, 1992).

Mawer, W., *Adventures in Sympathy: Being the Story of the PHS Since 1821* (A. Brown & Sons, 1935).

McBride, A.G., *The History of the Dreadnought Seamen's Hospital at Greenwich* (Seamen's Hospital Management Committee, Greenwich, 1970).

McCarthy, T., *The Great Dock Strike* (1889).

McLeod, H., *Religion and the Working Class in Nineteenth-Century Britain* (London: Macmillan, 1984).

McMillan, A.S., *The Royal Alfred Story* (London: 1965).

Mearns, Andrew, *The Bitter Cry of Outcast London* (London: J. Clark & Co., 1883).

Middleton, R., *Memoirs of Mr George Cussons of London* (London: 1819).

Miller, R.W.H., *From Shore to Shore: a History of the Church and the Merchant Seafarer*, published privately, 1989.

Miller, R.W.H., *Priest in Deep Water: Charles Plomer Hopkins and the Seamen's Strike* (Cambridge: The Lutterworth Press, 2010).

Miller, R.W.H., *One Firm Anchor: the Church and the Merchant Seafarer, an Introductory History* (Cambridge: The Lutterworth Press, 2012).

Miller, R.W.H., *Dr Ashley's Pleasure Yacht: John Ashley, the Bristol Channel Mission and All That Followed* (Cambridge: The Lutterworth Press, 2017).

Mitchell, C., *The Long Watch* (Sailors' Children's Society, 1961).

Mitchell, G., *Revival Man: the Jock Troup Story* (Christian Focus Publications Ltd, 2002).

Mooney, P., *Maritime Mission: History, Development, a New Paradigm* (Zoetermeer, the Netherlands: Uitgeverij Bockencentrum, 2005).

Parsons, G., *Religion in Victorian Britain, Vols I, II and III* (Manchester University Press for the Open University, 1988).

Pike, G.H., *Among the Sailors During the Life and Reign of the Queen* (Hodder & Stoughton, 1897).

Pilch, Barbara, *Windows on a Life: the Story of Margaret Harker* (Blofield, Norfolk: Images Publications, 2006).

Playen, C., *Reminiscences of a Voyage to Orkney and Shetland and Scotland in the Summer of 1839* (Copenhagen: J. Manson, 1840)(translated into English by Catherine Spence in 1896).

Plumridge, J.H., *Hospital Ships and Ambulance Trains* (Seeley, 1975).

Pritchard, Stanley, *Fish and Ships* (Mowbray, 1980).

Reckitt, Sir J., *Lifeboat and Anchor* (Port of Hull Society and Sailors' Orphan Homes, 1907).

Redford, W., and Knight, M.J., *Jacob's Ladder: the Rise of a Catholic Community, 1848–1912* (St Mary on the Sea, Grimsby, 1996).

Riddle, T. Wilkinson, *For Flag and Empire: the Story of the British and Foreign Sailors' Society in Peace and War* (Marshall Brothers, 1915).

Robinson, R., *Trawling: the Rise and Fall of the British Trawl Fishery* (University of Exeter Press, 1996).

Rompkey, R., *Grenfell of Labrador* (University of Toronto Press, 1991).

Rowley, Jennifer C., *The Hull Whale Fishery* (Lockington Publishing Co., 1982).

Runciman, J., *A Dream of the North Sea* (James Nisbet & Co., 1889).

Scarth, J., *Into All the World* (London: Griffith, Farran, Okeden & Welsh, 1890).

Schofield, A.T., *Behind the Brass Plate* (Sampson Low, c.1915).

Skinner, B.G., *Henry Francis Lyte: Brixham's Poet and Priest* (University of Exeter, 1974).

Smith, G.C., *The Boatswain's Mate* (Southey & Wileman, 1886).

Starkey, D.J., Reid, C., and Ashcroft, N. (eds), *England's Sea Fisheries: the Commercial Fisheries of England and Wales Since 1300* (London: Chatham, 2000).

Thompson, Paul, Wailey, Tony, and Lummis, Trevor, *Living the Fishing* (London: Routledge & Kegan Paul, 1983).

Triplow, Nick, Bramhill, Tina, and Shepherd, Jade, *The Women They Left Behind* (Fathom Press, 2009).

Trombley, Stephen, *Sir Frederick Treves: the Extra-Ordinary Edwardian* (London: Routledge, 1989).

Walrond, M.L., *Launching Out into the Deep: or the Pioneers of a Noble Effort* (London: SPCK, 1904).

Walton, J.K., *Fish and Chips and the British Working Class, 1870–1940* (Leicester University Press, 1992).

Williams, T., *Priscilla Lydia Sellon* (London: SPCK, 1965).

Wood, Walter, *North Sea Fishers and Fighters* (Kegan Paul, Trench, Trubner & Co., 1911).

Yelton, Michael, *Peter Anson: Monk, Writer and Artist* (Anglo-Catholic History Society, 2005).

Young, G., *A Picture of Whitby and its Environs* (Whitby: R. Rodgers, 1817).

Yzermans, V.A., *American Catholic Seafarers' Church* (The National Catholic Conference for Seafarers in the United States, 1995).

Articles

Anon., 'Copering the North Sea', *Chambers Journal*, 4 April 1885, p.323.

Anon., 'The Gravesend Sailors' Home', *The Nautical Magazine*, 1886, pp.794-803.

Anon., 'History of Grimsby', *Fish Trades Gazette*, 1920, pp.21-87.

Anon., 'The History of Trawling: Its Rise and Development to the Present Day', *Fish Trades Gazette*, 19 March 1921, pp.21-69.

Anon., 'With Scots Fisherfolk at Yarmouth', *Weekly Scotsman*, November 1949.

Anon., 'A Brief History, 1864–2014, St Magnus' Church, Lerwick', *St Magnus Church*, 19-20 June 2014.

Anson, Peter, 'Seamen's Welfare in Scottish Ports, c.1949', paper in the Anson
    Archive, Apostleship of the Sea, Hull History Centre, U DAPS/12/1/HIST.
Anson, Peter, 'A Plea for Catholic Seamen: Catholic and Protestant Activities, a
    Contrast', *The Catholic Federalist*, August 1920.
Anson, Richard F., 'The Recent Revival Among the Scottish Fisher-folk', *The Month*,
    November 1922, pp.414-24.
Cabantous, A., '*Religion et Monde Maritime au Havre dans la Seconde Moitie du
    XVIIIeme Siecle*', *Annales de Normandie*, 1983, 33, 3.
Colles, W.M., 'The Police of the North Sea', *Blackwoods Magazine*, April 1888,
    pp.571-80.
Duthie, John Lowe, 'The Fishermen's Revival', *History Today*, December 1983, p.27.
Friend, Stephen, 'George Charles Smith, 1782–1863', *IASMM Newsletter*, Autumn
    1991.
Friend, Stephen, 'The Origins of Organised Seafarers' Missions', *IASMM Newsletter*,
    Spring 1992.
Friend, Stephen, 'The North Sea Liquor Trade, c.1850–1893', *International Journal of
    Maritime History*, vol. XV (December 2003), no.2.
Friend, Stephen, 'Biography of E.J. Mather', *The New Dictionary of National
    Biography* (OUP, 2004).
Hargreaves, R., 'Fisherfolk', *The Nautical Magazine*, April 1974, pp.199-205.
Heath, P., 'North Sea Fishing in the Fifteenth Century: the Scarborough Fleet',
    Northern History, vol. 3 (1968).
Kennerley, A., 'Seamen's Missions and Sailors' Homes', *Exeter Papers in Economic
    History*, 1987, no.17.
Kennerley, A., 'British Seamen's Missions in the Nineteenth Century', in *The North
    Sea: Twelve Essays on Social History of Maritime Labour, Stavanger Maritime
    Museum*, Association of North Sea Societies, Stavanger, Norway, 1992, pp.79-95.
Kverndal, R., 'The Origin and Nature of Nordic Missions to Seamen', *Norwegian
    Yearbook of Maritime History*, 1977, pp.103-34.
Kverndal, R., 'Women on the Waterfront', *Maritime Mission Studies*, vol. 2 (Spring 2000), p.21.
Miller, R.W.H., 'The Salvation Navy', *IASMM Newsletter*, Spring 1996.
Miller, R.W.H., 'The *Société des Oeuvres de Mer*: Welfare Work Among French
    Fishermen off Newfoundland and Iceland', *Newfoundland and Labrador Studies*,
    2005, no. 20, 2, no 49.
Morley, C.R., 'The Origin of the Fish Symbol', *Princeton Theological Review*, viii
    (1910), pp.93-106, 213-46, 401-32.
Mortished, R.J.P., International Labour Office, 'Developments in Welfare Work for
    British Seamen', *International Labour Review*, September 1944, p.333.
Robinson, R.N.W., 'The Fish Trade in the Pre-Railway Era: the Yorkshire Coast,
    1780–1840', *Northern History*, vol. 25 (1989).
Ross, Ella, 'The Church and the Herring-Fishers', *World Dominion*, July-August
    1953, pp.197-202.
Rule, J., 'The Smacksmen of the North Sea', *International Review of Social History*,
    vol. 3 (1976), pp.383-411.
Sharp, C., 'Forbes Alexander Phillips: for Twenty-Five Years Gorleston's Fighting Vicr Was
    in the News', *Norfolk Fair*, June 1969, pp.44-7. St Magnus Church, Lerwick 2014.
Sutherland, J.J., 'The Hospital Ship, 1608–1740', *Mariner's Mirror*, October 1936.

Thompson, P., 'Women in the Fishing: the Roots of Power Between the Sexes',
    Comparative Studies in Society and History, XXVII (1985), p.7.
Walpole, Spencer, *Fisheries Exhibition Literature* (Wm Clowes & Son), vol. 1 (1884),
    pp.9-10.
Wright, R.F., 'The High Seas and the Church in the Middle Ages, Parts 1 and 2',
    Mariner's Mirror, 1967, pp.3-32; and pp.115-35.
Yarham, E.R., 'Blessing the Water', *The Nautical Magazine*, April 1972, pp.214-6.

University Theses

Choi, Jonah Won Jon, 'Shalom and the Church Maritime', DMin, New York
    Theological Seminary, 9 May 1996.
Friend, S., 'The Rise and Development of Christian Missions Amongst British
    Fishing Communities during the Nineteenth Century', MPhil, Leeds University,
    January 1994, 'A Sense of Belonging: Religion and Identity in Yorkshire and
    Humber Fishing Communities, c.1815-1914', PhD, Hull University, May 2010.
Jun, David Chul Han, 'An Historical and Contextual Approach to Seafarers by Korean
    Churches with Special Reference to Muslim Seafarers', DMiss, Fuller School of
    World Mission, Pasadena, California, 7 June 2001.
Kverndal, R., 'Seamen's Missions: a History of the Church Maritime', ThD, Oslo
    University, 1983.
Kennerley, A., 'The Education of the Merchant Seaman in the Nineteenth Century',
    MA, University of Exeter, March 1978, 'British Seamen's Missions and Sailors'
    Homes, 1815–1970, Voluntary Welfare Provision for Serving Seafarers', PhD,
    CNAA, September 1989.
Lummis, T., 'The East Anglian Fishermen, 1880–1914', PhD, University of Essex, 1981.
Miller, R.W.H., 'Charles Plomer Hopkins and the Seaman's Union, with Particular
    Reference to the 1911 Strike', MA, University of Warwick, 1992, 'Ship of Peter:
    the Catholic Sea Apostolate of the Apostleship of the Sea', MPhil, Institute of
    Marine Studies, University of Plymouth, April 1995, 'The Man at the Helm: the
    Faith and Practice of the Medieval Seafarer', PhD, University of London, 2002.
Oubre, S.K., 'The Apostolatus Maris: Its Structural Development, including its 1997
    Reorganisation', in part fulfilment of the Licentiate in Canon Law Catholic
    University of America, Washington, DC, 1998.
Robinson, N.W., The English Fishing Industry, 1790–1914: a Case Study of the
    Yorkshire Coast', PhD, Hull University, 1984.
Yzermans, V.A., American Catholic Seafarers' Church: a Narrative History of the
    Apostleship of the Sea', The National Catholic Conference for Seafarers in the
    United States, 1995.

Libraries

(The reference sections of the following libraries have been used.)

The Anson Library, Buckie, Scotland
The British Museum Library
Barking Public Library

Brixton Public Library
Cambridge University
Canvey Island Library
The Centre for Business History, Glasgow, Scotland
University of East Anglia Library
The National Library of Scotland (Edinburgh)
Gravesend Reference Library
Great Yarmouth Public Library
Gorleston Public Library
Grimsby Public Library
Guildhall Library, Aldermanbury Lane, London
Hull Public Library
Leeds Public Library
Leeds University Library
Lowestoft Public Library (Lowestoft Reference Library)
North Shields Public Library
Penzance Public Library
York Minster Library

Miscellaneous

The following are a selection from the very large number of people and papers consulted:

Ballantyne Papers: Many of the family's papers are in the possession of the grand-daughter, Mrs Karasek, now living in Tetford, Lincolnshire. Other documents are owned by Mr Eric Quayle at Zennor Church, Cornwall, and Professor Norman Holmes Pearson of Yale University. The manuscript of 'The Young Trawler' is in the RNMDSF Archives.

Criddle, M., Scrapbook about the work of Henry Cook's Mission, Gosport.

Friend, Stephen, Women's Voices Project, York St John University (DVD, 2005–2010).

Friend, Stephen, The Great Yarmouth Printing Co. Annual Report, 1898 (Great Yarmouth Library).

Friend, Stephen, The National Archives, Kew ('The Pure Water Co.', DCs Ref. no. BT31, 4220/27314).

Friend, Stephen, 'Great Yarmouth's Maritime Trail', pamphlet published by the Maritime Museum of East Anglia.

Hull History Centre

The New Dictionary of National Biography.

Revised Standard Version of the Bible.

Wilkinson, G., Jock Troup and the Fisherman's Revival, DVD, 2012.

Correspondence

Malcolm Criddle of Gosport
Derek Farman of Norfolk

Mrs Karasek, R.M. Ballantyne's grand-daughter
Alston Kennerley
Roald Kverndal
Charles Lewis, Curator of Norfolk Museum's Service
The Rev. Robert Miller
Dr Ronald Rompkey
Patricia O'Driscoll
The Mather family letters, RNMDSF Archives
Dr W. Blake Odgers, 'Case for Counsel's Opinion', 1 January 1889, RNMDSF
    Archives
Letter from Mr Hewlett, Dashwood's solicitor, 21 January 1889, copy in RNMDSF
    Archives
Letter to Dr Gilbert Smith, RNMDSF Archives
Letter to Sir Andrew Clark from E.J. Mather, 29 February 1888, RNMDSF Archives
Letter from R.M. Ballantyne to Mr Frank Wilson, 9 November 1889 (in possession
    of Mrs Karasek)
Letter in the Family Welfare Association archive file in the MDSF Archives (now in
    the GLC Archives)
Alan Stewart, grandson of W.F. Stewart
Skipper Harry Thorpe, 'From Cabin boy to Mission Skipper' (1958 tape recording)
    (copy in possession of Stephen Friend)

Websites

www.iasmm.org
www.warrenpress.net/FolkstoneThenNow'Fishermen-sBethel

Index

Index of Names

General Index

BV - #0011 - 211218 - C0 - 234/156/17 - PB - 9780718895143